100 THINGS
NORTH CAROLINA
FANS
SHOULD KNOW & DO
BEFORE THEY DIE

Art Chansky

TRIUMPH
BOOKS

Library of Congress Cataloging-in-Publication Data

Chansky, Art.
  100 things North Carolina fans should know & do before they die / Art Chansky.
      pages cm. — (100 things...fans should know)
    ISBN 978-1-60078-984-7
  1. University of North Carolina at Chapel Hill—Basketball—History.
  2. University of North Carolina at Chapel Hill—Basketball—Miscellanea.
  3. North Carolina Tar Heels (Basketball team)—History. 4. North Carolina Tar Heels (Basketball team)—Miscellanea. I. Title. II.
  Title: One hundred things North Carolina fans should know and do before they die.
    GV885.43.U54C42 2015
    796.323'6309756565—dc23
                                    2015012444

This book is available in quantity at special discounts for your group or organization. For further information, contact:
   Triumph Books LLC
   814 North Franklin Street
   Chicago, Illinois 60610
   (312) 337-0747
   www.triumphbooks.com

Printed in U.S.A.
ISBN: 978-1-60078-984-7
Design by Patricia Frey
Photos courtesy of Robert Crawford unless otherwise indicated

To the memory of Dean Smith, the greatest combination of coach and mentor in the history of college basketball.

Contents

Foreword

There are so many great facts and stories to know about Carolina basketball that this book could be titled *One* Thousand *Things North Carolina Fans Should Know & Do Before They Die*. One of my earliest Carolina "things" came when I was 13 years old and in junior high school. My social studies teacher got on me for not bringing in my homework on time. She said, "You know, Charlie Scott is a great basketball player at Carolina, and I bet he does his work on time."

From that point on, Charlie was one of my idols, and I tried to make him my example for what kind of a player and student I wanted to be. And then a few months later, he scored 40 points against Duke to lead Carolina to another ACC championship.

Something else I will never forget about UNC was when Dean Smith and his assistant coaches came to my home for their recruiting visit. They spent the first 30 minutes talking about everything *except* basketball, and my mother said, "Wasn't it nice of that school to send a dean down here to see little Phil?" Of course, Smith turned out to be a lot more than just my coach; he was my friend and mentor for life. And I am so sad he is no longer with us.

Making the decision to go to Carolina was the best decision I have ever made in my life. I have so many friends I met in school, in and out of basketball, that I still see today. I have been blessed to both play for the Tar Heels and to coach under Coach Smith and Coach Guthridge and, eventually, Larry Brown in the NBA. The Carolina basketball family is more than talk—it is real.

When I played in the NBA, other pro players would ask me if all the Carolina basketball family stuff was true. I laughed and said it was. Most of them did not stay in contact with their former college coaches and teammates and did not go back to their campuses during the offseason like so many Tar Heels do. Even today, you never know who will be in the gym during the summer, playing pick-up with current and former players or guys like me who are too old to play but still love to watch and hang out with all the guys who came after me and even a few who came before me.

One thing I remember at Carmichael Auditorium was that old hand-operated wooden scoreboard at the corner of the court. I wondered why it was there with the big electronic scoreboard over-head. Well, it was all about tradition. Of course, the Smith Center has a very fancy locker room for the players now, but we loved our cramped locker room in Carmichael and how the taller guys had to bend their heads when we ran out to the court through that short locker room door. None of our big men wanted to get cracked in the head before the game even started.

And I loved the old Blue Heaven so much with the students sitting behind both benches and going crazy. You always heard them throughout the game and when you came to the bench you could see them and hear them call your name. Those were the best days of my life, and I will cherish them forever.

After pro ball Coach Smith let me come back and be one of his assistants. He was a veteran coach who did not go on the road recruiting until it was time to offer a player a scholarship. But during my first few years, he went out recruiting with me all the time to teach me the ropes. And when he walked into a gym, there was always a great hush that came over the crowd. I was honored to be walking in with him, and it was fun to meet the young men who would someday wear the Carolina uniform.

Today, I am just a fan and I never miss a home game. It is much harder to be a fan than a player or a coach because you have no control over what happens on the court. As a player you could make a play and live with the consequences. Same thing as a coach. But sitting in the stands, you just have to watch what happens and hope it's for the best.

Sometimes I show up at the Smith Center an hour ahead of game time and marvel at how the staff and operations people get the arena ready for a game. Everyone has his or her job, so when it comes time for the team to run out, everything is just right. Someone even is in charge of bringing out the game ball, which reminds me of the story Coach Smith used to tell about his first game at Carolina. He thought he had everything prepared but forgot to assign someone to bring out the game ball, and they could not start the game without it. That may be the only thing he forgot during his Hall of Fame coaching career.

I hope you enjoy reading these kind of stories about Coach Smith and the other important people, places, and events in *100 Things North Carolina Fans Should Know & Do Before They Die*.

—Phil Ford

Acknowledgments

Thank you to all of the people who have written and/or helped me publish the reams of information on the history of Carolina basketball. Far too numerous to compile a complete list, I am especially grateful to former and current sports information directors at UNC Rick Brewer, Steve Kirschner, and Matt Bowers; journalists Chip Alexander, David Glenn, Dane Huffman, Al Featherston, Scott Fowler, Alfred Hamilton, Jr., Adam Lucas, Barry Jacobs, Larry Keith, Curry Kirkpatrick, Joe Menzer, Ron Morris, Lee Pace, Ken Rappoport, Ken Rosenthal, and Mark Whicker; and broadcasters Jones Angell, Woody Durham, Jim Heavner, and Mick Mixon.

Thanks to my wife, Jan Bolick, and her son, Ryan Watts, for their support. And thanks to fellow alums and friends who for years have engaged in a running dialogue of our favorite common subject, Tar Heel basketball.

Hailing from Boston, I remain a staunch Bruins, Celtics, Patriots, and Red Sox fan. Growing up, the college basketball I knew was Providence College and Connecticut, long before their Big East days. When I came to Carolina, the Tar Heels turned me on to big-time college hoops, and there has never been quite anything that compares to Carolina and ACC Basketball.

I remember meeting Dean Smith for the first time as a sportswriter for *The Daily Tar Heel* and later as sports editor when I got to ride on the team plane to away games. At the end of the 1970 season, he boarded the bus for the airport, and the Tar Heels began singing Happy Birthday to their coach. "No, no," he stopped them, "wait till next year when I will be the big 4–0." That was 45 years ago!

Through those years I worked for and with some of the best people in journalism and broadcasting: my former *DTH* and *The*

Atlanta Constitution colleague Owen Davis; *Durham Morning Herald* columnist Keith Drum (whom Smith claimed didn't know much about basketball until Drum became an NBA scout and could help Smith's players get drafted); and former Tar Heel player Dennis Wuyick, with whom I co-created *The Poop Sheet* in 1977 (now known as the *ACC Sports Journal*). Then, of course, my fraternity brothers, friends, and former Tar Heel players Jim Delany, Eddie Fogler, and Rich Gersten, who have taught me much about this great game and told me more than a few times when I got things wrong.

It was fun knowing Smith and Bill Guthridge, though outside of their fabled Carolina basketball family no one ever really *knew* them. Anyone, including writers and broadcasters, who claim otherwise, are not telling the truth. They protected their players to the point of having to joust with journalists who sought to know more than the limited access they were granted. Most of us not connected with the university had to observe and report from the outside looking in, and sometimes that led to more opinion and subjectivity than Smith liked.

I have been privileged to write four books on Carolina basketball, from *March to the Top* in 1982 to *Light Blue Reign* in 2009, and two books on the famed Carolina-Duke rivalry. Working with my Duke counterpart, Johnny Moore, on our first Triumph book, *The Blue Divide,* was a great pleasure and even more fun.

Lucky to have lived through the transition from hot type to offset printing to the world wide web, I worked with the late and legendary Jim Shumaker, editor of the former *Chapel Hill Weekly,* and got in on the ground floor of the Internet with the original GoHeels.com website, which proudly claimed from 1997–2002 to "never have been and never will be the official website of Carolina Athletics." Of course, GoHeels is exactly that today, having been sold to UNC's multimedia rights holder Learfield in 2002.

The first GoHeels rose to prominence in a time of turbulence at UNC, when John Swofford became commissioner of the ACC, Smith soon retired, and Mack Brown moved on to Texas—all in the span of six months. The Internet in those days, as now, had to fight for journalistic credibility, largely because it gave a voice to anyone who wanted to chime in with blogs, on message boards, and by tweeting out to the world. Not to mention, of course, Facebook.

Thankfully, respected publishers like Triumph Books still exist and want to print and market books like *The Blue Divide* and this *100 Things* edition and the Duke version written by Johnny Moore. Thanks to expert editor Jeff Fedotin, a self-proclaimed Dukie who, I have to say, seems very partial to Carolina, as well, and Triumph's Noah Amstadter, senior acquisitions editor. It has been great fun working on both books. Hope you enjoy this one.

1 Dean Smith's First NCAA Championship

The 1981 Final Four helped Dean Smith's returning players get ready for all the distractions that can occur. After staying in a hotel far outside of Philadelphia in 1981, Smith decided to house the team in the middle of New Orleans' French Quarter in 1982. With a veteran, conscientious team, Smith knew his players would be ready when the time came. Until then he wanted them to take their minds off the games and be close to their families.

Smith was concerned that most people expected top-ranked Carolina to easily beat Houston in the semifinals. Even though the Cougars were unranked, they had All-American Clyde Drexler and a great young center named Akeem Olajuwon (later Hakeem). Ironically, Smith got even more worried after the Tar Heels jumped out to a 14–0 lead because Smith believed that the other team relaxes, begins playing better, and could eventually go ahead. UNC didn't let up, but Houston started making some shots it had been missing, and Carolina missed some that would have put the Tar Heels further ahead.

Sam Perkins played a sensational all-around game, hitting 9-of-11 shots and all seven of his free throws and grabbing 10 rebounds. Jimmy Black's defense on Houston point guard Rob Williams was a big factor, but Carolina couldn't stop Lynden Rose, who wound up with 20 points. Smith called for the delay game at the six-minute mark, and if Houston had not continued its great offensive rebounding, it would have been an easy win. Smith cited James Worthy's driving dunk out of the Four Corners as one of the most spectacular plays he had ever seen, and his team advanced to the championship game for the second straight season—the first team to do that since UCLA in 1972 and '73.

Smith was well aware that society measures success through winning and losing. Having lost to Indiana the year before, his team had to defeat Georgetown to have a successful season in the eyes of many people. He didn't feel that way but wanted to win very much for his players, all of his coaches, and for all friends of the university, who wouldn't have to answer all those questions anymore about their coach not winning the big one.

Georgetown coach John Thompson, one of Smith's assistants on the 1976 Olympic team in Montreal, was a close friend of the Carolina coach. Thompson's adopted son, Donald Washington, played at UNC for two years in the early 1970s. Smith considered Thompson a remarkable man who did so much for basketball and for Georgetown, an excellent coach, and a motivational leader who would have his team ready for the championship game.

As much as Smith was concerned with their freshman center Patrick Ewing, he was even more worried about the Hoyas' leader Sleepy Floyd. He hadn't played well against Louisville in the semifinals, but Smith knew Floyd was a great competitor who would be looking forward to facing Worthy again. They had played against each other for the state championship while attending rival high schools in Gastonia, North Carolina.

The contest was intense. Georgetown never led by more than four points. Carolina's biggest lead was three. The momentum swung back and forth, and the pressure inside the Louisiana Superdome made it difficult for some fans to breathe. Floyd's short jumper hit the front of the rim and hung in the air before dropping through, giving the Hoyas a 62–61 lead with just under a minute to play. Would the Tar Heels lose again in their seventh trip to the Final Four under Dean Smith?

They brought the ball across midcourt and began to set up their offense for the last shot. Smith jumped up and signaled for Black to call a timeout with 32 seconds remaining, and the team huddled around its head coach. Part of the lore about Smith's coaching was his composure in such situations, and his assistant coaches said they never remembered him so cool, in so tight a squeeze. "The pressure was there. I could feel it all the way down the bench," recalled assistant Eddie Fogler, "but I honestly don't think he did."

Smith calmed the players, reminding them plenty of time still remained in the game. He told them to look for the first good shot and to cover the backboard. If the shot missed and Georgetown got the rebound, he said to foul them right away. That would stop the clock and force Georgetown to make two free throws or give Carolina another shot for at least a tie. Smith could make 30 seconds seem like an eternity to opponents.

Smith figured the Hoyas would surround Worthy and Perkins (who had already combined for 38 of the team's 61 points) with a zone and make the Tar Heels beat them from outside. He looked at his freshman, Michael Jordan, before the huddle broke. He seemed to know Jordan would get his first chance at immortality. "Knock it in, Michael," he said, tapping Jordan on the knee.

Sure enough, Black's skip pass over the Georgetown zone went to Jordan on the left wing; the skinny kid, who went on to become the greatest player of all time, went straight up and, indeed, knocked it in. Georgetown threw the ball away in the final seconds, and Carolina won 63–62 for its first national championship in 25 years—since McGuire's Miracle and the undefeated 1957 team.

2 Michael Jordan

As hard as it is to imagine, Michael Jordan grew up a David Thompson and N.C. State fan. He actually rooted *against* Carolina as a grade schooler. And until his junior year at Laney High School in Wilmington, North Carolina, the UNC coaches weren't that inclined to change his mind. Then the young Jordan became "Magic" Jordan. After not starting as a sophomore at Laney, Jordan began to blossom. Torn between basketball and baseball as a little boy, he now went virtually everywhere with a large leather ball under his arm.

It was still there when Dean Smith first visited the Jordan home in the fall of 1980. Through the entire two-hour visit, Jordan sat in the middle of his living room floor, cradling a basketball. When Smith and assistants Bill Guthridge and Eddie Fogler arrived at the two-story colonial house, Michael and his father were outside working on one of the family cars. But the Carolina coaches already knew about the closeness of the Jordan family. They had met James and Deloris Jordan the previous summer when Michael took the UNC basketball camp by storm.

Guthridge, at least, had not been surprised by Jordan's remarkable improvement. He saw Jordan as junior and rated him as an outstanding prospect then. After watching Jordan work out one afternoon that summer in Carmichael Auditorium, assistant coach Roy Williams called him "the best 6'4" high school payer" he had ever seen.

Because James Jordan had not missed one of his son's basketball or baseball games since the eighth grade, Smith was hopeful that Wilmington's proximity to Chapel Hill would work to Carolina's advantage. Still unknown to most college recruiters, Jordan blew

Even after completing his glorious NBA career, Michael Jordan still maintained a close relationship with Dean Smith.

UNC's secret after one week at Howard Garfinkel's Five-Star Camp later that summer of 1980. Jordan was voted MVP and instantly turned into one of the hottest prospects in the country.

But due to UNC's early mining of this gem, Jordan turned down Duke, Maryland, South Carolina, N.C. State, and virtually every other major college that had recruited him and committed to Carolina before his senior year, enjoying a stress-free season further honing his game and looking forward to going to Chapel Hill.

After a month or so on campus, Jordan was summoned to Smith's office before official practice started. The 1981–82 UNC media guide had already gone to press and his profile listed him as "Mike" Jordan. Smith had heard that Jordan's nickname in high school was Magic and told him that Magic *Johnson* already owned that distinction. *What about just "Michael Jordan" and make a name for yourself with that?*

Jordan would make a distinction and then some, becoming the fourth player after Phil Ford, Mike O'Koren, and James Worthy to start his first game as a freshman despite missing almost two weeks of practice with a sprained ankle. He quickly became one of the Tar Heels' top offensive rebounders and their best perimeter shooter, scoring in double figures in his first six college games against the nation's toughest schedule.

He soon was a fixture for Carolina fans, dancing around the lane, looking for an opening, and finally going to the basket with that ever-present tongue wagging from the side of his mouth. Any die-hard Carolina fan could tell you that Phil Ford stuck his tongue out—but only on free throws.

By midseason, Jordan was taking a lot of the big shots that had belonged to Al Wood the previous three years. And when the inevitable shooting slump arrived, Jordan was so determined to shake it that he stayed after practice every day for a week to take 82 extra shots because it was 1982. Walter Davis had begun the superstituous procedure during his own slump in 1977: shoot 77 extra shots after practice on the suggestion of Guthridge. So when Jordan's shot stopped falling, Coach Gut told him to do the same.

By the home stretch of the championship season, Jordan had ACC Rookie of the Year honors locked up. He shot better than 50 percent in February and March, attempting more field goals than any other Tar Heel while opponents were sagging inside on Worthy and Sam Perkins.

That is precisely what happened on Jordan's final shot of the season. Worthy flashed through the lane, drawing the Georgetown defense to him and leaving Jordan alone on the left wing. Jimmy Black threw the cross-court pass, and Jordan made history by sticking his tongue out and sticking the jumper in. That game-winning shot of the national championship, actually far easier than the lefty layup he arched over Georgetown's Patrick Ewing moments earlier, was etched into Carolina basketball forever. "I really didn't feel any pressure," Jordan said in the championship locker room. "It was just another jumper over the weak side of the zone."

Psycho T's Records

Tyler Hansbrough never thought seriously about turning pro before his college eligibility expired. He was having too much fun in Chapel Hill, wanted to beat Duke four straight times in Cameron Indoor Stadium, and sought a national championship. It was a fairly easy decision: *Should I stay all four years at UNC and try to become the all-time leading scorer and rebounder in the history of the school or leave a year early for the NBA, where my size might not allow me to play in the post?*

Coach Roy Williams could not even get "Psycho T" to make a statement regarding the 2008 NBA Draft. When Williams asked him, Hansbrough was pumping iron in the UNC weight room, still trying to get over the embarrassing loss to Kansas in the 2008 Final Four. "I'm not leaving," Hansbrough told his coach who then asked the sports information office to issue a statement. Although Williams was happy he would have his All-American big man back for a fourth year, he felt guilty about not pushing him out like his mentor Dean Smith did with James Worthy and Michael Jordan. Smith would always say, "What if they stayed another year and got hurt?"

Sure enough, Hansbrough began the 2008–09 season sidelined by a potential stress fracture. Among Williams' biggest concerns was that Hansbrough would not be healthy enough to reach the records he could break after returning to the lineup for his senior season. The workhorse from Poplar Bluff, Missouri, had become the standard for staying in school after a third straight season of making unanimous All-ACC and consensus All-American teams and winning almost every Player of the Year award given out.

After sitting out four games in November, Hansbrough returned for the ACC–Big Ten Challenge in Detroit. He had 25 points and 11 rebounds in only 27 minutes as Carolina trounced tired and dinged-up Michigan State 98–63 at Ford Field. The Heels went home with Hansbrough only 34 points away from Phil Ford's 31-year-old scoring record at UNC of 2,290.

Williams orchestrated the timing of the occasion by taking Tyler out of the Saturday evening game against Oral Roberts after he had scored 26 points and Carolina on the way to a 100–84 victory. Thus, the big moment would come in the first half against Evansville the following Thursday on ESPN. Ford, an assistant to Carolina icon Larry Brown with the Charlotte NBA franchise, could be in attendance because the Bobcats were off that night.

Contrary to Smith who rarely feted individual achievements with ceremony, Williams wanted to halt the game on Hansbrough's record-breaking point, acknowledge the legendary Ford (who would be seated at courtside), and let the 22,000 fans and national TV audience participate. Hansbrough deserved the recognition, and it wouldn't hurt recruiting either. Still, Williams worried that he might have gone overboard. He nixed the scripted celebration and hurried Hansbrough through the whole gig. *Here's the ball, go hug Phil, listen to the PA announcement, wave to the crowd, and let's get on with the game.* "He hijacked the ceremony to make sure we'd get it done quickly," veteran sports information director Steve Kirschner said, laughing. "He wanted it for Tyler, and it was good for recruiting, but he did not want to seem inconsiderate to anyone else."

Hansbrough finished with 20 points versus Evansville to easily pass Ford. He wound up the season with 2,872 points, a mark that will likely never be broken or even approached at Carolina. Later in the season, he surpassed Sam Perkins (1,167) as the UNC rebounding leader and finished with a new career mark of 1,219, probably another untouchable record.

The Unexpected Championships of 1957 and 1993

The 1957 and 1993 national championships were won by Tar Heel teams consisting of better college players than eventual pros. Both are heralded as the finest coaching jobs of coaches Frank McGuire and Dean Smith, deceased colleagues who coached together in Chapel Hill and eventually were named to the Naismith Hall of Fame.

The 1957 Tar Heels, hailed as "McGuire's Miracle," went 32–0 and carved out what is still the greatest story in the history of a sports-crazy state. The team was led by five starters from the New York area—Pete Brennan, Bob Cunningham, Tommy Kearns, Joe Quigg, and Lennie Rosenbluth—coined "Four Catholics and a Jew" in the days when PC stood for "privileged character" rather than "politically correct." Though Brennan, Kearns, and Rosenbluth went on to play briefly in the pros, the zenith of their basketball careers came during the memorable season in which the Tar Heels defeated every team they faced while only playing eight games at their home court, Woollen Gym. Including the Dixie Classic, a road game at N.C. State, and three games in the ACC Tournament, they actually played seven games on the Wolfpack's home court that season. They also won twice at the Boston Garden, Madison Square Garden, The Palestra in Philadelphia, and Memorial Auditorium in Kansas City, Missouri.

Those last two games in Kansas City were legendary. Carolina defeated No. 11-ranked Michigan State and All-American Jumpin' Johnny Green in triple overtime in the national semifinals on Friday night, March 22, when Brennan saved the game by driving the length of the floor after a missed free throw and sank a jump shot that sent the game into the second overtime. Brennan finished with 14 points, Cunningham had 19, and Player of the Year Rosenbluth had 31 in the eventual 74–70 victory.

Twenty-four hours later, the top-ranked Tar Heels faced No. 2 Kansas and seven-foot All-American Wilt "the Stilt" Chamberlain. Carolina may have been used to playing away from home, but with 10,000 Jayhawks fans screaming all night, this was the ultimate road game. UNC took a 29–22 halftime lead mostly by double and triple-teaming Chamberlain. But with Rosenbluth in fouled trouble and eventually fouling out in regulation, Chamberlain broke free to score most of his 23 points and tie the game in regulation. The first overtime was 2–2, and the second overtime was scoreless, as both tired teams played very cautiously in the days before the shot clock. In the third overtime, Kansas took a 53–52 lead in the final seconds before Quigg was fouled from behind after Chamberlain blocked his shot. Quigg stepped to the line and made two free throws and he batted down an entry pass to Chamberlain on the Jayhawks' last possession.

Smith joined McGuire's staff as an assistant coach in 1958. Upon succeeding McGuire three years later, he continued to embrace the 1957 champions as if they were his own. Smith won his first national championship with players named Michael Jordan, Sam Perkins, and James Worthy—all future NBA stars. But Smith's second NCAA title team defined him—as 1957 did for McGuire—as one of the greatest coaches of all time. The 1993 Tar Heels had their own All-American center, Eric Montross, and a superb supporting cast of forwards George Lynch and Brian Reese and guards Donald Williams and Derrick Phelps. But this was a team in which the sum was better than the individual parts. Like the 1957 team, the 1993 champions did not have any players who went on to become stars in the NBA. Yet Smith molded them into one of the most efficient teams in NCAA history.

Carolina finished first in the ACC and drew the No. 1 seed in the East Regional. After blowout wins in the first two rounds, the No. 4-ranked Tar Heels survived heart-stopping games in the Sweet 16 against No. 12-ranked Arkansas and the regional final against No. 7-ranked Cincinnati to move on to the Final Four in New Orleans, where the 1982 team had won it all. UNC defeated Kansas (coached by Roy Williams) in the semifinal and then faced Michigan's Fab Five sophomores for the national championship two nights later.

Carolina led 42–36 at the half but found itself in a one-possession game within the last minute of play. A few minutes earlier, Smith had daringly emptied his bench to rest his five starters for the home stretch. It worked as the Tar Heels clung to their lead and won after a tired and trapped Chris Webber called a timeout that Michigan did not have. Donald Williams, the Most Outstanding Player of the Final Four who hit 10-of-14 three-pointers on the weekend, sealed the 77–71 victory with free throws. Critics called Carolina lucky that Webber called the ill-fated TO with his team trailing by only two points, but it was Smith's rested defense that had forced Webber into the corner where he picked up his dribble, panicked, and called timeout right in front of his own bench. "Call us lucky," Smith said, "but also call us champions."

5 2005 National Champions

The journey from the 8–20 season in 2002 under coach Matt Doherty to the national championship of 2005 under Roy Williams was surreal for Jackie Manuel, Melvin Scott, and Jawad Williams, who went from the pits as freshmen to the mountaintop as seniors.

The Tar Heels had improved in 2003 to 19 victories, but that still wasn't enough to earn an NCAA Tournament berth or save Matt Doherty's job. Even when Roy Williams arrived for the 2003–04 season, too much selfishness remained amongst the team, and it took Williams an entire year to correct the mind-set. Carolina did win enough games (18) to make it back to the Big Dance for the first time since 2001, but that only lasted two games before the Heels were sent home by Texas.

After months of meetings, scrimmaging, and working out in the offseason, plus the addition of freshman recruit Marvin Williams, the Tar Heels looked good enough to open the 2004–05 season with a No. 4 national ranking. But that didn't last long; without point guard Raymond Felton, serving a one-game NCAA suspension for improper participation in a summer league, Carolina lost its opener to unranked Santa Clara in Oakland, California, on the way to the Maui Classic.

Upon arriving in the islands, Williams put the team through what would be the toughest practice of the season. "It was as mad as I've ever been in coaching," Williams said. Carolina beat Brigham Young by 16 in the Maui Classic opener and survived Felton's sprained wrist to win the tournament by beating Tennessee by 13 and Iowa by 14. Almost overnight, the Tar Heels had turned into a team that had people inside the UNC athletic department privately predicting would win the national championship and that books would be written about it.

It all stemmed from Williams' thought of the day—"Not I, but we"—before that grueling practice. Two important non-conference games followed, a victory at Indiana in the homecoming for Sean May, the hometown Hoosier who spurned the IU program by signing with the Tar Heels after Bob Knight was fired. The angry crowd notwithstanding, Carolina won 70–63 behind 50 points from Felton, Rashad McCants, and Jawad Williams. An admittedly nervous May missed five of his seven shots and grabbed only four rebounds.

Carolina posted its best win to date after returning home to face eighth-ranked Kentucky in the wild Smith Center. Behind 28 points by McCants and 19 rebounds from May, the Heels went up 15 at the half and cruised to a 91–78 victory. Having fallen all the way to 11th in the rankings, the Heels climbed back to No. 3 before ACC play opened. After a lopsided loss at fourth-ranked Wake Forest, they won 12 of their last 13 ACC games, and the only blemish was a one-pointer at Duke when Felton could not get off the potential game-winning shot.

In the rematch on Senior Day for Manuel, Scott, and Jawad Williams, Carolina scored the last 11 points of the game in the dramatic rally that nearly tore the Teflon roof off of the Dean Dome.

After Marvin Williams won the game with an offensive rebound and old-fashioned three-point play, Coach Williams called it the loudest crowd he had ever heard anywhere, as the Tar Heels snapped a four-game losing streak to the Blue Devils, won the ACC regular season, and maintained their No. 2 ranking while locking up a No. 1 seed in the NCAA Tournament.

Though McCants had missed the last four regular season games with an illness, the team went to the ACC Tournament in Washington, D.C., with confidence. But after rallying late to beat Clemson in the opener, Carolina lost to Georgia Tech for the second straight tournament. Roy Williams brought the Heels home and sent them right to practice. They responded by easily beating Oakland and Iowa State in Charlotte to move on to the NCAA Sweet 16 in Syracuse, which was the site of Dean Smith's last regional championship in 1997.

But the two games were agony. A controversial traveling call against Villanova helped UNC in the regional semifinal, and only 29 points and 12 rebounds by May, plus McCants' three-pointers and his timely block in the closing minutes, saved Carolina against Wisconsin in the regional final. The Tar Heels were on to the Final Four but not before hearing some tough talk from their coach. "If you play defense in St. Louis the way you played it here, we'll be coming home after the semifinals," Williams told them before they boarded the bus for the airport.

The first day after returning home included a session in "the Pit"—the practice gym with the rims taken off the backboards. It was nothing but defensive drills for 35 minutes. They did it Tuesday as well. They also signed a handwritten note in the locker room that read: "I pledge to my teammates and my coaches that I will give 100% mentally and physically on every defensive possession these next seven days. I cannot imagine letting my teammates down in this nor can I imagine the hurt I will cause myself."

14

North Carolina celebrates its first title of the Roy Williams era after defeating Illinois 75–70, a game in which Sean May had 26 points and 10 rebounds.

In St. Louis, the Tar Heels used defense to shake off a bad first half against Michigan State and run away from the Spartans on Final Four Saturday. They held Tom Izzo's team under 34 percent shooting and reached UNC's first national championship game in 12 years. Carolina led Illinois on Monday night by 13 at the half but broke down defensively in the second half and allowed the Illini to tie the game before Felton drilled a critical three-pointer and the Heels held on to win 75–70. It was Roy Williams' first national championship after four trips to the Final Four with Kansas. He was bear-hugged at the buzzer by May, the Most Outstanding

Player of the Final Four who finished with 26 points and 10 rebounds.

May was also bear-hugged by the mercurial McCants, who was removed from the game down the stretch after committing a costly turnover and taking a bad shot. His coaches just didn't trust him in such a tight situation. In a comment that would not truly resonate until nine years later, when McCants implicated himself in the UNC academic and athletic scandal and pointed a finger at his coach, he said to May as they rolled around on the Edward Jones Dome floor, "Do you believe that motherfucker kept me out for the last three minutes?" May jumped up and said to McCants, "You're crazy, man. We just won the national championship!"

6 2009 National Champions

Despite 10 straight victories that sent the Tar Heels into first place in the ACC, including their fourth consecutive win at Cameron Indoor Stadium, Roy Williams remained frustrated with their defense. They allowed non-contender N.C. State to shoot 54 percent and keep the game much closer than it should have been. Afterward, the media peppered ol' Roy on why he had stubbornly stayed with his man-to-man all season and not trapped more, switched more, or pressed more.

He had set up this confrontation himself, saying that not switching keeps players from being lazy and he coaches to "get your butt through the screens" at the top of the key. By not practicing changing defenses, he admitted the Tar Heels were not very good at it when they tried.

Having three times explained that "we're frickin' bad at it," he accidentally dropped the f-bomb in his next answer. He apologized repeatedly for the remainder of the press conference and immediately called his athletic director and chancellor to apologize. They thanked him for his sincerity, and Williams watched his language for the rest of the season.

He was still furious after the Tar Heels flubbed away a 16-point lead at Maryland, which halted the winning streak at 10 and left Duke only one game back in the ACC race. The Heels let the Terrapins rally by shooting quickly and poorly when they should have milked the clock, a surprising lack of poise this late in the season for an experienced team.

Carolina came back with its biggest ACC blowout, a 30-pointer against last-place Georgia Tech in which Hansbrough went 8-for-8 from the foul line and, appropriately, set the all-time NCAA record for most free throws made.

The Tar Heels were ready for their—and Hansbrough's—home finale against Duke until Ty Lawson slammed his big toe into a basket support two days before the game and limped out of practice on crutches. Once the news hit the message boards and Internet, the tale of Ty's toe had fans fretting that the Heels would lose to the Blue Devils, wind up tied for first in the ACC, and leave their NCAA seeding resting on Lawson's lameness.

After taking a painkilling shot and getting fitted for an oversize shoe and steel plate to protect the toe, Lawson somehow made three key plays in the final minutes and finished with 13 points, nine assists, and eight rebounds in a tense, eight-point victory against Duke. Carolina wrapped up the regular-season title, and Lawson wrapped up ACC Player of the Year honors; he later won the Bob Cousy Award as the nation's best college point guard and joined Hansbrough on several All-American teams.

Even though a No. 1 seed in the NCAA tournament seemed assured, the story of Ty's toe did not end there. The next day, his

The 2009 Duke-Carolina Games

Tyler Hansbrough's Senior Game against Duke in Chapel Hill was supposed to be the grand swan song for UNC's all-time leading scorer and rebounder. The Smith Center was packed to the highest row, and dignitaries and celebrities were spotted all over the building. Michael Jordan—the managing partner of the NBA's Charlotte Bobcats— arrived with head coach Larry Brown, assistant Phil Ford, and Bobcats players Raymond Felton and Sean May. In addition, former Democratic presidential candidate John Edwards attended with his wife, Elizabeth.

Carolina had defeated Duke for the fourth straight year at Cameron Indoor Stadium, sparked by Ty Lawson scoring 21 of his 25 points in the second half of the 101–87 win, and was expected to beat the Blue Devils again, win the ACC regular season outright, and secure a No. 1 seed in the NCAA Tournament, regardless of what happened the next weekend at the ACC Tournament in Atlanta. But a loss would give Duke a tie for first place and leave the Tar Heels' best path to the Final Four in Detroit up in the air, not to mention ruining Hansbrough's and Danny Green's (and what would turn out to be Lawson's and Wayne Ellington's) last home game.

With Lawson getting the feel of his jerry-rigged jammed right big toe and both teams shooting 56 percent, Duke held to a 39–38 halftime lead. Carolina took the lead for good early in the second half on Green's three-pointer but still clung to a 70–68 advantage when Lawson took over the game. He drove and dished to Green for another three-pointer and then went to the hoop, scored, and got fouled to put the Heels ahead 76–69 with a minute left. He then sealed the 79–71 win with two free throws.

Hansbrough, who had 17 points, two three-pointers, and eight rebounds, left the game after fouling out with 13 seconds remaining, waving to an adoring crowd and shaking hands with Williams as he approached the Tar Heel bench. He had already become Carolina's all-time leading scorer but would relinquish his ACC Player of the Year award to Lawson in 2009. As the rivalry has ebbed and flowed, it was UNC's sixth win over Duke in the last seven games and the Tar Heels' third outright regular season title in five years. Their dominance over the stretch was aided by their superior rebounding, winning the board battle against Duke in this game 37–22.

Once it was over, Hansbrough got emotional as he addressed the crowd during the Senior Day postgame festivities and thanked his teammates for "the best four years of my life." It was the send-off he had hoped for when he put off the NBA to come back to school for one more run at a national championship. "It's a hard game to play," Hansbrough said. "You're thinking about everything. You're thinking about your after-game speech. You're thinking, *Oh man, this is my last game in the Dean Dome*, and you start to think your college career is coming to an end. Then you're still trying to focus on the game and get the win."

foot was so swollen and painful that Williams thought he might have lost his indispensable point guard for the entire postseason.

Lawson sat out the ACC Tournament in Atlanta, and Williams wrote "Find a Way" on the white board in the locker room before Friday's quarterfinals against Virginia Tech. The Tar Heels survived the Hokies in the last minute for the second straight season, but without their motor, they could not muster enough offense the next day against Florida State when Hansbrough passed Sam Perkins as UNC's all-time leading rebounder.

Despite losing, they had begun building defensive intensity that would carry over to the NCAA Tournament, where Carolina routed Radford, ran away from LSU, smoked Gonzaga with almost perfect offense, and doubled-down on Blake Griffin to outclass Oklahoma. Four straight wins by double figures continued Carolina's assault on the NCAA Tournament record book and secured Williams' third Final Four trip in his six seasons at UNC—and the school's NCAA record 18th in its 99th year of basketball.

The Tar Heels then closed off the lane to deny Villanova's penetration in the national semifinals at Ford Field in Detroit, defeating the Wildcats soundly to reach the NCAA championship game and soften memories of the Kansas catastrophe the year before. The last obstacle proved to be widespread sentiment in support of Michigan State after the Spartans surprisingly ran away from UConn in the first semifinal. Coach Tom Izzo had adopted the city's 22 percent unemployment and the state's suffering economy as his causes, saying he hoped his team could be an inspiration for all of Michigan. "We have a cause, too, and it's to win the national championship, period," Williams said. But it didn't exactly end there. He went a little further, as he is wont to do when the cameras and recorders are running. "If you told me that if Michigan State wins, it's gonna satisfy the nation's economy, then I'd say, 'hell, let's stay poor for a little while longer.'"

That, obviously, was a joke, but some saw it as insensitivity by the Carolina coach. Unintentional insult is one thing. Abject foolishness is another.

CBS analysts Seth Davis and Greg Anthony *both* predicted Michigan State to win. Weren't these guys supposed to be experts? One upset pick was good theater, for sure, but both men picking the Spartans stretched their credibility.

Top-ranked since preseason, Carolina had already blown out the same team on the same court in December. The Tar Heels had compiled the biggest NCAA Tournament point differential in 13 years as five previous opponents tried to run with the best running team in college basketball. Izzo himself suggested his Spartans would be the sixth.

"Detroit, defense, and destiny" were the reasons for an upset given by Davis, a Duke graduate. He should have known that, while most of Motown favored Michigan State, a hostile atmosphere was really more helpful to the Tar Heels. The fans were too far away from the floor to be much of a factor, but Roy Williams used Frank McGuire's old us-against-the-world motivation to keep his team focused on getting off to a great start. "Remember what happened last year," he harped all weekend about the embarrassing loss to Kansas in the 2008 Final Four. "I *love* playing on the road," he had said Sunday; his latest Carolina team had played 22 true away games and won 20 of them.

As for the defense Davis mentioned, it belonged to the team wearing white and not green. The old coaching adage that good offense beats good defense made the high-scoring Heels a solid favorite anyway. Michigan State's only hope was to get the Tar Heels into a physical showdown from the start, and that did not happen—thanks, mainly, to junior Wayne Ellington.

Ridiculed and reminded throughout the season of its offense-only rap, Carolina capped two weeks of lock-down D. Their unselfish offense was vintage Roy Williams. Lawson and Ellington seized the perimeter and made the Big Ten Player of the Year (Kalin Lucas) and Defensive Player of the Year (Travis Walton) look like they couldn't cut it in the ACC. Lawson's seven steals in the first half tied a Final Four record. (His eighth in the second half broke it.) Ellington's 17 points catapulted Carolina to an NCAA title game high of 55 in the first half and a 21-point lead at the break.

By choosing to play at the highest level, the Tar Heels gave Michigan State no chance to avenge the earlier loss at Ford Field. The Spartans wore the look of defeat long before the ho-hum second half. The game began to feel like one of those December nights at the Smith Center when the Tar Heels were winning big. The eventual 17-point victory was so one-sided that lots of viewers switched over to *Dancing with the Stars* and tanked the TV ratings. The players on the bench, hidden by the elevated court, actually talked about what they might do after the game. The coaches cracked smiles in the closing minutes, rarely seen on the Carolina sideline.

Williams enjoyed a bear hug with Hansbrough, whose entire demeanor seemed to slip into another place as he realized his dream was actually going to happen. He let everything out, looking and sounding as awkward as he sometimes did throughout his spectacular four years at UNC. But he didn't care and told the media so afterward. "Write anything you want now because we have the championship," he said to the microphones in his face, half smiling and wearing the whole net that he and his teammates had just cut down.

The Lennie Rosenbluth and Phil Ford of his era, whose retired No. 50 would join theirs in the Dean Dome rafters, Hansbrough, along with the rest of his senior class, had won a school-record 124 games and accomplished the only goal left, as he and his teammates atoned for the one big embarrassment in their college careers.

The loss to Kansas had stuck in all of their craws like bad garlic. "We wanted to redeem ourselves," offered Ellington, the Final Four Most Outstanding Player who finally found his stroke and looked like he would never miss a shot during the last 10 games of the season. "We learned from our past experience that it was important to come out strong," added Lawson, who made 15 free throws while Michigan State fouled and fouled in frustration.

This championship game was dramatically different from UNC's previous four, which were grinding pressure-cookers. Never had Carolina performed like this with the NCAA title on the line, playing a first half so commanding that the second was all but an afterthought.

In their previous 16 Final Fours from the McGuire era on, the Tar Heels had won close championship games (1957, 1982, 1993, 2005), lost with disappointing performances (1977, 1981), or gotten wiped out (by UCLA in 1968). Even more often, they had fallen with a thud after sorry semifinals (1967, 1969, 1972, 1991, 1995, 1997, and 1998). They had knocked down some walls but never blown them away like they did on April 6 in Detroit.

In becoming the first team to win all six games by 12 points or more, the Tar Heels, clearly the best team in the country, were dominant up to and through the final game of the season. No doubts remained at the end. This might have been Carolina's proudest moment. And a Dean Smith disciple got it done, the assistant who had now won 55 NCAA tournament games in 21 seasons and climbed to within 10 of Smith's 65 in 36 years. "Roy Williams and Dean Smith don't fit in the same sentence," Williams insisted. "I'm not being humble. I really believe that."

The Luck Involved with Lennie Rosenbluth

When Frank McGuire left St. John's after the 1952 season to coach elsewhere, he trumped Everett Case with an ace in the hole named Lennie Rosenbluth. At 6'5" and maybe 175 pounds, Rosenbluth was swarthy and almost spider-like, so skinny that as a sophomore and junior he couldn't make his high school team loaded with meaty war veterans. He became a "vagabond player" with any organized team that would have him.

After improving so much that he starred in the *Daily Mirror* AAU tournament, Rosenbluth was called back by his high school coach and started for the rest of his junior year, leading James Monroe High School into the city playoffs at Madison Square Garden. That's where he met Harry Gotkin, who invited him to the Catskill Mountains that summer, getting a chance to play regularly for Laurel Country Club when three older teammates were severely injured in a car accident; one of them eventually died.

Red Auerbach of the Boston Celtics, among the college and pro coaches vacationing in upstate New York and scouting the summer games, watched Rosenbluth average 20 points with his uncanny shot and invited him to his team's training camp on Cape Cod. The shy 17-year-old roomed with Celtics star Bob Cousy, held his own on the court against big men Easy Ed McCauley and Bones McKinney, and landed a contract offer from Auerbach. "For a kid to play with the Boston Celtics?" Rosenbluth said. "Yes, I was ready to go."

However, the NBA banned Boston from signing a high school player, sending Rosenbluth back to New York City for what was to be his senior year in high school. By then the New York City high school coaches were on strike, relegating Rosenbluth's prep career to a half-dozen games and leaving him with little formal training in the sport of basketball. Instead, he played for Gimbals in the New York industrial league and joined the Carlton YMCA club, an African American team, led by future college and pro star Sihugo Green, that won 65 straight games. The coach was Hy Gotkin (Harry's cousin), whose younger brother Davey had gone off to N.C. State. They all arranged a tryout for Rosenbluth with Everett Case and the Wolfpack in April of 1952.

After a long train ride to Raleigh, touring the campus with Davey Gotkin and meeting Case for breakfast, Rosenbluth showed up in old Thompson Gym and found pick-up games going on two different courts. He didn't know where everyone came from; some were N.C. State players and some from other colleges. Some were high school kids, which was Case's way of hiding what were really illegal tryouts. "I told Case I was out of shape from not playing," said Rosenbluth, who also smoked at the time. "He said, 'Don't worry about it, just get in there and play.' I ran the court three or four times and couldn't breathe; I was dying. We were playing against State's varsity, and they're running up and down the court, and it was hot as the dickens in there. I just couldn't do it."

Case then spoke with Rosenbluth's father, Jack, a former minor league baseball player who had ridden the train down with Lennie. "Scholarships are hard to come by, and I don't want to waste one; I can't use Lennie," Case said.

Jack Rosenbluth couldn't understand it because Case had invited him to Raleigh for the Dixie Classic and 1952 NCAA Tournament after having worked out his son against the State players during the NIT the previous March. They called Harry Gotkin, one of Case's chief scouts, who was furious and told them to come back to New York. Upon returning, Gotkin took Rosenbluth to the St. John's athletic banquet, which was also a testimonial dinner for the departing McGuire, who had met Rosenbluth several times at Madison Square Garden.

McGuire knew Case favored faster players from Indiana over the more rugged kids from the Northeast. He figured Rosenbluth was raw and hadn't developed many bad habits and he would be well-suited for his instinctive, freelance system. Revealing he would be coaching at either North Carolina or Alabama the next season, McGuire offered Rosenbluth a scholarship as long as he could qualify to get in school. "No matter where you go, I'm going with you," Rosenbluth responded, shaking McGuire's hand. Years later, he said of the moment, "I was just grateful to be getting a scholarship and going somewhere."

So instead of playing and starring for N.C. State, Rosenbluth wound up as one of McGuire's boys. Old-time Wolfpackers have pondered what Rosenbluth himself called a "dumb mistake" ever since. UNC fired Tom Scott after his sixth season and two 12–15 records, failing to finish in the top eight and qualify for the Southern Conference Tournament both years. Worse than that, Scott had become Case's whipping boy, losing all 15 of his games against State, which was in the midst of a dominating 161–39 run and six straight Southern Conference championships. And they weren't close encounters, either, as State won by margins ranging from 26 to 40 points.

Carolina-Duke *football* might have still been the most important rivalry at the time, but clearly the Tar Heels were looking for someone to end the insufferable basketball embarrassment to the perennially powerful Wolfpack. Chuck Erickson and Billy Carmichael had remembered McGuire from his dramatic NCAA upset wins over State and top-ranked Kentucky the prior season.

One early draw for kids considering Carolina turned out to be that freshmen were still eligible in the Southern Conference, and McGuire managed to have his scouts line up a couple of New York-area high school players to come with him.

Unfortunately, Rosenbluth wasn't one of them. He lacked the credits in math and foreign language for admission to UNC. So McGuire suggested he spend a year a Staunton Military Academy in Virginia, where Rosenbluth played a postgraduate season in 1953. By then, McGuire was on the way to winning 17 games at UNC and establishing himself as somewhat of a miracle worker in the eyes of Tar Heel fans.

8 Big Game James

James Worthy made his mark on Carolina basketball during a six-week stretch in which he dominated college basketball and led the Tar Heels to the 1982 NCAA Championship. But Worthy had been involved with the UNC program for more like six years.

Since he was a sophomore in high school, Worthy was on Carolina's can't-miss list of prospects. And that was a tough list to make. "Worthy was one of the only high school players whom I knew would be a great college player, too," Dean Smith said of the 6'8" star from Gastonia, North Carolina, who was a man among boys at Ashbrook High School.

Smith first saw Worthy as a seventh grader at the Carolina Basketball School summer camp and from that point on he heard the rumors that Worthy would wear light blue some day. But when it came time to officially recruit Worthy, it was not a cinch that he would come to Chapel Hill or even stay in his home state.

Actually, Worthy had become so familiar with UNC basketball that it might have been a disadvantage when Michigan State and Kentucky began recruiting him. They could tell him things about their programs that Worthy did not know. Worthy basically knew the Carolina Way by heart. Despite Magic Johnson leading Michigan State to the national championship during Worthy's senior year in high school, Smith was more worried about Kentucky. Wildcats assistant coach Leonard Hamilton (now the head coach at Florida State) was from Gastonia and knew the Worthy family well. Worthy's older brother, Danny, worked in Lexington, Kentucky, for a few years, and the Big Blue recruiting machine was in full throttle to steal away young James.

In the end Worthy saw no logic in spurning his state university and in January of 1979, ended years of speculation by signing with the Tar Heels. But Worthy missed the last 15 games of his freshman season after snapping his ankle late in a home loss to Maryland. And Smith was always concerned that the rod and screws inserted into that ankle would hamper him for the rest of his career.

It was to become a test of endurance that Worthy shared with few people outside the program, a throbbing pain that plagued him through most of his sophomore season. "James comes from a religious family, and while we were devastated, he was more philosophical about it," said assistant coach Eddie Fogler. "His attitude was, 'Hey, it happened, and I'll make the best of it through rehabilitation.'" He missed every third practice, and the ache was especially bad on damp and rainy days. He developed tendinitis in the ankle, and his confidence withered because he didn't know if he could do the things he had always done as a thundering, slam-dunking basketball player.

Despite the pain Worthy slowly regained his confidence and showed old glimpses of his greatness late in the 1981 season. In the NCAA West Regional in Salt Lake City, Worthy and Utah All-American Danny Vranes engaged in an epic battle over 40 minutes before the Tar Heels defeated the Utes on their home court with a loud and boisterous crowd roaring through the entire game.

Al Wood's 39 points against Virginia and Ralph Sampson got the Tar Heels through the national semifinals in Philadelphia, and they awaited the NCAA championship game against Indiana on the day President Reagan was shot by John Hinckley outside a Washington hotel. After it was announced that Reagan was out of trouble, the game was played, but Worthy's foul trouble at the end of the first half and the beginning of the second benched him as the Hoosiers went on to win behind All-American guard Isiah Thomas.

Worthy was one of the players who called the team together for breakfast the next morning before returning to Chapel Hill and pledged to get back to the Final Four the next season and win it. In the offseason the rod and screws were removed from Worthy's ankle, and as a junior, he regained his old form and confidence as the Tar Heels opened the season ranked No. 1 and stayed there much of the year.

Like a true All-American, Worthy was at his best in big games. His first 12 minutes against Virginia in the 1982 ACC Championship in Greensboro, North Carolina, rank as the most impressive stretch of the season for any college basketball player. He made his first eight shots, beginning with a slam dunk off Sam Perkins' opening tip, and sparked Carolina to a 12-point lead over the third-ranked Cavaliers.

His personal *coup de grace* of course was against Georgetown in the national championship game at the Louisiana Superdome, scoring 28 points on 13-of-17 shooting, including four consecutive dunks in the second half. Worthy was always ready to play, but the

Carolina coaches remember him as more intense before that game than any in his career.

The 63–62 win against the Hoyas was to be Worthy's finale as a Tar Heel. He took Smith's advice and turned pro after his junior season, and the Los Angeles Lakers made him the No. 1 pick in the 1982 NBA Draft. Smith was worried that if Worthy returned for his senior season he would reinjure that ankle and, prophetically, Worthy did get hurt as a rookie with the Lakers. By then he had signed his multimillion-dollar guaranteed contract.

In the NBA Worthy became a perennial All-Star for the three-time NBA champion Lakers and earned the nickname "Big Game James." Worthy was also voted to the NBA's 50th Anniversary All-Time Team after he retired in 1994. His stay at UNC was hampered by injuries and cut short by turning pro, but without the kid who had been on their radar for six years, the Tar Heels would never have won Smith's first national championship.

9 Roy Comes Home

When Roy Williams became Carolina's head basketball coach on April 14, 2003, it was one of the most important and fortuitous hires UNC has ever made.

Important because, amid much controversy, the Tar Heels had missed the NCAA Tournament the previous two seasons, and the basketball program that Dean Smith had built into a nationally visible, much-envied, multimillion-dollar enterprise was tilting in a steady breeze created by Duke's dominance and the rest of the Atlantic Coast Conference. Fortuitous because when in 2000 Williams first turned down the UNC job, he'd meant what he said about ending his Hall of Fame career where it started: at Kansas. Luckily for Carolina, Williams had grown unhappy with several decisions made by the KU administration over the previous three years and he was no longer resigned to staying there forever.

Williams also came home because "the family business needed me" and he needed to be closer to the remaining members of his family in the mountains of North Carolina. His father, Babe, and older sister, Frances, would die within Williams' first four years back at Carolina.

As in 2000, Williams took a week to huddle with his wife, Wanda, his children, and his closest friends before making his decision. He knew he had let down millions of UNC alumni and fans three years earlier and wanted to be sure he was still welcome back in Chapel Hill. He also had to find the right words to tell his Kansas players that he was leaving to "go home."

He asked his mentor, Coach Smith, three questions:

"Do you think everyone there will be pleased with me coming back?"

"Would I be their first choice?"

"Are you sure you want me to take this job?"

The last question was important because of all those Tar Heels he had disappointed in 2000. Williams felt the worst about saying no to the man who had given him his start in college basketball.

When Smith answered "yes" to all three questions, Williams said he would meet with his Kansas players the next day and be ready to fly to Chapel Hill that evening. "I couldn't turn Coach Smith down a second time," Williams said.

The special bond Williams had with his former players and coaching colleagues at both schools made leaving Kansas so painful and returning to Carolina so heartfelt. At his introductory press conference in Bowles Hall, Williams wore a tie bearing crimson and blue colors because he wanted everyone watching that night of on ESPN and the next morning to know how much his 15 years as a Jayhawk had meant to him.

But he had a going-forward message for his old and new Tar Heel family members. Turning to the players who had endured 36 losses over the past two seasons, Williams raised an open hand and then closed his fist. He promised if they played together and listened to him, they would be successful. Within one year the Tar Heels were back in the NCAA Tournament. Within two they won the university's fifth—and Williams' first—national championship. Welcome home, indeed.

10 How Frank McGuire Came to North Carolina

As the 1951–52 college basketball season began after Frank McGuire's annual summer vacation with the family to the Catskill Mountains, he sensed it could be his last season at St. John's, and UNC was in his sights after having spent almost two years in Chapel Hill during Navy Flight School in the early 1940s.

He also saw the recruitment of his first black player, sophomore guard Solly Walker who was the most valuable high school player in New York City, as a galvanizing force on his team and preached that they all stick together, especially for their fifth game of the season against defending national champion Kentucky in Lexington, where Walker was sure to hear taunts and slurs.

The powerful Adolph Rupp, who had already chased the most successful football coach in Kentucky history, Paul "Bear" Bryant, off to Texas A&M, had told McGuire that he "can't bring that boy here." But McGuire said he was coming with his entire team and they would all eat and stay together at the same hotel. St. John's took a train from Grand Central Station. They all checked into the hotel in downtown Lexington without incident, and Walker played against the Wildcats in Memorial Gym, where he was jostled by the Kentucky players and harassed by their fans. The result was an 81–40 defeat, the most lopsided loss of McGuire's coaching career.

By the time the teams had a chance to meet again two months later, things had changed to the point where McGuire gave a successful audition to schools that might be looking to hire him as their next coach. Recovering from that blowout, the Redmen won 14 of their next 15 games to help secure NIT and NCAA bids for the second straight year. The NCAA assigned the Johnnies to Raleigh for the East Regional to face Southern Conference champion N.C. State on its home court, and the winner would meet top-ranked Kentucky for the right to advance to the national semifinals in Seattle, where the NCAA was sending Final Four teams for the first time.

McGuire expected the rough reception in redneck Raleigh to be hardest on Walker, and they wound up eating one meal together in the hotel kitchen before McGuire arranged for a local parish priest to take Walker in for the weekend.

The on-court assignment, however, was right in McGuire's wheelhouse, and he knew his improved, battle-tested team was capable of pulling off twin upsets. Wearing his silk suit and tie with a handkerchief perfectly pointed in his breast pocket, McGuire strutted into Reynolds Coliseum in his alligator shoes.

The state of North Carolina took notice when the Redmen held off coach Everett Case's Wolfpack by 11 points, as the red-clad crowd of 12,400 howled at Walker throughout the game. Watching from the stands were UNC athletic director Chuck Erickson and comptroller Billy Carmichael Jr., who were trying to decide whether to fire basketball coach Tom Scott after his second straight losing season.

In the rematch against Kentucky, McGuire used the first game to his advantage because the Redmen had already faced Kentucky All-Americans Cliff Hagan and Frank Ramsay and seven-foot center Bill Spivey. He also assured his team that the fans wouldn't be as bad as they were in Lexington because they didn't care who won. And then he riled them up by revealing that Rupp had already chartered a plane to the Final Four in Seattle and that hundreds of Kentucky fans had made hotel reservations out there. "We rose to the occasion and played our best game against Kentucky," McGuire said afterward. "Great players seem to hit their peak in crucial games, and that was the case. Our guy, 'Zeke' Zawoluk, did everything you could ask by scoring 32 points and holding his own against their big men inside."

St. John's won 64–57 in a game that wasn't that close. Of McGuire's 550 college career victories, one at each of his three schools topped the list: the 1952 win against Kentucky that catapulted the Redmen into their first Final Four; North Carolina's triple-overtime win against Kansas and Wilt Chamberlain five years later for the national championship; and the 1971 ACC Championship win for South Carolina against UNC and his former assistant, Dean Smith.

After the adventure of flying across the country in a small plane that had his players just happy to be back on the ground in Seattle, the Redmen defeated Illinois in the semifinals and then faced Kansas and 6'9" All-American Clyde Lovellette, who led the nation in scoring with a 28.6 scoring average and was unquestionably the best player at the first Final Four. The game was a foreshadowing of five years later, when McGuire and North Carolina would face Kansas again and the next Jayhawks giant, Chamberlain.

Just as it would be in Kansas City in 1957, McGuire's *team* was the equal of Kansas but had to figure out how to handle KU's big man in the middle. St. John's had already eliminated the top two ranked teams in Kentucky and Illinois but had not faced anyone with Lovellette's size and physical gifts. Kansas coach Phog Allen had an offense where everything ran through the future Hall of Famer who was so big that it was almost impossible to keep the ball out of his hands.

McGuire tried to counter by rotating Zawoluk and teammate Jack McMahon, but they gave away too many inches and could not contain Lovellette. Behind his 33 points and 17 rebounds, the Jayhawks built a big lead in the championship game. They led by 14 at halftime, and the margin allowed reserve guard Dean Smith to come off the bench and quarterback the delay game that ran out the clock.

Following the 80–63 Kansas victory, McGuire sought out Lovellette and the victorious Jayhawks and congratulated them all warmly. Smith's hand was among those McGuire shook. Disappointed, McGuire knew he had lost to a better opponent but had also propelled St. John's basketball to a new level, establishing it as more than just a strong New York City team. He also had won the first of his three national Coach of the Year awards at three different schools.

He wasn't sure where he was going, but after five years and posting a 102–36 record at his alma mater, he knew it was time to leave home. McGuire visited Alabama, where Floyd Burdette had just resigned after six years as coach, finishing second in the Southeastern Conference behind Kentucky the last two years. But North Carolina wasn't in the Deep South, and McGuire already had a few friends in Carolina and familiarity with the area. To someone reared on the asphalt of New York, the sand sidewalks and easiness of Chapel Hill touched McGuire in a way the town has for many before and since.

After getting a call from Raleigh entrepreneur Joe Murnick, McGuire met in New York with the vivacious Carmichael, a UNC graduate and one-time Tar Heel basketball player who made millions on Wall Street and then returned home after the stock market crash of 1929. Carmichael served in various roles for the Consolidated University, which included N.C. State, but he loved his alma mater most and wanted to give Case some competition. In charge of the purse strings, Carmichael offered McGuire the job as head basketball coach.

In the same year America elected war hero General Dwight David Eisenhower as president and television became the medium of choice with the *I Love Lucy* show, UNC hired its own dynamic change agent. "My decision was based on what was best for my family," McGuire said. "I didn't think of anything else. We could live in a house for the first time and have a swimming pool where Frankie could exercise. And we could go around town without it being such a hassle. It was just much better family surroundings than in a big city."

In some ways Frankie McGuire, Frank's mentally disabled child, set off a chain reaction that led to a college dynasty. There was even a Frankie McGuire Day in South Carolina, where he lived most of his handicapped life until his death in 2008, hyperbolizing him as the most important person in the history of basketball.

How Smith Met McGuire

The first season of basketball at the new Air Force Academy had been over for two weeks, and Air Force assistant coach Dean Smith was back in Topeka, Kansas, with his wife and two baby daughters, visiting his family. On Wednesday night, March 6, 1957, he listened on the radio to Max Falkenstien's call as Kansas defeated Kansas State in Manhattan by seven points to clinch the old Big

Seven Conference championship and reach 20 wins for the first time in five years.

Since he had been in the Air Force for almost four years, Smith planned to stay through the weekend and catch KU's last home game against Colorado to see KU's Wilt Chamberlain in person for the first time. He had worked with KU coach Dick Harp and the seniors on the current KU team during his postgraduate year and followed their success closely, believing that the Jayhawks were the best team in the country.

Something else was on Smith's mind. His boss, Bob Spear, had invited him to the annual college coaches' convention at the end of the month in Kansas City, where the NCAA Tournament semifinals and championship game were also being played. Spear told Smith they would stay in a hotel suite with three other coaches, among them Frank McGuire, whose UNC team was ranked No. 1 and still undefeated that season.

Spear wanted Smith to go because McGuire might be looking for an assistant coach to some day replace the aging and ailing Buck Freeman. It dawned on Smith that if Kansas and North Carolina kept winning, they could end up playing against each other in what was yet to be officially called the Final Four. The Tar Heels did go on to win the ACC championship and earned their first NCAA Tournament bid in McGuire's UNC tenure.

Spear was older than Smith, 26, and already well connected in the profession. He attended the NCAA coaches' convention at the national semifinals each year but always went alone and met up with coaching colleagues. This time he shared a two-bedroom suite at the Continental Hotel in Kansas City with three other head coaches he knew from the service—Ben Carnevale of the Naval Academy, University of Denver coach Hoyt Brawner, and McGuire, whose Tar Heels were playing that weekend.

Smith was the fifth wheel and slept on rollaway cot in the living room. His mentor, Spear, especially wanted Smith to broaden his coaching contacts and to see if he and McGuire hit it off. Freeman, McGuire's old college coach at St. John's who followed his protégé south, was slowing down and couldn't do as much scouting and recruiting anymore. McGuire wanted to spend more time on the road and knew he would have to replace Freeman sooner than later with a coach who could run things while he went recruiting.

The fact that Kansas had also reached the 1957 Final Four made the blind date somewhat uncomfortable because Smith was also there cheering for his school and several players he knew so well, plus his mentor Harp, to win the national championship. McGuire and Smith met briefly on Friday afternoon before the semifinals. Their paths had crossed once before after the 1952 national championship, when McGuire coached St. John's and Smith rode the bench for Kansas; it was hardly a match made in heaven—wise-ass New Yorker versus proper Kansan. "Whoever heard of anyone named Dean?" McGuire said. "Where I come from, you become a dean. You're not *named* Dean."

The morning after the Jayhawks spanked San Francisco (from where Bill Russell had already graduated) and advanced to the championship game against UNC, which had survived Michigan State in triple overtime to keep the legend alive, McGuire asked Smith perhaps the most important question of his young life to that point. "So, Dean," McGuire said over omelets in the suite, "who will you be pulling for tonight?"

Smith swallowed hard and smiled thinly. "I'm going to stay with the alma mater," he told McGuire.

"That's what I thought you would say," McGuire responded.

After breakfast Smith went for a walk and called his father in Topeka. "I might have blown my chance at the North Carolina job," he said, "because I told Coach McGuire I'd be rooting for the Jayhawks tonight."

"No, I don't think so," Alfred Smith said. "My guess is that Coach McGuire respects that kind of honesty and loyalty."

It's fair to say that North Carolina basketball would look different today if the outcome on March 23, 1957, had been different. The Tar Heels won 54–53 in their second triple-overtime victory in two nights. Smith sat depressed, chin in palm, watching the Tar Heels cut down the nets. He went into the Kansas locker room to console Harp and then walked back to the hotel. McGuire entered the suite with Spear, Carnevale, and Brawner. The Tar Heel players—all showered and dressed in their blazers and ties—trickled in shortly after ready to hit the town as national champs.

McGuire asked each of the coaches to say something to his team, and Smith replied that he was so upset with the outcome of the game that he didn't feel like talking. McGuire insisted, almost as if he were putting Smith through another aspect of the interview process. "You guys had it at the end," Smith recounted saying in his autobiography. "Congratulations. But I certainly wasn't cheering for you."

At breakfast the next morning with Smith, McGuire began by talking about Freeman, his old coach at St. John's who he had hired at North Carolina and saved from a life of alcoholism. He was also a brilliant assistant, better with X's and O's than McGuire, and so dedicated to the players' welfare that he checked their curfews in the middle of the night and followed them to the movies when they skipped class during the day. Whether he stayed one more season or not, Freeman's condition was worsening. McGuire said it was up to Buck, but sooner or later he would need an assistant who could conduct practice while he was recruiting in New York. McGuire didn't seem to mind that Smith was from Kansas with no connections in the Northeast. He had already been in North Carolina for five years, had it in his contract that he could spend summers at his lake home in Greenwood Lake, New York, and was clearly itching to log more time on the recruiting trail. His disabled son, Frankie, was now six and doing so well that McGuire could leave home for longer stints while his wife, Pat, managed the three children.

Feeling awkward to be considered by the school that had just taken down his beloved Jayhawks, Smith answered uncomfortably that he didn't expect to remain in the Air Force long term but that his official discharge was not until April of 1958. McGuire said that was okay; if Buck stayed on one more season, the offer would still be good the next year. Smith remained torn between his love for Kansas, where he might have a chance to return and coach under Harp, and the truth that working for McGuire with the defending national champions would be a great learning experience. They shook hands, agreed to stay in touch, and see what happened.

At the 1958 Final Four in Louisville, Smith again shared a suite with Spear and McGuire. Although McGuire was disappointed to miss the NCAA Tournament again, it gave him more time to spend with Smith. The same four head coaches—McGuire, Spear, Carnevale, and Brawner— took Smith to dinner that was more like a fraternity rush. Spear thought Smith should leave Air Force and spread his wings, Carnevale had already coached at North Carolina, and Brawner believed working with McGuire would bolster Smith's resume beyond going back to a system he knew at KU.

McGuire, who had also talked to his former player Al McGuire about the job, decided he wanted Smith and, with typical Irish bluster and charm, promised to make him the highest paid assistant in the country. Smith agreed to visit Chapel Hill in April, and that pretty much sealed the deal. "When I arrived I fell in love at first sight," Smith wrote in his autobiography. "The town was in its full springtime glory with dogwoods and cherry trees in blossom and petals floating in the breeze and dusting the footpaths."

After conferring with his wife, Ann, who was back in Denver and pregnant with their third child, Smith accepted. McGuire took him scouting for houses so it would be easier for Ann to choose when she arrived in North Carolina. The two coaches ate virtually three meals together and played golf and handball, getting very close very quickly.

McGuire taught Smith an early lesson that in all organizations there are circles within circles, and you fight to take care of the people closest to you first—a principle on which Smith built autonomy at UNC that far exceeded what McGuire had, sprouting a multi-branched tree that grew into the fabled Carolina basketball family. Those in the so-called inner circle got pushed for the best jobs and highest draft picks, and Smith was more reticent about helping anyone else without Carolina ties. Smith was McGuire's assistant for three seasons before chancellor Bill Aycock elevated him to head coach when McGuire resigned in August of 1961.

12 NBA Draft Master

Twenty-seven of Dean Smith's players were selected in the first round of the NBA draft over 37 years—from Billy Cunningham in 1965 through Vince Carter and Antawn Jamison in 1998. Brendan Haywood, whom Smith recruited before he retired, was drafted in the first round in 2001. Among the obvious first rounders and can't-miss pros were Cunningham, Charles Scott, Bobby Jones, Phil Ford, James Worthy, Michael Jordan, Sam Perkins, Brad Daugherty, Jerry Stackhouse, and Rasheed Wallace. Others, of less renown, at the very least earned good livings as pros.

For every Bob McAdoo, the NBA Rookie of the Year and MVP, was a Dudley Bradley, who never averaged in double figures in college or the NBA. For every Mitch Kupchak, who continually overcame injuries to win an NBA title, was Tom LaGarde, who never fully recovered from a blown knee his senior year to reach his

Twenty-seven of Dean Smith's players were selected in the first round of the NBA draft, including All-Stars (from left to right) James Worthy, Michael Jordan, and Walter Davis.

full pro potential. For every Walter Davis, another NBA Rookie of the Year and six-time All-Star, was Mike O'Koren, whom *USA TODAY* once called the NBA's best all-around player, but didn't play in an All-Star Game. For every Kenny Smith, who set NBA records for three-pointers, there was a Joe Wolf, a career journeyman whose biggest claim to fame was lasting 11 years with seven different NBA teams. For every Hubert Davis, a great shooter who made it, there was an Al Wood, a better shooter who never reached pro stardom. And for every Rick Fox, who turned out to be a better pro than college player, there was an Eric Montross who turned out not as good.

The common denominator? They all played for Smith and were considered anywhere from sure shots to good gambles by the various NBA teams that drafted them in the first round. Smith cajoled some pro coaches and general managers into picking his players, such as J.R. Reid in 1989 and Pete Chilcutt in 1991. Others needed no convincing. "You don't have to teach Carolina players much," Pat Riley was already saying in 1986. "They come to us with fundamentals, running, passing, moving without the ball…and they understand the pressure at the top, that they are expected to produce night after night."

No coach put anywhere near as many players into pro basketball as Smith did while he was at UNC. Smith's legions filled more roster spots, played more minutes, scored more points and—largely due to Jordan—made more money than the respective alumni of any other college program in the Smith era. Eleven different Tar Heels were members of 17 NBA championship teams between 1967 and 1998. In all, 75 of Smith's Tar Heels were drafted somewhere by someone in the NBA, and dozens more played in the old CBA and overseas. Smith's consuming goal was that any of his graduates who wanted to continue playing basketball would find a job in short pants. He was successful almost all of the time, particularly with players trying to squeeze out one or two years of (more) active duty.

Smith got the late Geoff Crompton, who barely played two full seasons in college, onto the roster of the Denver Nuggets, who in 1978 were coached by former UNC star and assistant Larry Brown. Darrell Elston, a one-year star in college, played one season in hte NBA and one in the old ABA. John Kuester, overshadowed by four fellow starters in 1977 who would all be first-round picks, was a third-round pick and lasted three years as a pro player before holding several college and pro head coaching jobs, including with the Detroit Pistons. Scott Williams' name wasn't called on draft day, but Jordan convinced the Bulls to sign him as a free agent in 1990, the first of three straight world title seasons for the Bulls. Williams left Chicago for Philadelphia in 1994 with three championship rings and lasted 11 more years in the NBA with five other teams.

George Lynch, whose heart far exceeded his talent, rode the coattails of Carolina's 1993 NCAA Championship to a big pro contract with the Lakers, and that sustained him when he got traded three years later. And Kevin Salvadori, hardly considered a legitimate college star, played two years in the NBA. Like Chilcutt three years before him, Salvadori was a longshot as a high school recruit before redshirting as a freshman. They both developed rapidly and made substantial money playing pro ball when hundreds of other players with similar, if not greater, ability never got the chance.

13 Antawn, the Duke Killer

Antawn Jamison was first-team All-ACC all three seasons he played at UNC and the ACC Player of the Year and MVP of the ACC Tournament as a junior, when he was also national Player of the Year. After his junior season, the Charlotte native was selected as the No. 4 pick in the 1998 NBA Draft by Toronto. (Shortly thereafter, he was traded for his teammate and classmate Vince Carter, drafted No. 5 overall by Golden State, and both enjoyed long, fruitful NBA careers.)

But Jamison saved his best performances for Duke. He was 5–2 in seven games against the Blue Devils. As a freshman Jamison had 23 points and 14 rebounds and 11 and nine in two wins over Duke.

As a sophomore he "slumped" to 10 and four in his first loss to the archrival and then came back with 33 points and 11 rebounds in the rematch in the regular season finale as Carolina went on to win the 1997 ACC Tournament, where junior Shammond Williams won the MVP by averaging 20 points and five assists in the three games.

And in his last season, Jamison recorded 35 points and 11 rebounds, 23 points and 13 rebounds, and 22 points and 18 rebounds (the latter despite a sore groin) in the two regular-season games and ACC Tournament championship, respectively, against Duke. That means Jamison averaged 22.4 points and 11.4 rebounds in his career against the Blue Devils. Think the Dukies were glad to see him go?

In fact, after Jamison departed, Duke went on to win 15 of the next 17 games against the Tar Heels. For his career Jamison averaged 19 points and 10 rebounds, and earning national Player of the Year in 1998, which is why his retired jersey (No. 33) is on the front row in the rafters of the Smith Center.

14 The L&M Boys and the Class of 1969

On January 4, 1967, in Winston-Salem, North Carolina, the Tar Heels opened their milestone ACC season against Wake Forest. The score was tied at 74, and the Deacons had the ball with less than a minute remaining. Bobby Lewis was dogging Wake guard Paul Long, trying to disrupt Long's dribble with his spindly arms and legs. Finally, with the clock winding down and the Deacons fans on their feet and howling, Lewis flicked the ball away into the open court.

Retrieving it, Lewis pitched ahead to a breaking Larry Miller, who caught up to the ball just as he was going under the Wake basket. With a move he had honed on the playgrounds of Pennsylvania, Miller spun the ball up off the left side of the backboard in one motion and kept running. Still at full speed and looking back over his shoulder, he watched the ball glance off the glass and into the basket, and then the muscular Miller collided with UNC sports information director Jack Williams, who was on the runway to the locker room. Williams went down like a load, and Miller never broke stride. He crashed through the locked dressing room door, taking it off at the hinges. Miller yelped once, took off his uniform, and hit the showers. By the time a wounded Williams walked in with coach Dean Smith, Miller was slicking back his wet pompadour in the mirror.

For sure, it was going to be some kind of season for the Tar Heels.

* * *

"You have to say we were lucky that Rusty Clark and Bill Bunting were born in this state," Smith said many times over the years, "because they and the others we recruited that year represented the turning point of our program."

Clark, Bunting, Dick Grubar, Joe Brown, and Gerald Tuttle—the famed Class of 1969—gave Carolina the height and quality depth it lacked in Smith's first five seasons. But their biggest gift to Carolina basketball was the freedom that allowed the reigning stars of the team to play where—and how—they would be most effective.

In 1967, when the Tar Heels won their first ACC championship and Final Four trip under Smith, it was the "L&M Boys"—senior Lewis and junior Miller—who really took the pressure off the highly touted sophomores. Not the other way around, as is popularly thought. "The sophomores were put in the best possible position because they were joining two fabulous players and didn't have to be the stars right away," said Larry Brown, SMU's current head coach and Smith's assistant in '67.

Lewis and Miller, Smith's first two marquee recruits, had played out of position up to that point in their college careers because they were needed on the front line. A wiry leaper who regularly won dunking contests from kids almost a foot taller on the Washington playgrounds, the 6'3" Lewis had played the pivot for the UNC freshmen in 1964, power forward next to center Billy Cunningham in '65, and small forward in '66 when the bullish Miller moved up to the varsity. That's the year Lewis set the single-game Carolina scoring record of 49 points against Florida State that still stands.

As a senior, he went outside to the big guard spot, unselfishly passing the ball more than shooting it. While setting up his taller teammates, he averaged six less shots as his scoring dropped from 27 points a game to 18.5. "Bobby made the biggest sacrifice of all, no question about it," Miller said 30 years later. "His game changed the most to accommodate the team, to make us better."

The presence of the seven-foot Clark and 6'9" Bunting allowed Miller to move to the wing, where he was a triple threat. He could shoot his left-handed jumper, feed the post, or take it to the hole. As a junior he averaged 22 points a game and won the first of two straight ACC Player of the Year awards.

"When Coach signed Bobby and Larry, people took notice and said, 'Whoa!'" Brown said. "The pieces were falling into place, and I knew we were going to be really good in 1967 because I had coached the freshmen coming up. But I was kind of surprised we played so well together early."

Miller and Lewis had lost to the freshmen in an open scrimmage before the season started, after which Brown had been scolded by his boss for creating so much spirit on the frosh team that it caused disharmony in the overall program. But Miller welcomed the sophomores when they moved up to the varsity. "I recruited those guys when they visited because I wanted to win," he said. "We just had the chemistry, and things jelled. It seemed like we could beat anybody we played."

Carolina won 16 of its first 17 games, losing only to Princeton when Clark sat out with the flu. Among the victories was a 59–56 upset of Duke in Durham, which signaled the changing of the guard in the ACC.

After five years of some narrow losses on the court, Smith's luck seemed to be changing as well. With the score tied 56–56 and the clock ticking, he was trying to get a timeout when Clark hit Miller for the winning lay-up. "I can't tell you how happy I was that nobody had seen my timeout signal," Smith said after the game.

Of course, Vic Bubas wasn't letting the mantle go without a fight even after Carolina won the rematch in Chapel Hill by 13 points to clinch first place in the ACC standings for the first time under Smith. Duke had been the media darling for years, and when the teams met for a third time a week later in the ACC Tournament championship game in Greensboro, most members of the press were still picking the Blue Devils to win.

Trying to keep the Heels loose and away from the speculation that Carolina couldn't beat Duke three times in the same season, Smith had opened practice the week of the tournament by playing volleyball with them in Carmichael Auditorium. "I made sure to have Rusty Clark on my team," Smith quipped. "He's some volleyball player."

The Tar Heels beat Duke a third time, earning the ACC's only entry into the NCAA Tournament and ending the Blue Devils' dominance in the league. It would be 11 years and three head coaches before Duke won another ACC championship. "People today don't understand what kind of pressure that was," Miller recalled. "You had to win three games in three days or you weren't going anywhere, no matter what you did in the regular season. I had to tell my parents, 'You can't come down here for the tournament.' I couldn't sleep. I couldn't eat. My stomach was in knots."

Miller, who had been in a late-season shooting slump, hit 13-of-14 shots in the final for 32 points. "I remember the one I missed, too," said Miller, who also had 11 rebounds against Duke. "It was from the corner, and when I let it go, I thought it was in. It was just one of those games when I was in a frame of mind. I knew it was in the bag."

Lewis scored 26 points, continuing his late-season surge after Smith and Miller had both told him to shoot more. "I haven't been stupid enough to try to completely turn Lewis into a playmaker," Smith had told Frank Deford of *Sports Illustrated* in February.

Lewis' personal best as a senior was during the NCAA East Regional in College Park, Maryland, near his hometown, when he won the MVP after leading the Tar Heels against Princeton, avenging the earlier loss, and Boston College. Afterward, Lewis' sister threw a giant "Final Four" party for the team and some Carolina fans.

Like Lewis, who played a few years with the San Francisco Warriors in the NBA, Miller had a solid career with several teams in the old ABA. He owns the ABA single-game scoring record of 67 points when he played for the Carolina Cougars. Clark, who still has the single-game UNC record of 30 rebounds against Maryland, turned down pro basketball to attend medical school and became a successful thoracic surgeon in his home town of Fayetteville.

Bunting, from New Bern, played a while in the ABA and works for a government housing agency in Raleigh. His college career improved steadily each year, and that's underscored by the relatively amazing improvement of his field goal shooting from 43 percent as a junior to 60 percent as a senior—when he took 164 more shots than the previous season.

The popular Grubar also had a short stint in pro basketball, but the knee injury he suffered in the 1969 ACC Tournament finals never healed enough for him to keep playing. The quarterback and matinee idol of the Tar Heels, Grubar returned to North Carolina after five years as an assistant college coach to enter private business.

The Class of 1969 was the only one in ACC history to win three straight regular-season titles outright and three consecutive ACC Tournaments. It compiled a three-year varsity record of 81–15 with five of the losses coming in three trips to the Final Four. Their ACC record was 45–6, and the class never lost to N.C. State, Wake Forest, Virginia, or Maryland.

15 The Secret of Silent Sam Perkins

Two hand-written notes led to two of the longest arms in college basketball coming to Carolina.

One note was scribbled on a piece of paper by Dean Smith during the summer of 1979 at the National Sports Festival in Colorado Springs. After watching a gangly kid play on an All-Star team that lost two straight games, Smith jotted down, "Has quickness, size and ability…a must for recruiting."

The other note arrived the same summer and came from Julius Girmindl, the coach at Shaker High School in Latham, New York. Girmindl wrote Smith in long hand. "I have a 6'10" player who is interested in attending North Carolina next year. Could you send some literature?"

It was one of hundreds of inquiries the Carolina basketball office received each year. But this one stuck in Smith's mind, and in September, coach Eddie Fogler was on what would be the first of many flights to Albany, New York, to watch Sam Perkins play. Fogler could not believe what he saw. The youngster had speed, quickness, shooting touch, and, yes, arms that hung to his knees when he stood up straight. "Just watching him warm up," Fogler said, "you could see how talented he was. Then when you meet him, *wow, what a great individual!*"

But how was it, Fogler wondered, that such a 6'10" high school senior was so unknown? The story is one of the more interesting in sports.

Samuel Bruce Perkins grew up in Bedford-Stuyvesant, the poorest section of Brooklyn. He lived with his grandmother, Martha, a Jehovah's Witness who cared far more about Sam staying home and studying than hanging out on the playgrounds. Consequently, Sam Perkins wasn't even on his basketball team his sophomore year at Tilden High School.

It was then that Perkins met Herb Crossman, a 31-year-old recent graduate of Fordham University who was soon to take a job outside of Albany. Crossman was walking past Tilden one afternoon when he saw an exceptionally tall youngster get off a school bus in the company of a couple of girls. Crossman, who coached a recreation league team called the Brooklyn Hoopsters, made several attempts to find the identity of the big fellow, then 14 years old. Finally, one of his players from Tilden said the mystery kid must have been "Kareem," a nickname given because of his height. Crossman's informant added, "He doesn't even know how to play." Crossman thought that could be fixed and recruited Perkins for the Hoopsters.

Quickly recognizing that Perkins was an extraordinary person and potentially a great athlete, Crossman knew that getting him out of Brooklyn was Sam's best chance for success.

Crossman asked Martha Perkins if he could become her grandson's legal guardian and take him to the suburbs of upstate New York. She agreed.

Some athletes have the natural aptitude for a sport, and Perkins was one of them. He became an instant star at Shaker High School, often dominating games in his first year of organized basketball. Perkins didn't attend any All-Star camps that summer and, because few college coaches were there, did not attract much more than Smith's attention at the National Sports Festival. Thus, Perkins wasn't rated highly by the numerous prep scouting services.

Coaches, though, began to notice, and the schools on Perkins' priority list were: UCLA, North Carolina, Syracuse, Duke, Notre Dame, and San Francisco. Any player narrowing his choices to those schools must be pretty good or suffering from delusions of grandeur. They found the answer at the Dapper Dan Roundball Classic after Perkins' senior year. He dominated that game, blocking shots, running the court like a deer, shooting that soft, lefty jumper. Coaches from around the country went bonkers, but they couldn't get a foot in the door. Perkins was down to six schools, and six it would stay.

On a sunny Saturday in the late spring of 1980, while the Beach Boys were playing a concert in Kenan Stadium, word leaked out that Perkins had indeed picked Carolina as his college choice. He would join a team that had sophomore James Worthy, junior Jimmy Black, and senior Al Wood. A fellow freshman signee was another New York product, Matt Doherty.

Quiet and polite throughout his entire career, Perkins was nicknamed "Silent Sam" by more than one UNC fan for the statue that sits on campus overlooking Franklin Street. At Carolina he would lull opponents to sleep with the same "lazy" demeanor. Then, whoosh, a little jump hook from the keyhole; swish, an arching jumper from the baseline; bam, a two-handed jam after beating his man down court; and, swat, another rejection by the long arms of the lane.

When the ACC added its experimental three-point line during his junior year, it was a bomb, as Perkins stepped outside to drain 12 treys on unbelieving opponents. He was on his way to making three straight All-American teams, becoming only the fourth player in UNC history to that point to do it. (Jack Cobb was the first way back in the 1920s.)

The best-kept secret in recruiting had become a national celebrity since his sophomore year when he teamed with Worthy, Black, Doherty, and Michael Jordan to lead the Tar Heels to the 1982 national championship. By then the coaches who had lost Perkins realized what they had missed. Their loss was Carolina's all-time gain, as Perkins' jersey hangs in the rafters of the Smith Center with the other royalty of Tar Heel basketball.

16 Phil Ford and the Everlasting Heroes

Arguably, Phil Ford remains the most popular athlete ever in the state of North Carolina. David Thompson was the *best* college player from the Tar Heel State and led N.C. State to the 1974 national championship, but he didn't have Ford's spunk. Thompson also had the Wolfpack's 1973 probation from his recruitment hanging over his head. Ford is remembered for two special games: beating State and winning ACC Tournament MVP as a freshman in 1975 and scoring 34 points while playing with an injured left wrist to upset eventual ACC champion and Final Four-bound Duke in his 1978 Senior Game.

After winning national Player of the Year, Ford was the second pick in the draft by the Kansas City Kings, won NBA Rookie of the Year, and was a three-time All-Star before his career ended due to injuries and alcoholism. Ford recovered and was on the UNC coaching staff for 12 seasons and today shares his unabridged story with kids, high school and college players, and families. His battle with addiction has not kept him from remaining one of the most revered sports heroes in the state.

* * *

Sam Perkins played on the 1982 national championship team and starred for the top-ranked Tar Heels of 1984, but he is beloved for more than his 2,145 career points and 1,167 rebounds (both in the top three in UNC history). Perkins stayed four years because he liked being a student more than a basketball player. Before the 1983 NCAA Regional Final against Georgia, he famously and innocently said that he didn't know what league the Bulldogs were in.

Perkins was the fourth pick in the 1984 NBA Draft by the Dallas Mavericks and had a 17-year pro career for four different teams. Unlike UNC teammates James Worthy, who makes his home in Los Angeles, and Michael Jordan, who can't go anywhere in public, Perkins visits Chapel Hill regularly and moves around town easily with a big smile.

* * *

Eric Montross has become even more of a hero since his two-All-American seasons and the 1993 NCAA Championship at Carolina. He was the ninth pick by the Boston Celtics, made the Rookie All-Star game, and second-team All-Rookie Team in 1995, but he bounced around for five more NBA teams before retiring after his eighth season.

He returned to Chapel Hill, where he heads up the Dean Smith Fund for the Rams Club, holds a unique Father-Son camp during the summer with a long waiting list, and is the analyst on the Tar Heel basketball radio network. Approachable and extremely popular, Montross is considered one of Carolina's top ambassadors.

17 The Clemson Streak

Along with the Tar Heels winning their third straight Southern championship, the 1926 season is remembered for two historic winning streaks—one that came to an end and one that began. The streak that ended was UNC's 27 consecutive victories against the so-called North Carolina Big Five opponents, which dated back to March 5, 1921, when Carolina defeated Trinity for the state championship. This amazing streak came to an end on Wednesday, January 20, at Wake Forest when the Baptists nipped the Tar Heels 29–28.

Five days earlier, however, an even more impressive streak began, one that continues 87 years later. On Friday, January 15, 1926, Clemson visited Chapel Hill for the first time, and Carolina, after jumping to a 23–0 lead, routed the Tigers 50–20. That game would represent the first win in a streak that would reach 57 games on January 26, 2014, when UNC defeated Clemson 80–61 in the Smith Center. Carolina is 57–0 against Clemson in Chapel Hill, an NCAA record for the longest home winning streak against a single opponent.

But here are 10 UNC-Clemson Games in Chapel Hill when the streak could have ended.

Date: 1/3/36
Score: UNC 24, Clemson 23
Record: 3–0
Location: The Tin Can
Leading Scorer: Earl Ruth
The streak almost ended before it got started. Down 24–21 with less than a minute to play, Clemson guard Ed Kitchens hit a shot from the corner to pull the visitors to within one point. The Tigers

then controlled the center jump (which in those days occurred after every basket), but very little time remained. Clemson forward Popeye Crawford heaved the ball from near midcourt, but it was wide of the basket allowing the White Phantoms to escape with a 24–23 win.

Date: 2/2/74
Score: UNC 61, Clemson 60
Record: 23–0
Location: Carmichael Auditorium
Leading Scorer: Walter Davis
Clemson led 49–43 with eight minutes to play, and it looked like the streak would end at 22 straight. With 1:14 remaining and Clemson clinging to a 58–57 lead, Darrell Elston hit a 20-footer over the Tigers' zone to give the Heels a lead they wouldn't relinquish. Elston's two free throws with nine seconds remaining made the score 61–58, virtually securing the victory. (There was no three-point basket in those days.) Clemson's Tree Rollins scored at the buzzer for the final 61–60 margin. "We feel very fortunate to win," Dean Smith said afterward in an understatement.

Date: 1/9/75
Score: UNC 74, Clemson 72
Record: 24–0
Location: Carmichael Auditorium
Leading Scorer: Walter Davis
Carolina was coming off two straight losses in the Big Four Tournament. Clemson was on a roll, and just about everyone believed the Tar Heels would lose this one. Things went as expected in the first half as the Tigers jumped to a 30–14 lead. The Heels cut the lead to five by halftime, setting up a second-half battle between the two ACC rivals. With 1:05 remaining and Clemson leading 72–71, freshman Stan Rome was fouled and went to the

line for a one-and-one free throw. Rome missed, Mitch Kupchak rebounded, and Walter Davis hit a jump shot on the break to give UNC a 73–72 lead. Clemson worked the clock, and with time running out, Rome drove and charged into Kupchak, giving Carolina possession. John Kuester hit one of two free throws with two seconds remaining to secure UNC's 74–72 win. The Tigers contributed to their own demise in this one, going an abysmal 14–32 from the free throw line.

Date: 1/26/80
Score: UNC 73, Clemson 70
Record: 27–0
Location: Carmichael Auditorium
Leading Scorer: Al Wood

Probably the best team in Clemson basketball history ventured into Carmichael Auditorium for a regionally televised game on Saturday, January 26, 1980. Led by Larry Nance and Billy Williams, the '80 Tigers would make it all the way to the West Regional final before losing to UCLA. But on this Saturday, the streak would continue as Rich Yonaker and Al Wood led the Heels to a hard-fought 73–70 win.

Date: 2/21/87
Score: UNC 96, Clemson 80
Record: 33–0
Location: Smith Center
Leading Scorer: Jeff Lebo

The third-ranked Tar Heels and the No. 10-ranked Tigers entered the game with identical 24–2 records and fighting for first place in the ACC standings. The game represented a legitimate opportunity for the Tigers to break the dreaded streak, but the league-leading Tar Heels would have none of it. Led by Jeff Lebo (24 points) and Joe Wolf (21 points), Carolina won going away 96–80.

Date: 1/26/97
Score: UNC 61, Clemson 48
Record: 43–0
Location: Smith Center
Leading Scorer: Antawn Jamison

It was Super Bowl Sunday of 1997, and the Tar Heels were struggling. After traveling to Europe at the end of December, a road-weary Carolina team opened the conference schedule by losing its first three ACC games. When the Tigers came calling at the end of January, the Heels were coming off a loss to Florida State and stood 2–4 in the conference and 11–5 overall. The whispers were growing louder: Dean Smith was slipping. On January 26, 1997, anyone who predicted that Smith would break Adolph Rupp's record less than two months later would have been fitted for a straitjacket. But as had happened so many times before, the Heels got well at home against Clemson and turned the season around in the process. Led by Antawn Jamison's 22 points and Vince Carter's great defense on Clemson point guard Terrell McIntyre, Carolina won 61–48. UNC would then go on to win 16 of its next 17 games before losing to eventual national champion Arizona in the national semifinals at the Final Four in Indianapolis.

Date: 2/27/02
Score: UNC 96, Clemson 78
Record: 48–0
Location: Smith Center
Leading Scorer: Adam Boone

The 2002 Tar Heels suffered through the worst season in the history of UNC basketball. If ever there was a year when Clemson felt confident playing in Chapel Hill, 2002 was it. Carolina entered the game having lost 13 of its last 15, was last in the ACC standings, and going nowhere. There was no reason to believe the Tar Heels would protect the home court and keep the streak alive. But they did. Motivated by the streak (i.e. not wanting to be the first UNC team to lose to Clemson at home), the 2002 Heels played their best game of the season and won going away 96–78 behind 23 points and 10 rebounds from guard Adam Boone.

Date: 1/14/03
Score: UNC 68, Clemson 66
Record: 49–0
Location: Smith Center
Leading Scorer: Rashad McCants

Another one that got away from the Tigers. The Tar Heels trailed 49–43 with 13:44 left and looked dead in the water. At that point, Jawad Williams hit three straight shots over a one-minute span to get his teammates and the Smith Center crowd back in the game. With the score tied at 56, Rashad McCants took control, hitting two three-pointers and a follow shot to give the Heels a 64–60 lead with 1:56 remaining. The Tigers pulled within one before Raymond Felton helped seal the win at the free throw line.

Date: 2/10/08
Score: UNC 103, Clemson 93 (2OT)
Record: 53–0
Location: Smith Center
Leading Scorer: Tyler Hansbrough

This one was probably the cruelest of them all, as Clemson led the entire game. After Demontez Stitt's layup with 8:56 to play, Clemson led 68–53, and the 52-game streak looked to be history. This, however, was a special group of Tar Heels, a group that would finish first in the ACC standings in 2007, 2008, and 2009; win the ACC Tournament in 2007 and 2008; win the East Regional in 2008 and South Regional in 2009; and win the national championship in 2009. Trailing by 15 the Heels proceeded to hit 11 of their next 15 shots, including four three-pointers to tie the score at

82 and force overtime. It took two overtimes, but Carolina finally prevailed 103–93.

Date: 1/26/14
Score: UNC 80, Clemson 61
Record: 57–0
Location: Smith Center
Leading Scorer: James Michael McAdoo

Yet another UNC-Clemson matchup in Chapel Hill where a struggling Carolina team got well against the Tigers. The Tar Heels entered the game 1–4 in the ACC and 11–7 overall, and Clemson was 4–2 and 13–5. The way the Heels had played in losses to Wake Forest, Miami, Syracuse, and Virginia, many expected a Clemson win. Once again protecting "the streak" motivated a UNC basketball team to play one of its best games of the season. It was never close as the Tar Heels turned a 37–21 halftime lead into a 31-point advantage midway through the second half to win handily 80–61.

Miller Time

The true turning point of Carolina basketball in the Dean Smith Era, which means the program's perpetuity, was the signing of Pennsylvania strong boy Larry Miller, the 6'4" left-handed brute who like most Pennsylvanians was earmarked for Duke. If Miller had gone ahead and signed with the Blue Devils in 1964, they would have retained their dominance in the ACC and as one of the top programs in the country. But after a succession of stars from Art Heyman to Jeff Mullins to Jack Marin to Bob Verga who led Duke to the 1963, '64, and '66 NCAA Final Fours, the talent pendulum swung toward UNC.

Smith had two great players in his early years at Carolina—Billy Cunningham and Bob Lewis—and Miller would make the third. Then, a year later, came the freshman class of 1966 with seven-foot Rusty Clark, 6'9" Bill Bunting, and 6'4" point guard Dick Grubar. Together with Lewis and Miller in 1967, the Tar Heels dethroned Duke as ACC champions and advanced to Smith's first Final Four and the school's first in 10 years—or since the undefeated season of 1957 under Frank McGuire.

After Lewis graduated, Charles Scott joined the UNC varsity as the school's first African American scholarship athlete, and the beat went on for two more Final Fours in 1968 and '69. But breaking the ice against Duke in 1967 was the key, and Miller was the focal point. Miller averaged 22 points and nine-plus rebounds per game and was neck-and-neck with Duke's Verga for ACC Player of the Year honors. When the teams met for the conference championship in Greensboro on March 11, 1967, in the then 9,000-seat Greensboro Coliseum, everything was on the line. The winner (and only the winner) would advance to the NCAA Tournament, and the victorious team's star would win the league's highest honor.

Earlier in the week, noting that Carolina had already beaten Duke in the home-and-home regular season series, *Greensboro Daily News* sports Editor "Smitty" Barrier wrote a column predicting the Blue Devils would win because they were tournament tested, and it was hard for any ACC team to beat another good team three times in the same season. Miller tore that column out of the newspaper and pasted it inside his locker during the week of practice, when Smith tried to keep the team loose by setting up a volleyball net one day and splitting up the squad for a match. Miller took the article with him to Greensboro folded it up and put it inside his sneaker before the championship game against Duke.

Verga had 20 points for Duke, but Miller was clearly the star with 32 points on 13-of-14 shooting from the floor. And he thought the shot he missed, a jumper from the right corner, was in all the way. Miller also had 11 rebounds to lead both teams. Lewis added 26 points for the Tar Heels who led 40–34 at the half and held on to win 82–73 as they established themselves as the new power in the ACC.

After the game in the cramped locker room underneath the Coliseum playing floor, Miller took the sweaty article out of his shoe and showed it to Barrier when he came in with the rest of the media. The player and sports editor shared a laugh. On Monday the ACC Player of the Year voting was released, and Miller edged Verga 52–48. Carolina went on to win the NCAA East Regional in College Park, Maryland, avenging a regular season loss to Princeton in overtime 78–70 and defeating Bob Cousy-coached Boston College. The Tar Heels advanced to the Final Four in Louisville where they let an early lead get away against Dayton and lost to the Flyers and their star Donnie May.

It was just as important for Carolina to stay on top in the ACC as get there, and in 1968 the Tar Heels repeated as regular season champions and ACC Tournament champs as did Miller as tournament MVP and ACC Player of the Year. They returned to the Final Four, this time in Los Angeles, defeating Ohio State in the national semifinals before losing to top-ranked and undefeated UCLA led by Lew Alcindor (later Kareem Abdul-Jabbar).

19 Kenny "The Jet" Smith

Virginia had been hot on Kenny Smith's trail since his junior year at Archbishop Molloy High School in Queens, New York. UVa assistant Jim Larranaga (now head coach at Miami) had played at Molloy and remained close with head coach Jack Curran. The late Curran was a legendary high school coach and very much a Dean Smith-type figure to Larranaga and others who had played for him.

This was in the fall of 1982 after UNC had won the national championship in New Orleans by edging Georgetown on freshman Michael Jordan's jumper. Virginia was certain it wanted Kenny Smith in its backcourt and urged him to sign early during the November signing period. But now UNC was considered the best program in the country. The Tar Heels would be losing point guard Jimmy Braddock, and there was a wide-open spot in the starting lineup. They had Buzz Peterson coming back as the heir apparent, but they still wanted to sign another point guard. Smith decided to wait and sign somewhere in the spring.

Dean Smith saw "The Jet" play in December and loved his speed, quickness, ball handling, and maturity on the court. Curran had known the Carolina coaches for years and previously recommended one of his players, unknown point guard Jimmy Black, in 1977. Curran was going to let his next star guard make up his own mind.

The Jet had a great senior season, and Carolina was anxious for him to play in the McDonald's All-Star Game that spring so he could meet Joe Wolf and Dave Popson who had already signed with the Tar Heels. However, Virginia's Ralph Sampson was receiving the Naismith Player of the Year award at the McDonald's banquet and during his acceptance speech Sampson praised Virginia and

Now known for his television presence on TNT, Kenny Smith drives by Duke's Tommy Amaker during Smith's freshman season, which was slowed by a wrist injury.

said it was worthy of any recruit's consideration—especially Kenny Smith. Rumors abounded that The Jet would indeed play for coach Terry Holland and the Cavaliers.

The following Tuesday, though, Smith bitterly disappointed Virginia and stunned the basketball world by signing with UNC. Larranaga was quoted as saying The Jet made a mistake. A more diplomatic Holland said, "I'm not sure Carolina knows exactly what it has."

If the Tar Heels didn't know, they found out quickly, as Smith won the point guard position and joined a lineup that included sophomore Brad Daugherty, junior Jordan, and seniors Sam Perkins and Matt Doherty. With Steve Hale, Curtis Hunter, Warren Martin, Peterson, Wolf, and Popson coming off the bench, UNC was an overwhelming preseason pick for No. 1 in the country.

With The Jet running point in this lethal lineup, the Tar Heels won their first 21 games, including an 85–72 win at Virginia. But during the 17th game of that opening streak, Smith was hit from behind while going up for a fast-break dunk by LSU's John Tudor. The Jet landed in the aisle at Carmichael Auditorium with a broken left wrist. He missed one month and eight games and, even though Carolina went unbeaten in the ACC with a 14–0 record, the team was never quite the same. When he returned for the last two regular-season games, The Jet played with a protective half-cast on his wrist. Carolina lost to Duke in the semifinals of the ACC Tournament and to Indiana in the Sweet 16 at the old Omni in Atlanta. Dean Smith was visibly upset when he left the postgame press conference because he thought he had the best team in the country. With The Jet healthy, he did.

Kenny Smith went on to make second team All-ACC as a sophomore and junior and first team as a senior in 1987, when the Tar Heels again went 14–0 in the ACC. He remains second in UNC career assists (768) behind only Ed Cota (1,030). He is also one of only 10 Tar Heel players to score at least 40 points in a game (41 at Clemson in 1987). Yet, The Jet says one of his greatest disappointments was that he could not lead the Tar Heels to the Final Four during his career. He was the sixth pick in the 1987 NBA Draft, played 10 pro seasons, and did win two NBA rings with the Houston Rockets. In the first game of the 1995 NBA Finals against the Orlando Magic, Smith made seven three-pointers, including a shot that sent the game into overtime. The Rockets won 120–118.

Kenny Smith is better known today as one of the best basketball analysts on TV, teaming with Charles Barkley, Shaquille O'Neal, and Ernie Johnson on TNT's popular *Inside the NBA* show and more recently has appeared during college games in the NCAA Tournament. He does not hesitate to show his love and loyalty for his alma mater and is happy to take occasional grief about it.

20 Lawson and Ellington Rise

Before practice started in November of 2005, Roy Williams had received commitments from mercurial Maryland mini-guard Ty Lawson and silky smooth Philly sharpshooter Wayne Ellington, who gave Carolina the type of backcourt that would send the Tar Heels to back-to-back Final Fours in 2008 and 2009. And they came within an overtime loss to Georgetown in the 2007 regional final of making it three in a row in a season marked by blood, tragedy, and a blown lead.

The regular-season ender against Duke seemed like the most uneventful game of the rivalry in years—until the last minute of play when Tyler Hansbrough took a flagrant elbow across the nose from Blue Devils freshman Gerald Henderson. Blood streaming from Hansbrough's face relegated to the backburner the fact that Williams had swept Duke for the first time since his return and notched his 100th victory as Carolina's head coach.

With cotton stuffed up his nostrils, "Psycho T" Hansbrough looked in the mirror and was so amused by his blood-spattered face and jersey that he asked a photographer to take a picture that became a Carolina classic. Henderson drew a suspension for one game of the ACC Tournament while Hansbrough adjusted to playing with a plastic mask that made him more of a cult hero among Tar Heel fans. Replica masks started selling over the Internet like the "Make It Wayne" T-shirts that popped up in Ellington's honor the next year.

As Hansbrough struggled with the apparatus all weekend in Tampa, his young mates took over to win UNC's 16th ACC Tournament but the first in nine years. Carolina had last cut down the ACC nets in 1998, three head coaches ago. Freshmen starters Lawson, Ellington, and Brandan Wright made the All-Tournament team with Wright joining Bob McAdoo (1972), Phil Ford (1975), Sam Perkins (1981), Jerry Stackhouse (1994), and Duke's Jason Williams (2000) as the only first-year players to win the Everett Case MVP award. That catapulted Wright to becoming UNC's second one-and-done after his freshman season (following Marvin Williams in 2005).

Hansbrough played the entire ACC Tournament and a first-round NCAA win over Eastern Kentucky with the mask, then threw it off during an early timeout against Michigan State and went on to score a season-high 33 points, the most by a Tar Heel in an NCAA tourney game since Al Wood's legendary 39 versus Virginia in 1981.

Carolina looked even tougher six days later while scorching Southern Cal in the second half of their Sweet 16 match at the Meadowlands despite a season-low five points from Hansbrough. By now a sophomore consensus All-American, Hansbrough came back with 26 points and 11 rebounds as his team held a 10-point lead over Georgetown and stood six minutes from reaching the 2007 Final Four in Atlanta.

Danny Green's missed 20-footer from in front of the UNC bench barely 10 seconds into the shot clock began a rash of quick shots that, coupled with poor defense, allowed the Hoyas to tie the game on Jonathan Wallace's late 3-pointer. Regulation ended with the Georgetown zone surrounding Hansbrough and a wayward jumper by Ellington. The outcome already blown, the stunned Tar Heels were outscored 15–3 in overtime. Green missed all six of his shots in that game, and Lawson and Ellington combined to shoot four for 20 against the Hoyas. "I was dumbfounded the way my team played for a four or five-minute stretch and, regardless of what I said and did, I couldn't reel them back in," Williams said. "[We] took bad shots, took hurried shots, couldn't get the basketball inside, and got out of character more than any team I've ever had. That team got tighter with every possession."

The Tar Heels, though, would redeem themselves with two straight Final Fours, including the 2009 NCAA Championship. The 2009 Tar Heels were the first team to win all six NCAA Tournament games by at least 12 points.

Lawson missed seven games of the 2008 season, which relegated him to honorable mention in the All-ACC voting and raised questions about his toughness, but he was still the Tar Heels' third-leading scorer and easily led the team in assists. Ellington was second to Hansbrough in scoring with a 16.6 average and shot 40 percent on 195 attempts from three-point range, making second team All-ACC and first team All-ACC Tournament.

After entering their names into the NBA draft to test their pro stock, Lawson and Ellington decided to return to school and joined Hansbrough to lead the dominating 2009 season as the Tar Heels were bent on avenging their embarrassing loss to Kansas in the 2008 Final Four and win a national championship.

Lawson had already been named ACC Player of the Year (helped by two sensational performances in sweeping Duke) and was spectacular in five NCAA Tournament games after missing the ACC Tournament and the first round of the NCAAs recovering from a jammed toe. His second half against LSU in Greensboro helped the Heels through their biggest scare and proved he was willing to play with pain. He came back to win MVP in South Regional wins over Gonzaga and Oklahoma. He made several All-American teams and won the Bob Cousy Award as the best point guard in America.

Ellington took over at the Final Four in Detroit, scoring 39 points and grabbing 13 rebounds in double-digit wins against Villanova and Michigan State to win the Most Outstanding Player award. Ellington not only scored 17 points in the first half of the national championship game, but he also made 8-of-10 three-pointers to set the Final Four record for shooting percentage from behind the arc. That he was only the third-leading scorer on the team among all five starters who averaged double figures demonstrates just how powerful the 2009 Tar Heels were. Ellington remains second in all-time three-point shooting at UNC with 229—four behind Shammond Williams.

Lawson and Ellington left for the NBA after their junior seasons, joining Hansbrough as first-round draft choices. Green was drafted midway through the second round and, arguably, turned out to be the best pro from that group after setting three-point shooting records in the NBA Finals with the San Antonio Spurs.

21 Felton, May, and McCants

When North Carolina gave Roy Williams his first NCAA championship in 2005 (after four trips to the Final Four in his 15 years at Kansas), Williams said in his postgame press conference that if, "Matt Doherty were here, I would hug him."

Doherty, who lasted three years as Carolina's head coach before being removed in 2003, had signed all five starters from the 2005 national champions—seniors Jackie Manuel and Jawad Williams (along with reserve Melvin Scott) and juniors Raymond Felton, Sean May, and Rashad McCants, the three best players on the team. Coach Williams had signed the sixth man, freshman Marvin Williams.

While Doherty has been popularly credited with recruiting Felton, May, and McCants, the truth is the three players were his to lose. A unique set of circumstances for each had them all but signed, sealed, and delivered to UNC before Doherty even succeeded Bill Guthridge, who retired during the summer of 2000.

Raymond Felton grew up in Latta, South Carolina, and was a Tar Heel fan for life. (In fact, his nephew Jalek Felton has already committed to UNC in the freshman class of 2017.) Dozens of schools recruited Felton, including Clemson and South Carolina, but all of them knew he wanted to play at Carolina. "I'm going to recruit the hell out of him," said Eddie Fogler when he was the coach at South Carolina, "but I'm telling you he's going to Chapel Hill."

Sean May's father, Scott, was the Player of the Year for Indiana's undefeated NCAA championship team in 1976. Growing up in Bloomington, Indiana, Sean was viewed to be following in his dad's footsteps at IU and would play for the same coach, Bob Knight. When Knight was fired in 2000 and took the Texas Tech job a year later, Scott May did not want his son to play for Knight's replacement, Mike Davis, at the school that had booted his old coach. And after visiting Lubbock, Texas, Sean May determined he did not want to play in that rural Texas town.

The perfect compromise was UNC, whose Hall of Fame coach Dean Smith was Scott May's coach on the 1976 U.S. Olympic team and whose own star from that team, Phil Ford, had remained Scott's friend. After conversations with Smith and Ford, Scott May was satisfied Carolina was the best place for his son.

McCants had been highly touted after playing his sophomore year at Erwin High in Asheville, North Carolina. But then McCants went north to finish his high school career at New Hampton (New Hampshire) Prep. Having fallen off Carolina's recruiting radar, McCants' New Hampton coach called Doherty and said his star player still wanted to be a Tar Heel.

So all three—the slick point guard, the big post man, and the torrid outside shooter—all signed with UNC and Doherty in the fall of 2001, and it's a good thing, too. The Tar Heels were about to suffer through a disastrous 8–20 season, breaking a few three-decade-long streaks of reaching the NCAA Tournament, winning at least 20 games, and finishing top three in the ACC. Doherty was under such heavy fire during that season that, had the big three waited until the spring to sign, they all might have reconsidered where they were going.

Felton made third team All-ACC as a freshman, and McCants led the team in scoring with a 17-point average, but May missed 24 games with a broken foot as the Tar Heels finished 19–16 after losing in the third round of the NIT. Doherty was let go in April, and Roy Williams took the job a week later.

In 2003–04, the Tar Heels returned to the NCAA Tournament but lost in the second round to Texas as Williams worked hard to correct bad habits and create a winning attitude on the team. The core five of that team had been signed by Doherty, but Williams turned them into champions the following season.

Calendar Boy

Roy Williams was the No. 3 assistant on the Carolina basketball staff for eight seasons, from 1978–79 through 1986, before Eddie Fogler left to take the head coaching job at Wichita State, and Williams was elevated to full-time, full-pay as opposed to being full-time with little pay in those years as the so-called restricted-earnings coach.

Before becoming a head coach, Roy Williams (second from the left) was the No. 3 coach behind assistants Eddie Fogler (third from left) and Bill Guthridge (coach on far right) under Dean Smith.

During that period he did a number of odd jobs to make money and help support his family—wife Wanda, who was an elementary school teacher in Chapel Hill, and two young children. Since his annual salary from UNC was $2,700, he was a paid speaker at various summer camps and drove tapes of the coaches' weekly TV show to stations across North Carolina every Sunday morning from November through March. "My wife and children wanted to eat," he said, only half-joking and then telling of a third odd job he had, developing a Carolina basketball calendar that he sold to businesses around the state. The calendar was basically an 18 x 23-inch poster with the individual pictures of that season's team members and the schedule of games.

Williams drove more than 10,000 miles in 10 weeks the first year and sold 9,000 calendars. "I'd go see a customer, get on my hands and knees, and ask him to buy 100 calendars," Williams said. "Then I'd put the name of his company across the bottom of the calendar."

Eventually, Williams refined and improved his business so that he was spending five weeks on the road, driving 5,000 miles, and selling 50,000 calendars. The money he made was more than 10 times his state salary from UNC. The calendar became a staple for Tar Heel fans, some of whom buy them every year and keep them as collector's items. "I was the best dad-gum calendar salesman in the country," Williams said years later.

The Carolina basketball calendar still exists but is no longer produced by the basketball office. It may never have started in the first place without Williams' ingenuity and hard work.

The Dean Dome

The Student Activities Center (SAC), which was renamed for Hall of Fame Coach Dean Smith not long after, was built in the early 1980s with $38 million in private donations, the most expensive on-campus arena ever financed that way. Gifts ranged from $5 to $250,000, the latter good enough for the rights to purchase four of the best seats in the house for the donor's lifetime and the lifetime of his or her oldest child—a private seat license good for two generations.

After the Tar Heels played in 8,800-seat Carmichael Auditorium for 20 years, the Dean E. Smith Center opened on January 18, 1986, with a 95–92 win against Duke. Carolina was rated No. 1 in the country, and Duke was No. 3 for the nationally televised event that felt more like a Final Four game than a regular-season meeting. Duke's Mark Alarie scored the first basket in what had already been dubbed the "Dean Dome," and Warren Martin dunked UNC's first basket in the new 21,800-seat home for the men's basketball team.

The Smith Center, built in a wooded ravine on the southern most point of campus along Route 15-501 and Mason Farm Road, took a long time for the planning, fund-raising, and eventual construction. More than 20,000 cubic yards of rock had to be dynamited out, and 150,000 cubic feet of dirt had to be redistributed. That part was only done halfway, as excessive blasting was needed to take out more rock on the west side of the construction site. Thus, the ground floor of the arena is only a semi-circle, creating storage and production problems since the day the building opened.

More than 2,000 individuals gave money, and every name appears on brass and granite plaques facing the north or main entrance to the building. Each name is in 3/8-inch letters. "It was the single largest effort in intercollegiate athletics," UNC athletic director John Swofford said at the time. Swofford, who moved on to be the commissioner of the ACC in 1997, spearheaded the capital campaign with Smith and the late Ernie Williamson, executive director of the Rams Club, and the late Hargrove "Skipper" Bowles, a UNC alumnus and 1972 North Carolina gubernatorial candidate.

The drive was centered around a traveling road show to Rams Club meetings around the state and North Carolina alumni gatherings throughout the country. It certainly did not hurt that Smith was building a national powerhouse that won the 1982 NCAA Championship during the heart of the fund-raising campaign. Swofford said at the time, "The key factor, of course, was the job that Dean has done with basketball here and the respect people hold for his program. And if you had designed a fund-raising campaign in heaven, you couldn't have come up with better timing after the team played for the national title in 1981 and won it the next year."

Although there was a discussion of a big arena in Chapel Hill dating from the national championship of 1957, and three-sided Carmichael Auditorium was attached to Woollen Gym in 1965, it wasn't until 1980 that the way was truly cleared for a major effort for a self-standing building in 1980, according to Swofford.

A 25-person steering committee was chaired by Bowles, and the meetings got under way with the help of an arena model provided by local architects, Joe Hakan and Glenn Corley. They were embarking on a mission that had never been done before: building the largest on-campus basketball facility in the country with completely private funding. Williamson remembered at the time,

"It was the most fantastic thing I've been involved with. We would go from town to town, and Dean would talk, and Skipper would talk. There were those on the conservative side who thought we could never do it, and many of those people came back to us later and said, 'Well, I guess you're going to do it and I'll get involved.'"

Don't Call It the Dean Dome

The nickname "Dean Dome" surfaced before the Dean E. Smith Center ever opened and, of course, combines the coach's first name with the fiberglass dome. "It makes me sound bald," Smith quipped.

"We were forbidden to call it that around him," recalled one of his former players.

Smith was criticized by some for allowing the building to be named after him while he was still coaching. "It's a great honor, don't get me wrong," he said, "but it was not one of my goals. You can't name it for all of the players, and the way it was sold to me, maybe I was the common denominator."

Those contributing the most money were allowed to purchase lifetime season tickets, and the amount of the donation determined the number and location of the seats. For example, the right to buy padded floor seats along the sideline opposite the benches was reserved for gifts of at least $250,000.

After more than half of the original $35 million goal had been pledged, ground was broken in the spring of 1982, a few weeks after Carolina had defeated Georgetown for the NCAA championship. A major upsurge came at the end of the campaign in 1984, when seating priority was being determined. In the month before the August 1984, deadline, more than $5 million came in from small donors, sending the final tally $3 million over the top.

The 300,000-square-foot octagon, which was officially dedicated and named for Smith the night before the opening game, had a state-of-the-art spring-loaded playing floor, almost 200 small speakers mounted throughout, four giant video walls that were installed in 1996, and, of course, 21,572 seats—not a single one more than 150 feet from the court. Upgrades to seating, lighting, and LED boards have been made since.

Swofford shook his head at the time when looking back on the unprecedented fund-raising drive. He said, "Carolina people are just phenomenal, and so was the supreme effort of Skipper Bowles. But Coach Smith was critical to the campaign, even though he clearly does not liking asking people for money. He just makes and impact on people nobody else makes."

Nearly 30 years after the Smith Center opened, a debate rages on at UNC over whether the building should be renovated for hundreds of millions of dollars or a new arena built for billions. A renovation would leave in place those private seat licenses that are now being used by the children of many original donors who could continue buying season tickets without having to make significant gifts to keep those rights. However, constructing a new arena, with a smaller seating capacity and including corporate luxury suites, would open up new revenue streams that are sorely needed by UNC athletics of the 21st Century.

The original seat licenses would end, and those who wanted to keep buying season tickets would have to make another large donation to the Rams Club. The premium seats of those who no longer wanted them would go to younger millionaires of the next generation, who were willing to pay for new private seat licenses that would be renewable every five or 10 years, creating new revenue streams that do not exist at UNC right now.

24 The Kansas Connection

Frank McGuire, Dean Smith and Kansas—yes, Kansas—are responsible for the longest-standing dynasty in any sport in America. McGuire, who died in 1994, came to UNC in 1952 when it was a football school. His St. John's team had just lost to Kansas in the 1952 NCAA Championship, in which reserve junior guard Dean Smith ran the Jayhawks delay game in the closing minutes of the 80–63 victory in Seattle. A month or so after that game, McGuire accepted UNC's offer to move south and coach the Tar Heels.

McGuire constructed his underground recruiting railroad from New York and by the 1956–57 season he had put together a juggernaut that won 32 consecutive games without a loss, winning the NCAA championship in Kansas City over Kansas and Wilt "The Stilt" Chamberlain in triple overtime. That same weekend he interviewed a young assistant coach from the Air Force Academy for a possible position on his UNC staff. Dean Smith enjoyed meeting McGuire but admitted during the interview that he would be rooting for his alma mater in the title game that night. McGuire liked that because Smith showed the same kind of loyalty he had.

Smith eventually landed the job with McGuire in 1958 and served three years on his staff before being promoted to head coach in the summer of 1961. McGuire had moved on to coach the Philadelphia Warriors for one season—the season that his center, Chamberlain, set the NBA record for scoring 100 points against the New York Knicks in Hershey, Pennsylvania.

Meanwhile, Tommy Kearns, the point guard on McGuire's 1957 champions, had become a stockbroker in New York and landed the wealthy Chamberlain as one of his clients. They had met in the center jump circle in Kansas City when McGuire sent the 5'11" Kearns out to jump against the 7'1" Chamberlain in what McGuire hoped was a psychological ploy.

Smith's Kansas connection stayed alive, and at least three times he turned down offers to return to Lawrence and his home state to coach KU. Meanwhile, he had used the tradition McGuire started to build his own powerhouse program and when he retired after 36 seasons had won more games (879) than any coach in major college history. During his coaching tenure at UNC, he used his Kansas ties to help two Tar Heel alumni become the head coach at his alma mater.

Former Carolina player and assistant Larry Brown coached the Jayhawks for six seasons, led them to two Final Fours, and won the 1988 national championship on the 50th anniversary of the NCAA Tournament with both McGuire and Smith in attendance. When Brown moved on, Smith recommended another of his former assistant coaches, Roy Williams, to the Kansas search committee. The then-unknown Williams stayed 15 years in Lawrence and posted a 418–101 record for a .805 winning percentage, winning more games than any KU coach except Smith's coach, the legendary Dr. Phog Allen (590–219). Williams also won nine Big 8/Big 12 conference championships.

The last season he had served as an assistant coach at UNC, Williams was joined on the Tar Heel bench by former Kansas head coach Dick Harp. In 1958, Smith chose the UNC position under McGuire instead of joining Harp at Kansas, where Smith would have surely become the next head coach there instead of at UNC. When Williams returned to Carolina as head coach in 2003, it closed the circle on a 50-year relationship between the two schools and two of the best basketball programs in college history.

The Tar Heels have won five national championships (compared to three for Kansas) and reached an NCAA high of 18 Final Fours (Kansas has 14).

Smith passed away at 83 on February 7, 2015, and his life was most widely celebrated in two states—North Carolina and Kansas—for the connectivity he represented between both. Frank McGuire, Dean Smith, Wilt Chamberlain, Tommy Kearns, Larry Brown, and Roy Williams—the Carolina-Kansas connection has thrived for a half century.

Age of Argyle

Dean Smith was speechless for one of the few times in his coaching life. The Tar Heels had just returned from New York, where they had lost to Georgetown in the old ACC-Big East Challenge (which preceded the ACC-Big Ten Challenge) in the Meadowlands. It was 1989, and after nearly 30 years on the job, Smith thought he knew how to react to anything that might be said about his team.

He would not have been upset over criticism about the 12-point loss to the Alonzo Mourning and Dikembe Mutombo-led Hoyas, who were better than a Carolina team trying to rebuild from losing J.R. Reid to the NBA a year early and Steve Bucknall and Jeff Lebo to graduation. He wouldn't have minded flack over the Heels' ragged play, which kept them on the verge of being blown out most of the game. Smith knew it might be a tough season given the personnel losses and lack of outside shooting. (His fears proved correct despite the continued emergence of Hubert Davis as Carolina wound up winning only 21 games, the fewest in 10 years.)

But this was not about how the Tar Heels played. It was about how they looked before they began the game. Smith had just learned that some Carolina alumni and fans from New York were saying his players' uniforms, particularly their bell-bottomed warm-up pants, were seriously out of style. In North Carolina, where the Tar Heels could dress in burlap sacks and still receive cheers, team clothing was never an issue. They had had the same style unis for more than 15 years, and no one cared because, after all, it was Carolina. But in New York, style did matter. And when word got back to Smith that his uniforms were so far from the cutting edge as to be obsolete, he took it to heart. The master of detail had somehow failed to notice that almost all basketball warm-ups—college and pro—were now made more like casual jogging outfits with classic ankle cuffs. The straight-tailored leg with the flare bottom was outsville.

This was no small concern to Smith, who had been the first coach in the ACC and among the first in the country to put his team into V-neck jerseys and colored shoes. In the early 1970s, Carolina donned blue Converse sneakers with its home white uniforms and wore white shoes with road blues. The Tar Heels also went through a period of wearing stretch knee socks with their numbers on one leg—except for George Karl, whose old gym socks hung over his shoes and seemed to flop along with his blond hair. Yes, Carolina taking the court with its white velvety warm-ups and blue shooting shirts under the jackets was the rage back then. Smith also had some players wear sweatbands on their wrists (white at home and blue on the road) because tennis players did that to keep their hands from getting too slippery.

It was also part of Carolina's image as a first-class program—along with the blue travel blazers and Smith's insistence that his teams stay in four-star hotels and eat at the best restaurants. The coach, himself, was always impeccably dressed either in stylish sport jackets or expensive Italian-cut suits. And when between the 1972 and '73 seasons, former players Larry Brown and Doug Moe convinced him to lose his hair cream and go for the blow-dry look, Smith willingly acceded to the dictates of fashion.

"Well, we haven't changed our uniforms in a long time. Maybe we should think about it," Smith said after a long pause. Wondering aloud how they should go about it, his eyes lit up at the suggestion that Chapel Hill native Alexander Julian give the Tar Heels a complete makeover. Julian, by then a well-known fashion designer in New York, had grown up hanging around the men's clothing store his family had on Franklin Street. A UNC grad and lifelong Tar Heel fan, Julian returned to North Carolina often and had received acclaim for designing the uniforms of Charlotte's new NBA team, the Hornets, two years before. "If we use Alex, I will need his word that he doesn't do this for any other college team," Smith said. "It wouldn't mean as much if other teams were wearing his uniforms as well."

Later that day, Smith's secretary Linda Woods placed a call to Julian in New York City. She found out that Julian was traveling in Europe and would be extremely difficult to reach. "Make sure he knows that it is coach Dean Smith who is calling," Woods said before hanging up.

Within an hour Julian had returned the call. "Dean Smith is a great hero of mine, and I've been a Carolina fan before I could walk," Julian said later. Then he added with typical dramatic flair, "Having Dean Smith ask you to redo the Carolina uniforms is like God asking you to redo the uniforms for the archangels."

Julian went through an elaborate process, including having Michael Jordan test different fabrics while practicing with the Chicago Bulls before the next season. Claiming that "some of the most beloved fabrics in America are Carolina blue," Julian experimented with chambray, oxford cloth, and faded denim in his design studio in Connecticut. His associates said Julian was part kid in a candy story and part mad inventor.

Julian introduced the first version of Carolina's so-called "designer uniforms" in the fall of 1991 at a press conference that featured Hubert Davis and George Lynch as models and attracted media from around the state and the nation. Julian himself was in Europe and could not attend. Although the denim warm-up jacket and shooting shirt proved too heavy—and the original nylon uniforms did not take to being washed so many times during the season—the staple of the new uniform became the famed argyle stripe down both sides of the jersey and shorts. The diamond-stitched pattern was in several shades of Carolina blue and defined the Tar Heels' contemporary designer look.

Champion Products, a division of North Carolina-based Sara Lee Corporation, worked with Julian to produce the prototype but was cut out when Nike signed a multimillion-dollar contract with UNC in 1993. Since then Nike has marketed authentic and replica Carolina uniforms, shooting shirts, and warm-ups to retail outlets all over the world. Well into 1990 licensed apparel carrying the various Carolina trademarks remained in the top five sellers among all colleges and universities. Some of the most popular items were the oversized replica jerseys and baggy basketball shorts, which were worn by teenagers all over the country.

Julian, who donated his work for "love of the university," eventually overhauled the UNC women's uniforms as well, trimming their jerseys and shorts in Carolina blue with a paisley stripe down both sides. Just like the Tar Heels had worn the argyle during Smith's second national championship season in 1993, the Lady Tar Heels broke out their new togs following their first and only NCAA title in 1994.

26 Vinsanity

Of the freshman class that entered Carolina in the fall of 1995, Vince Carter was by far the most highly rated and ballyhooed recruit. But it wasn't always that way for the Daytona Beach super athlete who has gone on to a decorated career in the NBA. Carter attended the Five-Star Camp in Pennsylvania the summer between his sophomore and junior years at Mainland High School. Kevin Garnett and Stephon Marbury were two of the much bigger prep names at that camp, but in the end, all the coaches would know Carter, too. "The hardest part was gaining respect from players like Stephon," Carter recalled after enrolling at UNC. "Guys would come in the lane and pass to the guys they knew."

Carter said he went to Five-Star to find out where he stood compared to other high school stars and found himself moving from the unknown category to a top 10 prospect in the country. He made the prestigious camp's All-Star team and was named Most Promising Prospect. When it came down to making a college decision, Carter had narrowed it to a pair of rival schools—Florida and Florida State and Duke and Carolina. He was one of the few recruits who got to visit with Mike Krzyzewski while the Duke coach was laid up with a bad back during the 1995 season. Carter visited Coach K at his home while Krzyzewski was lying on the couch. In the end what UNC and Dean Smith had already accomplished won out over what other coaches were promising they could do if Vince came aboard. And UNC assistant coach Phil Ford was the easiest of all the other rival assistants to talk to; he and Carter bonded immediately and became friends who shared both their basketball and personal stories. Florida's Mr. Basketball agreed that

Carolina's reputation athletically and academically and the chance to play for Smith, ultimately, made him sign with the Tar Heels.

Things weren't easy at first in Chapel Hill. Jerry Stackhouse had turned pro a year earlier than expected, forcing Carter from a more comfortable reserve role into a starting position. And he found Smith, though a great coach and thorough teacher, to be a tough taskmaster. Carter was used to getting by as a superior athlete. Smith wanted him to become a better basketball player. So the 6'6" leaper began as a relative disappointment compared to fellow freshman Antawn Jamison, who was thought to be going to prep school for a year before he made a high enough score on the SAT. Jamison was an instant star, averaging 15 points and almost 10 rebounds and making first team All-ACC as a freshman.

Carter averaged less than half those numbers and spent the end of the season in Smith's doghouse, eventually coming off the bench. Rumors circulated that he was unhappy and would transfer to Florida. Carter admitted that—after a prep career in which he just flew over people—he tried to get along on those skills alone. His mother, Michelle Robinson, doused the transfer rumors by telling Smith the tough love his freshman year was just what her son needed.

The rest is history. Carter nearly doubled his scoring average as a sophomore, moved to shooting guard as a junior, and turned pro (along with Jamison) after leading the Tar Heels to back-to-back ACC titles and trips to the Final Four. As a pro he has become one of the longest-standing stars in the NBA, finishing up his 17th season in the NBA with six teams, going from Rookie of the Year in 1999 to an eight-time NBA All-Star. The future Hall of Famer retained his amazing athletic ability while developing into one of the most spectacular stars in the NBA, whose jaw-dropping plays and dunks earned him the nickname of "Vinsanity."

27 The 1968 Team

A solid argument can be made that the 1968 Tar Heels were the best team in UNC basketball history. They went 12–2 in the ACC, won their second straight ACC Tournament, and defeated third-ranked and undefeated St. Bonaventure (with All-American center Bob Lanier) and eighth-ranked Davidson to reach the Final Four in Los Angeles. Then Carolina rolled over Ohio State to face UCLA, which is considered among the greatest college teams ever assembled.

The Tar Heels of 1968 were led by senior All-American Larry Miller, a two-time ACC Player of the Year and MVP of the ACC Tournament. The rugged, handsome lefty from Catasauqua, Pennsylvania, averaged better than 22 points and eight rebounds per game and went on to be a first-round draft choice of the Los Angeles Stars of the old ABA.

The three players who joined the lineup the year before to help catapult Carolina to its first ACC title under Dean Smith were now experienced juniors. The point guard was 6'4" Dick Grubar, who averaged eight points a game and led the team in assists. The power forward was 6'9" Bill Bunting, who also averaged eight points a game, and the center was 6'11" Rusty Clark, who had a spectacular double-double season averaging just under 16 points and 11 rebounds a game. Against Maryland, Clark also set the UNC single-game rebounding record with 30, a mark that still stands.

The Tar Heels lost Bob Lewis from the 1967 team but replaced him with sophomore Charlie Scott, the first African American scholarship athlete at Carolina, who made first team All-ACC by averaging 17.6 points and six rebounds a game in his first major college season. Junior forward Joe Brown and sophomore guard

Eddie Fogler came off the bench to give Smith a solid, seven-man rotation. The team was 22–1 going into the last week of the regular season, when it lost to South Carolina in Miller's last home game and then at 10th-ranked Duke in triple overtime.

After edging South Carolina in overtime and blasting N.C. State in the championship game of the ACC Tournament in Charlotte, the Tar Heels faced their toughest two games of the season at Reynolds Coliseum in Raleigh. First came St. Bonaventure with 6'11" Lanier. Despite a combined 46 points and 21 rebounds from Lanier and Bill Butler, Carolina held the Bonnies to 39 percent shooting and hit 52 percent of its shots to win by 19 points. Miller was spectacular with 27 points and 16 rebounds, Clark had 18 and 10, and Scott scored 21 points in perhaps Carolina's best game of the season.

Next up was eighth-ranked Davidson, the school Scott originally committed to, with star center Mike Maloy who had 18 points and 13 rebounds. But the Tar Heels held the Wildcats to 35 percent from the floor, rallied from a six-point deficit at the half, and won 70–66. Clark was the star with 22 points and 17 rebounds, while Scott and Miller combined for 34 points and 12 rebounds. UNC was off to its second straight Final Four.

Unfortunately, after beating Ohio State and holding its fourth straight opponent to under 40 percent shooting, Carolina faced the second-ranked Bruins of UCLA only a few miles from their campus in Westwood. UCLA had avenged its only loss of the season by routing Elvin Hayes and No. 1 Houston in the semifinals, and Smith allowed his team to watch the first half of that rout before going back to the hotel.

The next night, it was Carolina that shot under 40 percent and trailed the Bruins by 10 at halftime after holding the ball for much of the first 20 minutes. Smith thought he could keep the game close and draw UCLA All-American center Lew Alcindor away from the basket, but the strategy did not work, and the teams played at a regular pace in the second half with UCLA winning its second straight national championship 78–55. Alcindor, who later changed his name to Kareem Abdul-Jabbar, was unstoppable with 34 points and 16 rebounds. He did not need much help from the rest of the Bruins, even if they were the best college team ever assembled to date, as Lynn Shackleford, Mike Lynn, Lucius Allen, and Mike Warren combined for 31 points—three less than Alcindor.

UCLA and Houston were the two best teams in the county in 1968, but UNC may have fielded its best team ever. Smith was given a Carolina blue Cadillac convertible after the season by appreciative alumni and boosters who finally saw him as having escaped the shadow of his predecessor Frank McGuire.

28 Loyal Assistant

Bill Guthridge, the silent assistant who sat next to Dean Smith for 30 seasons, had his own team his first 10 years at Carolina, coaching the UNC freshmen and junior varsity squads. He was less anonymous before the freshman eligibility rule was reinstated for the 1972–73 season. Guthridge often coached some of the nation's most highly recruited frosh as they waited to join the varsity as sophomores. In 1970, for example, without injured scholarship players George Karl and Donn Johnston, Guthridge's five walk-ons upset N.C. State's seven scholarship players.

After another prelim against the Wolfpack, Guthridge chewed out one of the officials all the way to the locker room, only to find out that the varsity refs had been detained by a snowstorm and the guys who had just worked the freshman game would also be officiating the State-Carolina main event. On several occasions Guthridge whipped off his plaid sports jacket and slung it under the bench.

Then there was the junior varsity game against Old Dominion during the mid-1970s. The score was tied at the end of regulation, and TV commitments for the varsity game posed a problem with playing the overtime. Guthridge suggested to the ODU coach that they play sudden death. "He was afraid we'd get the tap from center, so I offered to give him the ball out of bounds," Guthridge recalled. "One of the refs said that was against the rules, so I proposed that we go ahead and play without officials."

The result was a double technical foul on Guthridge, who took his team off the floor while calling the ref every name in the book without saying anything dirty. "I've never heard him use a cuss word," said Mickey Bell, one of his freshman in 1972. "We were playing at Duke, and he wanted to get on the referees about a couple of calls. He stood up, all red in the face, and ready to unleash on them. When they ran by, all he could say was, 'You're... You're...You're a cheater! A cheater!'"

Like Smith, Guthridge hailed from Kansas. Unlike Smith, who attended Kansas University, Guthridge went to Kansas State, where he was a reserve guard on the Wildcats' 1958 Final Four team and roomed with eventual Purdue head coach Gene Keady. Guthridge's older sister went to KU and actually dated Smith, which is how the two men met. They remained friends, and Smith hired him to replace Larry Brown on his staff in the spring of 1967.

Guthridge's head-coaching record in college was 72–25, not including two varsity wins when he took over after his boss got thrown out. Smith was ejected at Clemson in 1972 and against Clemson in Greensboro in 1977. But for the most part, Guthridge was the key background figure in the Tar Heel program until Smith retired in 1997 and Guthridge took over for three seasons. Guthridge went 80–28, won an ACC championship, and took the

Tar Heels to two Final Fours. He won more games in his first two seasons than any college coach in history.

Besides recruiting and on-the-floor coaching at practice, his duties included scouting opponents, making travel plans for the team, and monitoring players' academic progress. Carolina was one of the few major college basketball teams that did not use an academic advisor during Smith's tenure. "We wanted to treat them like regular students," Guthridge said. "Once the players showed they could do the work, they had no restrictions like the rest of the student body. Others who didn't do as well had to keep up mandatory class attendance and keep going to study hall."

Beginning in the early 1990s, Carolina rented the private jets of several NBA teams to travel to away games, often making the trip the same day so the players missed a minimum of class time. The cost of renting a pro plane was expensive, but the UNC basketball program could afford it. Annual revenues from television appearances, ticket sales, and postseason tournaments usually exceeded $4 million, while the Carolina basketball budget grew to about $2 million a year under Smith and Guthridge.

Guthridge also ran Smith's summer camp called the Carolina Basketball School. It ran three sessions with about 400 campers per session, was always filled to capacity, and never advertised. The camp grossed more than a quarter of a million dollars, from which Guthridge and fellow assistant coaches Phil Ford and Dave Hanners were paid healthy stipends. "Dean Smith took care of me and my family," said Guthridge, who turned down head-coaching offers at Auburn, LSU, Vanderbilt, and Penn State during his years at Carolina. "He was very easy to work for. I had what I considered the best job in the country."

It was sad, but somewhat symbolic that Guthridge passed away on May 12, 2015, three months after his boss and friend. Coach Gut was 77.

29 Monster Montross

After Eric Montross led the 1993 Tar Heels to the NCAA championship and was projected as a lottery pick in the upcoming NBA draft, he had no intention of leaving UNC. Much like Tyler Hansbrough 15 years later, Montross was having too much fun in college and was learning too much. "I've said a million times I'm not going anywhere," Montross said.

"Are you kidding?" asked his father, Scott Montross, a prominent attorney in Indianapolis. "To have another year to be coached by Dean Smith and Bill Guthridge—for free?"

Montross brought his seven-foot frame and a lot of potential to Chapel Hill in the fall of 1990. Too much was expected of him from the outset—given that he'd excelled at the high school level, where he was seven inches taller than the tallest player who ever guarded him.

The transition was a big one for the big guy, who looked somewhat awkward and clumsy playing college basketball. He was mocked around the ACC, especially at Duke, where the Cameron Crazies called him Frankenstein and *The* (Duke) *Chronicle* left a big empty white space on the front page of the student newspaper in his honor the day of the Blue Devils' home game with Carolina.

But with the constant supervision of Smith and Guthridge, who tutored the UNC big men, and a year and a half of game experience, Montross began to emerge as a force in the middle toward the end of his sophomore season. By his junior year, he was much more of a complete player. Montross had developed a nice jump hook shot and counter drop-step move. He'd become consistent at the foul line. He could play defense without getting into foul trouble and had perfected his ability to keep opponents off the boards. "What sets

Eric Montross, a four-year player who led North Carolina to a national title in 1993, throws down a jam.

North Carolina apart is Montross," said Randy Ayers, head coach at Ohio State, which had ended the Tar Heels' 1992 season in the NCAA Tournament and then lost to them by 20 points the following December. "No one else has anyone like him."

As a junior Montross was named first team All-ACC and second team All-American by the Associated Press. He was second in the ACC in field goal parentage—61.5 percent, the best for a Tar Heel at that time since Brad Daugherty made 64.8 percent in 1984–85. He scored in double figures in 36 games (setting a UNC single-season record) and averaged 15.8 points and 7.6 rebounds. He shot 65 percent in six NCAA Tournament wins, culminating with the victory against Michigan and the Fab Five in the national championship game.

Montross was heavily recruited by Indiana, but he felt very comfortable in Chapel Hill and decided to leave home. Actually, his second choice was Michigan, where his parents went to school, and his maternal grandfather played for the Wolverines. His sister, Christine, went to Ann Arbor while Eric was at UNC.

But there was no doubt which team the entire family was pulling for when Carolina Blue met the Maize and Blue in the Superdome on April 5, 1993. "If it's anyone else besides Carolina, we're 'Go Blue,'" Scott Montross said of the Michigan chant. "But we're Tar Heels in this tournament."

30 Sheed and Stack

The first two players to leave Dean Smith's program after their sophomore years were Rasheed Wallace and Jerry Stackhouse, who were taken No. 3 and No. 4 in the 1995 NBA Draft. That makes them a bit different from the 22 top 10 draft picks since 1966 and the 35 first-round picks since 1980, both of which lead the nation.

Some say that Wallace and Stackhouse personify a recruiting shift by Dean Smith, who had players in the 1970s (Robert McAdoo) and the 1980s (James Worthy, Michael Jordan, J.R. Reid) who left school after their junior years, but none that Smith *knew* was going out early when he signed them. "I guess you can blame me for that," former assistant coach Phil Ford said, laughing. "We still wanted the best players, but it was clear the best players weren't going to stay for four years. And we told Coach Smith that."

Wallace was a high school All-American from Philadelphia. The 6'11" multi-talented athlete, who drew hometown comparisons to Wilt Chamberlain, was at first thought to be staying put and playing for Temple or Villanova. But the prospect of playing for the national championship every season at Carolina was too much for Wallace to pass up. "I'm a player just out of high school who needs a lot of polishing," Wallace said upon signing with the Tar Heels in the spring of 1993 after UNC had won the national championship. "That's why I picked North Carolina. Dean Smith has a proven track record of developing players."

Wallace got caught up in Smith's storied seniority system when he arrived in Chapel Hill. There was no question from preseason scrimmages in the Dean Dome that he was better than senior Kevin Salvadori, a reserve in 1993 who was vying to take the graduated George Lynch's spot in the starting lineup. But Smith always favored senior incumbents. Wallace played in all 35 games but did not move into the starting lineup for good until the 1994 regular-season finale at second-ranked Duke, which had already clinched first place in the ACC behind Grant Hill. Wallace had 14 points and five rebounds and put an exclamation mark on the 87–77 upset win with a ferocious down-the-lane dunk in the closing minutes.

Stackhouse, as well as the third freshman in that class, Jeff McInnis, only started a single game during the 1994 season. But, like Wallace, he got as many minutes as anyone on the team except senior center Eric Montross. That was okay with Stackhouse, who would have had to displace senior Brian Reese or junior Donald Williams, the Most Outstanding Player of the Final Four the year before. The Kinston, North Carolina, native and lifelong Carolina fan, Stackhouse said he was happy coming off the bench and was actually the third-leading scorer (12.2 points) behind Williams (14.3) and Montross (13.6) on the well-balanced team ranked No. 1 for much of the season. Wallace was the fourth-leading scorer (9.5).

Still, the logjam of Tar Heels expecting time gave them too many players, and the chemistry suffered throughout the season. They lost in overtime to Massachusetts early in the season; lost both games to Georgia Tech; lost at Clemson, at Virginia, and at Wake Forest. But their talent emerged when they saw Duke Blue, sweeping the Blue Devils who eventually reached the Final Four in Charlotte.

Carolina won the 1994 ACC Tournament and was ranked No. 1 headed into the NCAA Tournament, where they were shocked by Boston College in the second round at Landover, Maryland. Montross, Salvadori, Reese, and Derrick Phelps graduated, leaving the 1995 team basically to Wallace and Stackhouse.

That talented team did reach the Final Four before losing to Arkansas in the semifinals. The '95 Tar Heels finished in a four-way tie for first in the ACC with Maryland, Virginia, and Wake Forest and ended the season ranked No. 4 with a 28–6 record. Wallace (16.6 points) and Stackhouse (19.2 points) led the team in scoring and rebounding (8.2 per game for each). They both made first team All-ACC and All-ACC Tournament and numerous All-American teams. Clearly, both were ready for the NBA and projected lottery picks all season. They would leave UNC short-handed and inexperienced for the 1996 season, but that wasn't a good enough reason to stay. Stackhouse announced his decision to enter the NBA draft at a press conference with Smith in Chapel Hill. Wallace did it at his high school in Philadelphia with Bill Guthridge in attendance.

Since then Joseph Forte (2001), Ed Davis (2010), Harrison Barnes and Kendall Marshall (both 2012) have departed for the NBA after their sophomore seasons; Marvin Williams (2005) and Brandan Wright (2007) were one-and-dones.

31 Roy's Beginnings

The summer after his high school graduation, Roy Williams played what he thought was his last organized basketball game when he captained his All-Star team in the North-South game in Greensboro, North Carolina. Fortunately, after Williams enrolled at UNC, assistant coach Bill Guthridge liked his desire during tryouts for the 1969 freshman team, and Roy was able to put on the North Carolina uniform as the last man for a squad that featured the highly recruited Bill Chamberlain, Steve Previs, and Dennis Wuycik.

Williams barely knew who these big guys were. He hadn't followed college basketball very closely, certainly not recruiting, from his home in the mountains and never witnessed a game until he arrived in Chapel Hill. "Growing up, watching North Carolina play basketball just wasn't part of our family's deal," Williams said. "The first ACC basketball game I ever saw in person was when we played the preliminary game in the Charlotte Coliseum as a freshman."

He rarely got off that bench during the 1968–69 season, mopping up in 11 of the 17 games and taking a total of seven shots (he made two). In the team picture, the frail kid at the end of the back row shorter than both student managers looked more like the mascot than one of the players. Indeed, Williams' playing career was over.

Williams was a quantifiable gym rat and went to work for the campus intramural office, umpiring softball games so well he was promoted to supervisor of all officials and ran a Woollen Gym schedule that included more than 50 basketball and volleyball games a day between dormitory teams, fraternities, and graduate schools. A tiny figure in the corner of the press catwalk high above Carmichael Auditorium, he also picked up a few bucks keeping statistics for Smith during varsity games.

Williams worked 24 hours a week because he needed the money to stay in school, doing what his mother, Mimmie, had taught him. He got so good at managing student referees, controlling the highly contentious intramural games, and earning respect as the pint-sized czar of Woollen Gym that Guthridge again took notice and recommended to Smith that he ref games at the Carolina Basketball School, the summer camp for hundreds of young kids and a few hot-shot college prospects.

During those intramural days of winter, walking between courts at Woollen and the old Tin Can, Williams occasionally stopped at Carmichael Auditorium and poked his head through a portal to check out varsity practice. When a manager, who was supposed to keep everyone but players and coaches out of the building, told Dean Smith "it's Roy up there watching," the boss nodded and let him stay.

By the summer of 1973, Williams was in grad school and watching Smith's practices more regularly, sitting in the stands at Carmichael with a legal pad and treating it like a lecture from the grand master. After keeping varsity stats from afar as an undergrad, he was looking under the hood to find out how all of it worked so smoothly.

Smith and Guthridge also hired him as a full-time counselor at the Carolina Basketball School, and Williams impressed them with not only his energy, but also the same power of recall for which the head coach, himself, became famous. "In two days he knew every camper in his gym by name," Smith said. "After the first year, he was the head of a gym, which was the quickest I had ever put anybody in charge of his own gym."

Guthridge assigned Roy to referee an important camp game one evening that included a sought-after rising senior from Rocky Mount, North Carolina, named Phil Ford. The best point guard recruit in high school, Ford had dazzled fans at the *Raleigh Times* and Hillside holiday tournaments and already was a legend in the state. Smith sorely needed him to get the Tar Heels to the same level as the vaunted N.C. State teams, which featured two other native North Carolinians, David Thompson and Tom Burleson. And he wanted Ford, who was being pursued by schools from Lefty Driesell's Maryland to Frank McGuire's South Carolina, to have a good experience at the UNC camp. Williams' job was to make it a fun game.

Roy wasn't officially a part of Carolina basketball again but said, "They knew who I was." That was enough to keep the connection through the next five years, and Williams joined the UNC staff as a part-time assistant in 1978.

32 Visit the Carolina Basketball Museum

A can't-miss destination for UNC and college basketball fans is the Carolina Basketball Museum, located in the Williamson Athletics Center, two buildings down from the Dean Smith Center. It is a state-of-the-art tour through the fabulous history of Tar Heel basketball, beginning with a four-minute surround-sound movie that visitors watch before entering the museum.

Inside are artifacts, videos, photos, and panels that highlight the history of the Carolina basketball program. It also includes interactive presentations about UNC's 18 Final Four appearances, five NCAA championships, and 17 Atlantic Coast Conference Tournament titles, plus many of the greatest games and finishes in Tar Heel history.

It takes about an hour to thoroughly move around the museum from display case to display case, watch the several videos, including one from current coach Roy Williams and highlight reels of some of the most storied moments in the history of a storied program.

The late Dean Smith often wrote letters of congratulations to recruits who did not sign with UNC, wishing them well in the school they did choose. One notable item in the Michael Jordan display case is a letter from Duke coach Mike Krzyzewski to Jordan with similar sentiments about his signing with UNC in 1981, Coach's K first year at Duke.

National championship trophies are displayed—plus the rings won by the players on those championship teams. The Carolina Basketball Museum is constantly changing. Displays are updated, and new items are added when they are received from UNC alumni and fans who donate some of their most precious collectors' items to the museum.

Since the town of Chapel Hill no longer has a museum—some say because longtime residents are ashamed of their history of segregation—the Carolina Basketball Museum is the most popular and most trafficked museum in the town where the University of North Carolina is located. Attendees to home basketball games often arrive hours before tip-off and spend an hour at the museum, which closes on gamedays one hour before tip-off.

The normal hours are Monday through Friday from 10:00 AM to 4:00 PM and Saturday from 9:00 AM to 1:00 PM. The Carolina Basketball Museum is not open on Sundays. But if there is a home game that day, it is open for three hours the day of the game. Admission is free, and photos can be taken inside the museum. Parking is available across the street (Skipper Bowles Drive) on non-gamedays. On gamedays cars without parking permits must be moved four hours before the scheduled tip-off of the game.

33 Franklin Street Celebrations

The first major celebration after a basketball victory in Chapel Hill came on a beautiful Saturday in 1977 after the Tar Heels defeated Kentucky to reach the Final Four in Atlanta. UNC was a Cinderella team, having played the stretch run of the season racked with injuries. Tom LaGarde, Carolina's senior center, was lost for good with a knee injury, and Dean Smith had to go with three freshmen in the middle: Rich Yonakor, Jeff Wolf, and Steve Krafcisin. (Yon-Wolf-Sin, Smith called the trio that he hoped would combine to approach LaGarde's averages of 15 points and seven-plus rebounds per game.)

Carolina had plummeted in the rankings from No. 4 to No. 14 after losing three out of four ACC games in late January. So, despite a lineup that still included Phil Ford, Walter Davis, Mike O'Koren, and John Kuester, critics were writing off the Tar Heels after LaGarde went down. After losing by 20 points at 19th-ranked Clemson, Smith told the team there would be no practice the next day but to come back Monday ready to work. "I will tell you then how we are going to win the national championship," Smith said to suddenly wide eyes.

Carolina reeled of nine straight wins to end the regular season and finish first in the ACC. The Tar Heels exemplified their newfound durability and togetherness by winning at Duke on Saturday, February 26, to clinch first place in the ACC and the next day defeating No. 10-ranked Louisville in Charlotte in a made-for-national-TV game.

Alumni and fans were back on the bandwagon and ready for the ACC Tournament in Greensboro. Carolina, which had a first-round bye in the then-seven-school ACC, defeated N.C. State in the semifinals but lost Davis with a broken index finger that he slammed against the backboard skying for a rebound. With Davis playing only a few inspiring minutes using one hand the next night, the Heels rallied to beat defending ACC champion Virginia in a rough-and-tumble title game and advanced to the NCAA East Regional in College Park, Maryland.

There, with Davis back in the lineup, they rallied to defeat No. 10 Notre Dame in the Sweet 16 but lost Ford to a hyperextended elbow in the closing minutes. Ford could not go against Kentucky two days later, so Kuester ran Four Corners after Carolina had taken an early lead and, somehow, this M*A*S*H unit held off the No. 13-ranked Wildcats.

Students and fans raced out of bars, restaurants, frat houses, and dorms after Carolina's dramatic run to the Final Four. They threw rolls of toilet paper into the trees on campus and Franklin

Street and partied into the night. Spring had come to Chapel Hill, and the Tar Heels were still playing. Another such celebration ensued a week later when, behind freshman O'Koren's 31 points, No. 5-ranked Carolina edged No. 4 UNLV and All-American Reggie Theus 84–83. There were only sad faces on Monday night when UNC lost to Marquette in the national championship game.

But a tradition had been born in Chapel Hill, which had seen a smaller party 20 years earlier on a Saturday night when Frank McGuire's Tar Heels completed their miracle 32–0 season by beating Kansas and Wilt Chamberlain in triple overtime in Kansas City. But that game had ended close to midnight on the East Coast, and most of the people had to follow it on the radio, as TV was not yet prevalent.

After Al Wood scored 39 points against Virginia in the 1981 Final Four, thousands took to the streets to party after the upset of Ralph Sampson and the fifth-ranked Cavaliers, who had defeated Carolina twice during the regular season. They bought gallons of blue paint at the local hardware stores and drew giant "39" numbers on sidewalks and buildings.

Another big party followed the next year after the Tar Heels beat Houston in New Orleans to reach the national championship game against Georgetown. On Monday, the first full-fledged night-time celebration ensued after Michael Jordan hit the winning shot, and UNC defeated the Hoyas 63–62 to win Dean Smith's first national championship.

Duke was not very good in those days, and it took the Blue Devils becoming a national power through the late 1980s before beating them was worthy of a Franklin Street celebration. One occurred on Sunday afternoon, March 12, 1989, after Carolina edged Duke in a thrilling ACC championship game in Atlanta. The Blue Devils had won the 1991 NCAA title and were heading for a second straight when bloodied-but-unbowed Eric Montross led the 75–73 upset of top-ranked Duke at the Smith Center on the evening of February 5, 1992. And, of course, Carolina had the biggest party to date the next season when the Tar Heels defeated Michigan back in New Orleans to win Smith's second national championship.

These days, the Franklin Street Celebrations come only after beating Duke—home or away—or winning the national championship, like Roy Williams' teams did in 2005 and 2009. Town officials know when such a super party may break out, and they prepare thoroughly by bringing in police reinforcements from Carrboro, Durham, and Hillsborough. The fire department is also fully engaged because somewhere on the 100-block bonfires will be started. Only once did something unseemly occur when students turned over a parked car. An estimated 10,000 people have crowded the downtown during some of the biggest Franklin Street celebrations. They have become a tradition almost as great as Carolina basketball itself.

34 Golfing Adversaries

When Larry Brown left Dean Smith's staff at North Carolina to play in the brand-new American Basketball Association, Smith immediately tabbed Bill Guthridge as his new assistant coach. It was a natural choice and happened quite quickly.

Smith and Guthridge both grew up in Kansas. (Smith attended KU, and Guthridge Kansas State about seven years apart.) Smith was the seventh man on the 1952 Jayhawks that defeated Frank McGuire's St. John's team for the national championship, the year before McGuire left to become UNC's head coach. Guthridge also

Dean Smith sits between coaches Phil Ford and Bill Guthridge, his right-hand man for three decades.

played in the 1958 Final Four for the K-State Wildcats. Smith even went on a few dates at KU with Guthridge's older sister.

Smith and Guthridge, who both majored in mathematics in college, also served as assistants on the golf team after joining the basketball coaching staffs at their respective alma maters. When Guthridge arrived in Chapel Hill, he found out quickly that Smith was not only his equal on the golf course, but also was as fierce a competitor. And he was the boss.

In fact, their golf matches got so intense that Guthridge finally gave up the sport. Neither man liked to lose, and Smith was infamous for the mental games he played with opponents on the course. He was a stickler for the rules and often pointed out what he believed to be the slightest infraction by one of his opponents. For example, if he and his partner in a four-ball match had made it over the water on a long Par 3, Smith would say to his opponents as they were getting ready to hit their tee shots, "Well, there are two dry ones!" He also loved to wager on the course and was known to keep doubling the bet until the stakes got high enough for him to lock in his concentration.

So, as Smith's right-hand man who otherwise worked smoothly with the head coach, Guthridge did not want to risk his relationship with Smith over a competitive golf game. He put down the clubs and picked up a tennis racket, often playing with his wife, Leesie, and their children while remaining a fiery competitor on the basketball sideline.

Once Guthridge retired after succeeding Smith as head coach for three years (winning more games than any other college coach in his first three seasons and taking the Tar Heels to an ACC championship and two Final Fours), Guthridge took up golf again and learned that he had not lost much of his game over the past 25 years. He played 274 rounds that first year and soon became a single-digit handicapper again for the rest of his golfing career. He even played a few rounds with Smith and beat his old boss most of the time.

35 Woollen Gym

After playing in a less-than-adequate facility (the Tin Can) for 15 seasons, the 1939 basketball season saw the opening of the school's state-of-the-art gymnasium. The story of the gymnasium actually goes back more than a couple of decades earlier when UNC business manager Charles T. Woollen began to develop a plan to replace Bynum Gym. In 1918 Woollen went to work collecting data on gymnasiums and swimming pools. For 10 years Woollen worked on the project behind the scenes, preparing for the day when the university would have the resources to build a new gym.

By the mid-1920s students and faculty started to talk (read: complain) about the need for a new gym to replace the antiquated Bynum. In an editorial in the *Daily Tar Heel* on November 24, 1927, the paper opined, "One of the urgent needs of the university which demands attention is the growing necessity for a new gymnasium to care for the physical welfare of the increasing student body." From that point forward, the *DTH* would offer at least one editorial per year detailing the need for a new gym. All the while unbeknownst to the student body, Woollen continued to work on the project, gathering information and talking to architects. As a result he became one of the foremost gymnasium authorities in the southeast.

On November 26, 1933, Don Becker wrote in the *DTH*, "For some time the crying need on this campus has been a new and adequate gym. In an era when the national government is appropriating billions of dollars for reconstruction, it is not amiss to suggest that a part of North Carolina's share of public funds be invested in a new gym building for the university." Of course, Charles Woollen and university president Frank Porter Graham had already been working that angle, talking to anyone who would listen concerning federal funds for the project. Finally, on October 24, 1936, Stanley H. Wright, North Carolina public works administration director, announced that UNC would be receiving a grant of $283,090 (45 percent of the cost) for a new gym, an indoor swimming pool, and a women's dormitory. The university would then have to raise the remaining $346,000 needed to complete the project.

With the funds secured, construction began in April of 1937 and was completed a year later. On Friday March 25, 1938,

President Graham hosted a dinner at the Carolina Inn, officially dedicating the gymnasium and natatorium. Two months later the UNC board of trustees voted unanimously to name the new gymnasium the "Charles Thomas Woollen Gymnasium," in honor of the man most responsible for making the gym a reality.

Woollen Gymnasium opened in the spring and was ready for physical education classes when school started in September. On Monday, December 5, 1938, the first big event was held in Woollen as 12,000 people packed the gym to see president Franklin Roosevelt. A month later on Monday, January 2, 1939, the basketball Tar Heels played their first game in Woollen, defeating Atlantic Christian 59–17. Sadly, Charles Woollen had passed away on September 21, 1938, two-and-a-half months prior to President Roosevelt's appearance in the facility that honored his name.

Woollen was born in Guilford County on November 18, 1878, and arrived in Chapel Hill in 1901 as a 23-year-old freshman. He worked his way through school as registrar, proctor, custodian, purchasing agent, and secretary to the president. Graduating in 1905 Woollen never left the university he so dearly loved, working in some capacity at UNC until his untimely death in 1938.

In 1910 Woollen took over the management of athletic affairs and under his leadership, the athletic association moved out of the red and began to turn a profit. In 1914 Woollen became business manager of the university where he projected the development of service plants and oversaw the electric, water, telephone plants, the laundry, and the book exchange. It was during his time as business manager that Woollen was instrumental in the planning and development of what would become Emerson Field (1916), the Tin Can (1924), Kenan Stadium (1927), as well as Woollen Gymnasium (1938). The Tar Heels played in Woollen until moving into Carmichael Auditorium for the 1965–66 season.

36 McGuire Versus Smith

The 1968 season began just after Frank McGuire's wife, Pat, lost her battle to cancer in September, and Dean Smith was among the hundreds attending her funeral in New York. It was also a time of upheaval in America with much of the country growing concerned over Lyndon Johnson's handling of the escalating war in Vietnam.

On the court the Tar Heels again led wire to wire. UNC had clinched the ACC race by winning 12 consecutive conference games—20 straight overall—when McGuire and his South Carolina team visited Chapel Hill for the first time since the 104–70 blowout loss two years earlier that had miffed McGuire because he thought his protégé had run up the score.

This time Carmichael Auditorium was buzzing for Larry Miller's last home game. Smith took the microphone before the game and asked the crowd to treat McGuire and his team with respect. Miller, an All-American on his way to a second straight ACC Player of the Year award, expected to go out a winner. But the steadily improving Gamecocks had notched another successful season and, based on their earlier four-point loss to the Tar Heels in Charlotte, arrived confident of pulling an upset. McGuire's penchant for a dramatic entrance gave the game a surreal start, especially considering Smith's request.

Even after his team came out for its final warm-ups, McGuire hung back in the locker room until just before tip-off. When the now 53-year-old legend finally emerged in his requisite silk suit, nodding and waving to familiar faces in the stands and warmly embracing Smith at the scorer's table, the crowd's reaction electrified the auditorium. If McGuire was still a hero to some old guard in Carolina blue, younger or newer fans unaware of the back story only saw him as the enemy and a serious threat to Smith's hard-earned success.

South Carolina's senior class, labeled "the Four Horsemen," had added a pony in sophomore Bobby Cremins, a scrapper with unrefined skills. The Gamecocks shot well all night and led late when Smith told his team to foul Cremins and dare the 59 percent free throw shooter to protect the lead. Cremins went to the line 16 times and made 13, and South Carolina held on to win by one point.

After the game McGuire was animated when he talked to sportswriters. He had taken off his gold cuff links and held them between his fingers as he gestured, almost as if to say he was still the king. Sitting by his locker, Cremins was surrounded by men with notepads and pens for the first time in his career. He joined his coach as a hero to the state of South Carolina that night, and the future Georgia Tech coach would later tease Smith about giving him the chance not only to ice the game, but also become the desire of coeds who swarmed him when he got back to Columbia.

McGuire's team tied N.C. State for third place behind UNC and Duke but lost twice to the Wolfpack, which was now coached by former Everett Case player Norman Sloan. Press Maravich had moved on to LSU after his son, Pete, failed to score 800 on his SATs and could not attend State or play anywhere in the ACC. The Gamecocks, thus, got the fourth seed in the 1968 ACC Tournament in Charlotte, leaving them in North Carolina's bracket. They had to beat the Tar Heels to reach the championship game and at least be considered for the NIT, which with McGuire's old friendships and sentimental ties to the Big Apple, would have been a lock.

Despite falling behind early, South Carolina rallied with an 18–4 run in the second half that tied the game in the final seconds. Miller missed at the buzzer, but the Tar Heels won in overtime 82–79. The key to survival was another philosophical coaching difference. Smith's freestyle substitutions allowed his bench to contribute nine points. The Four Horsemen and Cremins scored all of their team's points, underscoring McGuire's longtime tendency of staying with his starters and possibly wearing them down.

In the championship game, Sloan's Wolfpack hung around in the first half. Smith walked into the locker room behind the end zone stands at the old Charlotte Coliseum and simply said, "You know what you have to do." He walked out, and his team blew open the game to win by 37 points, locking down its second straight championship.

Duke again got the NIT bid, inflaming McGuire's hatred for the ACC Tournament and leaving him to think that bolting the conference altogether would be an easier way into a postseason tournament. His former player at St. John's, Al McGuire, had proven that as coach at independent Marquette, which had its pick of bids from the NCAA or NIT. That Smith's team advanced to play another independent, St. Bonaventure with All-American Bob Lanier before defeating Davison to win the East Regional, supported Frank McGuire's theory that not having to win a treacherous conference tournament was the easier road to an NCAA bid.

McGuire went back to the Final Four and watched Smith coach the Tar Heels into the championship game against unbeatable UCLA with Lew Alcindor. After playing their own game of stall ball in the first half, the Tar Heels ran with the Bruins and were blown out, 78–55. Smith figured if they were going to lose anyway, why incur bad publicity of continuing to stall on national television? Even after being run over by the UCLA machine, the Tar Heels were able to find a silver lining. Assistant coach John Lotz even called it "a tremendous thrill to be in the field with UCLA."

As coach of the two-time ACC champions, Smith truly had arrived and he received the same gift as McGuire had after his undefeated, national championship season at UNC in 1957—a Carolina blue Cadillac—presented to him by some of the same Rams Club officials on the front steps of Carmichael. "I'm not the

Cadillac type," Smith said. "I accept the gift because I'm certain you're really expressing appreciation for the fine play of the team."

Smith drove the car to the airport, where he used an old McGuire maneuver of parking at the Airport Motel across the street from the terminal in exchange for giving the manager a few basketball tickets. He flew to Pittsburgh to wrap up the recruiting haul that would keep Carolina on top: star guard Steve Previs and rugged forward Dennis Wuycik were joining an incoming freshman class that also included Long Island's Bill Chamberlain, the second African American scholarship basketball player at UNC after Charlie Scott. McGuire had recruited some cocksure players from New York who quickly bought into their coach's hatred for the ACC.

The Tar Heels were well-seasoned and now had college basketball's most controversial player in Scott, a junior who received the third-most votes on the All-ACC team as a sophomore and had taken over for Larry Miller as the focal point of the 1969 team. Of course, Scott carried the extra burden of his skin color and the racist reaction it provoked.

Smith nearly went into the stands of the new Carolina Coliseum in Columbia, South Carolina, after a redneck, who called Scott a "big baboon," as the Tar Heels walked off the court. It followed a suspenseful, six-point victory for UNC, which avenged a loss 12 days earlier to McGuire's newly named "Iron Five." The South Carolina starters had played all 40 minutes in the game at Charlotte and stunned the No. 2 team in the nation behind 38 points from their cocky sophomore star John Roche.

McGuire apologized for the crass act, fearing that his school was not ready for its first African American player, Casey Manning, from the border town of Dillon, who was starring for the USC freshman team at the time. Just as Smith had made efforts to integrate before Scott, McGuire had tried to break South Carolina's color line earlier, recruiting such players as Gilbert McGregor, who became a star at Wake Forest.

South Carolina won the ACC Tournament in 1971, which marked the only ACC title for a school from the state of South Carolina. The Gamecocks went independent after that season, and that quelled the acrimony between the schools a bit. "When I came to college, most of what I had heard about Frank McGuire wasn't good because [the Gamecocks] were the big rivals and the bad guys," said Roy Williams, who was a freshman walk-on in 1969 and then kept statistics for Smith the next three years. "After learning more about the history, that he hired Coach Smith, it hit me that Frank McGuire really started the basketball success at North Carolina."

37 Eat and Drink at Four Corners Grille

Four Corners turned 35 in 2014. Not the stalling strategy—but the restaurant on Franklin Street. I know because I was there as one of the original owners, along with then-UNC assistant basketball coach Eddie Fogler and about six other limited partners who "always wanted to open a sports bar."

We weren't even 10 years out of college back then but believed Chapel Hill needed a sports-themed bar and restaurant. I covered the Tar Heels on the road, and Fogler recruited all over the country, and we agreed that we lived in just about the only big-time college sports town without one.

Liquor by the drink had passed in North Carolina in 1978, eliminating the brown bagging law that caused the laughable debate between the "wets" who wanted the law passed for new tax revenue and the "dries" who believed the new law would increase the number of alcoholics in the state. (It's laughable because I never knew a true alcoholic until I came here for school.) With brown bagging, people drove around with cases of liquor bottles in their trunks. Before entering a fine restaurant, they would grab a fifth and put it in a brown bag. And they sat at dinner until that fifth was empty, often staggering out to the parking lot. Passing liquor by the drink not only spawned thousands of new bars across North Carolina, it also saved a lot of lives. You could never drink as much alcohol in one night ordering from the bar as you could walking out of a place with an empty bottle.

Four Corners was the second restaurant in Chapel Hill with a mixed-drink license (Papagayo's, where R&R Grill is today, was the first.) Once we slapped those brass letters—FOUR CORNERS—on the front fascia a month before we opened, the town went crazy with anticipation.

The current owner, Kristian Bawcom, is dealing with an entire generation of customers who have no idea where the name of his bar and grill came from. After all, it's not even on *one* corner. He has an explanation on every menu:

Dean Smith is most associated with the "Four Corners" offense, a strategy for stalling with a lead near the end of a game. Smith's teams executed the Four Corners so effectively that in 1985 the NCAA instituted a shot clock to speed up play and minimize ball-control offenses.

And, because Dean Smith owned the strategy, people thought he also owned the sports bar. And who were we to dissuade anyone from believing that? Phil Ford, who popularized Four Corners during his Carolina career and whose giant picture holding up four fingers while dribbling the basketball greeted guests at the front door, was also supposedly a silent partner. As was Walter Davis, whose nickname sat atop the dessert portion of the menu: Sweet D's.

We had the most fun before we opened, designing shirts with a hand raising four fingers and coming up with the menu items.

Fabulous Phil was a roast beef sandwich with horseradish.

Worthy Burger was half pound patty that barely fit in your mouth.

Kangaroo Kid (for Billy Cunningham) was "corned beef with hot mustard that really jumps."

When Michael Jordan and his wagging tongue arrived, we featured a tongue sandwich until it became too expensive.

Four Corners was so popular from the day it opened that controlling the crowds became less fun. We served lunch, dinner, a late-night menu, and Sunday brunch because we sold too much alcohol. In those days, the North Carolina ABC board required restaurants with a mixed-drink license to make 50 percent of their revenue through selling food. This, of course, was impossible with a high-volume bar. Now, it is a 70/30 ratio, which makes a lot more sense. Eventually, business leveled off at Four Corners because another new bar seemed to open every week. And every new bar offered drink specials that drove students there until the next new bar opened.

But Four Corners was always, as it remains today, the eatery most associated with UNC sports. After we sold it, former Tar Heel basketball player Hughie Donohue took over for about eight years. Eventually some former students (a few of whom we had to cut off in the old days) bought it, and now it is better than ever under Bawcom's ownership.

It has a well-priced menu with excellent food and service and more than 20 high-def TVs where you can watch every sports event imaginable through every satellite package offered. It is still packed for Tar Heel games, but Sundays are special in the fall with hundreds of patrons wearing their favorite jerseys crowding in to watch the NFL game of their choice.

The old Four Corners had its moments that will never be forgotten. The night Carolina won Smith's first national championship in 1982, our managers covered the entire front of the building with plastic to keep from getting splashed with light blue paint. And there was the night that we finally had to ban the rowdy, top-ranked Tar Heel men's lacrosse team from the premises. That was no fun, but we did not have enough insurance to cover what might happen. It spawned the funniest moment I ever had at Four Corners.

A couple of days after coach Willie Scroggs' team won the second of their three championships (they also won six ACC titles and Scroggs retired with an overall record of 120–37), I was sitting on the upper level next to the front windows, where I could see who was walking down Franklin Street and, presumably, they could see me. Flush from winning it all again, a couple of lacrosse players spotted me at the place they could no longer go to celebrate. As one of the All-American players passed by, he stopped and stuck his head in the front door. Raising the middle finger of one hand at me, he shouted, "Hey, Carolina Lacrosse, No. 1!"

38 Cota the Cutter

When Ed Cota arrived at Tilden—his third New York City high school in three years—he was considered another of those playground legends who would be a no-show at practice. Even after Cota once missed 56 days, blew off summer school, and didn't regain his eligibility until almost a year later, his new coach, Eric "Rock" Eisenberg, saw something that other coaches had apparently missed.

A gifted player since his days at Mahalia Jackson Middle School, Cota's world fell apart in February of 1990 when his mother, Cecilia, and his stepfather, George Cedeno, were visiting Cedeno's native Panama. On the road from Panama City to Colon, a tire exploded and Cedeno flew out of the car, landing in a wheelchair for life. Cecilia spent six months in the hospital and wound up with an artificial hip and knee.

Forced to live with his grandmother, the 14-year-old Cota wandered aimlessly between school and the streets, spending as much time rolling dice as shooting hoops. He bounced around from Bensonhurst High, almost a two-hour commute via bus and subway, then to New Utrecht, and eventually to Tilden, where he told Eisenberg he wanted to try out for the team and then cut class for those 56 straight days. By the time he had his family back and decided to give basketball another serious shot, "Cota the Cutter" had a little more than one season of eligibility remaining. His senior year athletically was his sophomore year academically, when Cota scored 55 points in one game while leading Tilden deep into the public school playoffs. "No one really understood how much this accident had taken out of him," Eisenberg said. "They weren't dealing with the whole product; they were dealing with a kid who they thought had become a bum. A lot of high school coaches get hundreds of these kinds of kids, and most coaches don't take the time to isolate the one or two of their problems and deal with them. They say, 'The kid's a cutter, let's get him outta here.' No one isolated the problem that Eddie was in emotional shock."

Cota emerged as a bona fide college prospect as a senior, but he lacked almost two years of classroom work to graduate. Eisenberg knew that even with a successful appeal for another season at Tilden, Cota would have to finish in prep school if he wanted to keep playing basketball. "St. Thomas More in Connecticut is a real school," Eisenberg said. "A lot of the prep schools are fake, where the kids don't do a thing except get phony grades. So I called the coach, Jere Quinn, who I had heard great things about. He said he thought he could help, but he didn't know me so he had to check things out... Jere did a great job and helped Eddie become a better player, but it wasn't easy. Eddie missed home like crazy, like a junkie misses heroine, a fat person misses food, or an alcoholic misses alcohol. He was drawn back on weekends, sometimes he'd get back to school a day late, and Jere was pissed off. They'd dock him and take some privileges away."

By the guard's senior year, college scouts and recruiting analysts knew two facts about Ed Cota: he could play on the major college level and he would probably do it at North Carolina. When Eisenberg returned to a court that was ringed by other college coaches and mentioned to them that Dean Smith was making a special trip to New Jersey, it was a little like the Red Sea parting. "All the coaches took a step backward," Eisenberg recalled, laughing. "Collectively, they were all saying, 'well, if for some reason Eddie doesn't go to Carolina, tell him we're still interested.' I guess they figured if Dean wanted him, Dean was going to get him."

Just before Cota boarded a plane at LaGuardia for Chapel Hill, there was one more question that had to be answered, according to Eisenberg "He asked me, 'Rock, do you think I'm a North Carolina-type person?'

"I said, 'Eddie, I know you are, but you're the last person in the world who doesn't know that. You've got to find that out for yourself. Me telling you that you are doesn't mean anything. You're the one who's got to believe it.'"

As he settled in Chapel Hill, it took a while for Cota to find out. He studied enough to make a 3.0 (B average) his first semester, but basketball came harder than he had expected. He started the first game of the season, a disappointing loss to Arizona, when the team was outplayed and outhustled by the eventual national champions, and freshman Cota wound up taking more shots than any of his teammates.

Plagued by turnovers, he never stayed in the game long enough to get comfortable. One night, in frustration, he called his stepfather to complain. Cedeno then phoned Eisenberg, who immediately called Cota back. "I got Eddie, woke him up, and called him every name in the book for worrying his father like that," Eisenberg said. "I told him if he wanted to be stupid and leave Carolina, let me know…Fortunately, the very next day Coach Smith had a talk with him, and the rest is history."

Cota's gradual emergence—from an unsteady freshman to Smith's "sixth starter" coming in during the first five minutes of the game—helped transform the Tar Heels from a team going nowhere to perhaps the most efficient offensive machine in the school's history. Cota went on to become only the second freshman to lead the ACC in assists and missed breaking Kenny Smith's UNC single season record of 235 by two. And it's no coincidence that once the basketball was placed in Cota's hands, Shammond Williams started knocking down threes, Vince Carter began moving better without the ball, and Antawn Jamison and Serge Zwikker got precise pass after precise pass in the paint. "They must have scored on 65 to 70 percent of their possessions the last half of the season," guessed Eisenberg, who saw most of Carolina's games in person or on TV.

"Eddie's just a player who makes everybody around him better. No freaking ego. He's a '90s athlete with a '50s mentality."

Cota was named the 1997 ACC Rookie of the Year and a Freshman All-American. He earned second team All-ACC honors three years in a row, as a sophomore (1998), junior (1999), and senior (2000). As a sophomore, he broke the ACC record for most assists in a single season. He was named to the 1999 AP All-American team as an honorable mention. He earned three NCAA All-Regional team selections while helping UNC to three Final Fours in his college career. He was the first player in NCAA history to have 1,000 points, 1,000 assists, and 500 rebounds in a career. Cota finished with the third highest assist total in NCAA history and owns the record for most career assists at Carolina. Remarkably, Cota also played an NCAA record 138 games without ever fouling out.

Because of his six-foot size and lack of a long-range jump shot, Cota never made it in the NBA despite several tryouts. But he played professionally in Europe for five different clubs, twice making European All-Star teams. After retiring from basketball in 2008 at the age of 32, he settled in Chapel Hill, not New York City.

39 Hansbrough Indoor Stadium

Carolina fans now fondly refer to Duke's home court as Hansbrough Indoor Stadium—and for good reason. In his first visit to Cameron as a freshman on March 4, 2006, Tyler Hansborough personally ruined J.J. Redick's senior game by scoring 27 points and pulling down 10 rebounds to spark the second-half surge over

Tyler Hansbrough throws down a dunk against Duke in the Dean Dome, but it was in Cameron Indoor Stadium where Psycho T truly owned the Blue Devils, going 4–0 against them.

the top-ranked Blue Devils. Hansbrough also had a steal and two blocks, but it was the late three-pointer he made from the right wing with the shot clock running down that sealed the 83–76 upset, as Carolina earned its seventh straight win of the season and second place behind Duke in the ACC standings. This one was virtually a one-man show, as only two other Tar Heels (Bobby Frasor with 10 and Marcus Ginyard with 12) scored in double figures.

Hansborough also wrapped up first-team All-ACC as a freshman and went on to be the only player in ACC history to do it four straight years. He said he did not realize what had been accomplished until he stepped to the foul line with only seconds remaining and the outcome secured. "When I knocked down those free throws, it hit me that we'd just come in here and beat Duke," Hansbrough said. "It doesn't get any better than this."

Oh, yes it did. The following season, fifth-ranked Carolina went to Cameron on February 7, 2007, and defeated No. 16 Duke 79–73 with another late surge, erasing the Blue Devils' five-point halftime lead that stretched into double figures early in the second half. And this time, it wasn't just Hansbrough's 16 points. Freshman Brandan Wright led the team with 19 points and nine rebounds, and freshman Ty Lawson chipped in 15 points, eight rebounds, and four assists. Senior Reyshawn Terry keyed UNC's 37–29 rebounding advantage with 10 boards. "We started to get tougher as the game went on, as it was winding down," said Hansbrough, who scored 12 points in the second half. "That's maybe what we need to do at the beginning of the game, too."

Hansbrough made it three in a row at Cameron on March 6, 2008, but the top-ranked Tar Heels needed to score the last 10 points of the game to run away from No. 6 Duke 76–68. Carolina let an 11-point halftime lead slip away early in the second half before ramping up its defense and holding the Blue Devils scoreless over the last five and a half minutes of the game.

Junior Danny Green led the team with 18 points—two on his famous driving dunk over Duke's Greg Paulus—and had an amazing seven blocks. Hansborough had a spectacular double-double of 16 points and 15 rebounds while surpassing the 2,000-point career scoring mark in his junior season. Sophomore Wayne Ellington had 16 points, and Lawson added 10 points, three assists, and three steals as UNC wrapped up its second consecutive ACC regular season title.

The clean sweep came the next season when the third-ranked Tar Heels riddled Duke's defense in a 101–87 victory with another amazing second half run. Carolina, the first team in nine years to score 100 points against the Blue Devils, trailed Duke at the half by eight points before using 25–11 and 14–0 runs in the second half to win going away. And Hansbrough and Green became the only players since Wake Forest's Tim Duncan and Rusty LaRue to win four straight years in Cameron against Mike Krzyzewski's Duke teams.

This comeback was triggered by Lawson, who scored 21 of his season-high 25 points in the second half, many on drives right through the Duke defense. "We didn't think they could stay in front of us," Lawson said. "I just knew I could get to the basket." The Tar Heels won their eighth straight on the season and snapped Duke's 14-game home winning streak—since UNC's last visit there.

Ellington and Green added 15 points each, and Hansborough had 17 points and six rebounds to bring his four-year scoring average at Cameron to 19 points. Like he did as a freshman, Hansbrough hit a late three-pointer from the top of the key to put the final nail in Duke's coffin. "Each year it's been different," Hansbrough said. "Our freshman year, no one thought we could come in here and win. Tonight was one of those things where you didn't want to think about the record. We just wanted to come out and play."

40 Hubert Davis

The route Hubert Davis took to major college basketball, the NBA, ESPN, and back to college as an assistant coach with the Tar Heels was paved by a long-term family relationship. Davis' Uncle Walter had been a Tar Heel hero in the 1970s—the freshman who threw in the tying heave in Carolina's epic comeback from eight points down with 17 seconds left to play against Duke in 1974. Walter was also one of Dean Smith's favorites, a kid who struggled to become a good student and by the time he graduated a first-round NBA draft choice.

Before enrolling at UNC, Charlotte native Walter Davis had attended a year of prep school in Delaware. Homesick for the South, Walter often spent weekends visiting his older brother Hubert in suburban Virginia. Bill Guthridge came to recruit Walter and got to know Hubert, his wife Bobbie, and their three-year-old son, Hubert Jr. In a thank you note to the Davis family, Guthridge added a playful prophetic footnote: "At this time we want to officially begin the recruitment of Hubert Jr."

During Walter's four years in Chapel Hill, Hubert and Hubert Jr. were frequent visitors to Carmichael Auditorium and the Tar Heel locker room. In fact, Hubert Sr. drove the car with Walter and Phil Ford from North Carolina to Montreal for the 1976 Olympics, when the Team USA won the gold medal under Dean Smith. And Hubert Jr. spent the trip to and from Canada sitting in the back seat with the two Tar Heel stars.

Inevitably, young Hubert dreamed of following his uncle's path. Smith held a place in his program for Hubert Jr., who had grown into a fine athlete in his own right but was not considered a major college basketball prospect. After visiting with young Hubert

The Sullivans

When Ryan Sullivan accepted a scholarship to UNC, it was like a dream come true. He had been a Tar Heel fanatic even before his older brother Pat, who was recruited by dozens of schools and had Duke among his final choices. In fact, when Mike Krzyzewski visited the Sullivan home, Ryan refused to leave his bedroom and meet the Duke coach. That's how adamant he was about the Tar Heels and his brother playing in Chapel Hill.

When Ryan received a scholarship offer from Dean Smith, he thought he would *succeed* his older brother in the Tar Heel program. He never figured he'd get to play with him, even in practice. Well, it turned out that the Sullivans were almost together for Ryan's entire Carolina career, which lasted three seasons.

First, Pat decided to sit out what would have been his senior year in 1994, when the defending national champion Tar Heels had four starters and two key reserves back and three hotshot freshmen coming in. Then after Pat played as a fifth-year senior in 1995 while Ryan took his redshirt season, the older Sullivan turned down professional basketball in Europe to stay in Chapel Hill and consider his options to get into coaching. "I lucked out having him here, and now he might be here till I graduate," Ryan said. "It was a bonus having big brother around to help you out. I still had some questions, too, and he helped me with any of those."

Pat Sullivan rarely missed a game his first three seasons before back problems ended his career prematurely in 1995. His best year was the 1993 national championship season when he averaged 6.4 points, 2.4 rebounds, and was fifth on the team in assists, which was tops among reserves. Pat then began his coaching career, which led to him becoming a longtime assistant in the NBA.

While Pat coached a private high school in Raleigh, Ryan was a freshman Tar Heel reserve. When Pat joined the UNC basketball staff as video coordinator, Ryan hoped to make some of his brother's highlight films this season. "My shot's coming along, and my defense improved over the summer," said Ryan when he was a 6'3" sophomore who hoped to earn minutes in what was a thin Carolina backcourt.

Even though he never moved up the bench, Sullivan had no regrets about picking Carolina over a smaller school where he might have played more. "UNC is a beautiful school," he said. "I met a lot of great people and I got to be a basketball player here. What more can you ask for? I got to go to Hawaii twice, Seattle for the Final Four, and Europe the next year. No small school would have offered me that. This was the place to be."

and his father, Smith delivered much the same speech that he had given to Ranzino Smith five years earlier. Named for former N.C. State star Sammy Ranzino, Chapel Hill high school star Ranzino Smith longed to be a Tar Heel, and Coach Smith said he could have a scholarship but could not promise him any playing time. Ranzino was a high scorer in high school but was not very tall for a shooting guard, and the UNC coaches believed he would be a reserve coming off the bench at best.

Smith and Guthridge felt much the same way about Hubert Davis, but they were willing to offer him a scholarship because he was "family." In fact, they worried that Hubert might never get off the Carolina bench. "We're happy to have him, but I told Hubert it's going to be difficult to play at this level, and he understands that," Smith said in 1988. That statement was soon to become a point of humor around the Carolina basketball office. After one day of practice in October of 1988, a wide-eyed Guthridge said simply, "Hubert is a lot better than we thought." The following January, Davis got a chance to show everyone how much better.

Helping fill in for the injured Jeff Lebo, freshman Davis played 18 minutes at Duke and scored eight crucial points in UNC's 20-point upset of the No. 1-ranked Blue Devils. Three years later he had 35 points on the same Cameron Indoor Stadium court to complete his improbable journey toward All-American status and NBA as a first-round pick by the New York Knicks.

Hubert had a 12-year career in the NBA, playing for six teams and finishing with more than 5,500 points, 1,000 rebounds, and 1,000 assists. He always came back for the Carolina Basketball School each summer and loved coaching the campers. But ESPN hired him in 2008 to become a studio analyst, and he advanced to be a *GameDay* host each weekend during the basketball season. His reported annual salary was about $500,000.

In 2012 Roy Williams called Davis and asked him to drop by the UNC basketball office. Assistant coach Jerod Haase had left the staff to become head coach at UAB, but Davis thought that Williams was going to ask him to alter the schedule for Davis' summer camp that he conducted at the Smith Center. Instead, Williams asked Davis to replace Haase, even though he had no formal coaching experience. Davis was rendered speechless and said he had to go home and talk to his wife, Leslie. After Davis' retirement from the NBA, the family had settled in Chapel Hill.

Davis would be taking a substantial pay cut to leave ESPN, and instead of working six months a year, his new job would be the 24/7 life of a college basketball assistant coach. But it would also give him much more time to spend with his wife and three kids who did not see much of Hubert while he was constantly traveling for ESPN during the basketball season. Davis said yes and has been a staple of the Tar Heel staff since 2012. Some have speculated that he is being groomed to eventually succeed Williams as head coach. Whether or not that happens, Hubert Davis' amazing journey began as living proof of how inexact the science of recruiting can be.

41 Scoring Machines

The greatest scoring machine in UNC basketball history was not the school's all-time leading point maker, Tyler Hansbrough, or Carolina's second all-time scorer, Phil Ford. It was All-American and Player of the Year Lennie Rosenbluth, who only played three varsity seasons but does lead the Tar Heels in all-time scoring average at 28 points per game.

Rosenbluth, who played when freshmen were ineligible for the varsity, scored 40 or more points five times in his career—from 40 points against Duke in his last regular season game in 1957 to the 47 he scored against Furman as a junior in 1956. "Rosie" also scored 45 points three times, including setting the ACC Tournament single-game scoring record against Clemson on March 7, 1957, in Raleigh's Reynolds Coliseum.

Rosenbluth scored the most points in any season (895) in 1957 and remains the fourth all-time scorer in Carolina history with 2,045 points. Hansbrough (2,872), Ford (2,290), and Sam Perkins (2,145) all played four years at UNC. Had Rosenbluth played as a freshman, when he averaged over 30 points a game, he may very well have totaled more points than Hansbrough.

The UNC single-game scoring record still belongs to Bob Lewis, who tallied 49 against Florida State on December 16, 1965, the first year Carmichael Auditorium was open. Billy Cunningham has the second most points in a single game—48 against Tulane on December 10, 1964, the first of two straight seasons that the "Kangaroo Kid" led the ACC in scoring. Lewis and Cunningham both had two 40-point scoring games, but the Carolina player who scored 40 three times was Charles Scott, who twice scored 40 or more in the ACC Tournaments of 1969 and 1970. Five other former Tar Heels had one game in which they scored at least 40 points: George Glamack (45), Shammond Williams (42), Kenny Smith (41), and Harrison Barnes and Tyler Hansbrough (40 each).

Lewis leads the Tar Heels with the most consecutive 30-point games (five in his sophomore season of 1965). Scott scored 30 or more four straight times in 1970, and Rosenbluth had a streak of three in 1957, the Tar Heels' undefeated national championship season. Rosie also leads UNC with the most consecutive 20-point games—appropriately 20 in 1957. Scott did it 13 straight times in 1970, Rosenbluth did it 13 times in his junior year of 1956, Lewis scored 20 or more 12 straight times in 1966, and Larry Miller hit 20 or more for 10 consecutive games of the 1967 season.

Scott's 40 (28 in the second half) is the most by a Tar Heel in the ACC Tournament, the famous 1969 championship comeback win against Duke. In NCAA Tournament play, Hansbrough holds the UNC record for 325 points in 17 games. Al Wood in the 1981 Final Four against Virginia and Rosenbluth against Canisius in 1957 share the school record for most points scored in an NCAA Tournament game with 39. James Worthy still has the Carolina record for most points in a national championship game (28) against Georgetown in 1982.

Hansbrough's 40 against Georgia Tech in his freshman season (2006) remain the most points ever scored by a Tar Heel in the Dean Dome. Barnes scored 40 as a freshman against Clemson in the 2011 ACC Tournament in Greensboro. Four other UNC freshmen scored 31 points in a game—Antawn Jamison, J.R. Reid (twice), Mike O'Koren, and Walter Davis. Reid had 31 points in the NCAA Sweet 16 win against Notre Dame in 1987, and O'Koren scored his 31 against UNLV in the 1977 Final Four.

The 1938 Class

Over the past 60 years, Carolina basketball fans have had the pleasure of watching some great "classes" arrive in Chapel Hill, play together, win together, and graduate together—memorable classes like those of 1958, 1969, 1972, 1977, 1994, and 2009. However, ask even the most die-hard Carolina basketball fan to name the first of UNC basketball's great classes, and it's doubtful that any would say, "the class of 1938." Most Carolina fans are simply too young to remember Ruth, Bershak, Mullis, Grubb, and Potts, and the contributions these five men made to UNC basketball from 1934–1938.

As the freshman class arrived on campus in the fall of 1934, America was still in the grips of the Great Depression. Families all across the country were struggling to make ends meet, and attending college was a luxury few people could afford. It was in these difficult times that Earl Ruth and Pete Mullis of Charlotte; Foy Grubb of Spencer, North Carolina; Andy Bershak of Clairton, Pennsylvania; and Ramsey Potts of Memphis, Tennessee, made their way to Chapel Hill. These five would form the nucleus of a three-year run that saw the White Phantoms go 55–14, win three Big Five championships, finish first in the conference standings twice, and win the conference tournament once.

Ruth was the leader of the class of 1938. He arrived in Chapel Hill in 1934 after an outstanding athletic career at Central High in Charlotte. He was a three-year starter for the Phants and is the last UNC player to serve as team captain for two seasons—1937 and 1938. Following his time at Carolina, Ruth served as a lieutenant in the Navy during World War II before embarking on a long and distinguished career at Catawba College in Salisbury. From 1968–1974 Ruth served as U.S. House representative for North Carolina's 8th District. In 1975 president Gerald Ford appointed him as governor of American Samoa, and he later worked in the U.S. Department of Interior. Ruth passed away in 1989 at the age of 73. In 2012 a stretch of Highway 601 in Rowan County was renamed the "Congressman Earl Ruth Highway" to honor the late congressman.

Bershak was truly the Big Man on Campus during his undergraduate days at UNC. Though Bershak was a star on the Carolina basketball team, his greatest claim to fame was on the gridiron where he earned the title "the greatest end in the history of North Carolina." Following his senior season, Bershak was named to eight different All-American teams and chosen by the Detroit Lions in the fifth round of the 1938 NFL Draft. Unfortunately, Bershak was unable to play pro football due to his being diagnosed with nephritis in the spring of his senior year. Andy made the best of a tragic situation, remaining in Chapel Hill as an assistant football coach until the winter of 1943, when he moved back to Pennsylvania. Bershak passed away on Friday, November 19, 1943, the day before the annual Carolina-Duke football game. He was 27.

Mullis arrived on the Carolina campus in the fall of 1934 and became a legendary figure in the UNC physical education department. After helping coach Walter Skidmore win consecutive state titles at Charlotte Central in 1933 and 1934, Mullis decided to follow Skidmore to Chapel Hill. At UNC, Mullis played freshman basketball in 1935 and three years on the UNC varsity, starting at forward in his junior and senior seasons. Though he was only 5'8", Mullis distinguished himself with his long outside shot, his expert ball handling, and his competitive nature. During his three-year varsity career, Mullis never missed a game, starting 42 of 44 games in his junior and senior seasons. During his time as an undergraduate, Mullis also was a member of the swim team as a diver and served as freshman class president and president of the Monogram Club.

Upon graduation in 1938, Mullis entered graduate school at UNC and received his Master of Education in 1940. Following the hiring of Bill Lange as head basketball coach in 1939, Mullis was named Lange's assistant and assisted three UNC basketball coaches—Bill Lange, Ben Carnevale, and Tom Scott—from 1939 to 1952. Mullis was a member of the UNC physical education department from 1939 until his death in 1962.

Grubb was born in Davidson County and graduated from Spencer High School in 1934. At Carolina, Grubb lettered in both basketball and baseball and was secretary-treasurer for the Class of '38. Graduating with a B.S. in commerce, Grubb worked with financial institutions in Shelby and Morganton before serving as a lieutenant in the Navy during World War II. Following the war Grubb went to work with General Motors in Winston-Salem, North Carolina, before helping establish Mid-Carolina Bank in Greensboro. Grubb passed away in Durham on June 18, 2002, at the age of 87.

Potts' final game in a Carolina uniform was the loss to Washington & Lee in the 1937 Southern Conference Tournament. Potts was not in school in 1938 and thus did not play basketball. In 1937 Potts started all 23 games for the Phants and also served as captain of the UNC tennis team. The Memphis native graduated from Carolina in 1941 and, believing that the United States would eventually be drawn into the war in Europe, enlisted in the U.S. Air Force. During World War II, Potts completed 38 bombing missions and received the Distinguished Service Cross, the Silver Star, the Distinguished Flying Cross with Two Oak Leaf Clusters, the Distinguished Unit Citation, the British Distinguished Flying Cross, and the French Croix de Guerre. Oscar-winning actor Jimmy Stewart was Potts' operations officer on a number of the missions. Potts returned to the United States in 1946 and enrolled in law school at Harvard, graduating in 1948. He practiced law in Memphis before becoming a founding partner of the law firm Shaw, Pittman, Potts, & Trowbridge in Washington, D.C. Potts retired from the firm in 1986 and passed away in May 28, 2006, in Boynton Beach, Florida, at the age of 89.

43 Dean's Roller Coaster to the Record

Before the 1996 season, Dean Smith had said sarcastically of Adolph Rupp's record for all-time coaching victories that he was chasing: "When we win eight games this season and eight the next, I'll be a little closer."

Despite losing four of its last six games with a freshman-laden team, Carolina managed to win 21 games and move Smith within 25 of Rupp's 876 as he entered the 1997 campaign. Yet Smith found himself in another quandary. Winning at least 20 games each season was a given at Carolina (UNC had done it for 26 straight years), and even slight improvement over the last season meant that Smith might be upstaging his own team by tournament time. "I don't want the attention on me. I want it on the team," he said tersely before the opening game. "That's why I said several years ago that I'd get out before I broke the record. Luckily, it shouldn't be a problem this year...You can't count on 26 wins with any team."

Smith's 36th—and last—season on the bench turned out to be one of his strangest. While winning nine of its first 10 games against a soft schedule, his team continued the uneven play that had marked the last half of the previous season. Much of it came from a new backcourt of freshman Ed Cota and junior Shammond Williams, who had taken over from Jeff McInnis (turned pro) and Dante Calabria (graduated). Cota and Williams had both taken prep school years before coming to Chapel Hill, and both exceeded expectations. Cota was tagged as a non-shooting passer and Williams a shooter whom Smith said "scares me to death when he has the ball."

Overcoming Carolina's uneven start in ACC play, Antawn Jamison helped lead the Tar Heels to the Final Four during Dean Smith's last season on the bench.

The frontline had three sophomores, and while they had their moments, none was considered a superstar in the making. Antawn Jamison had gotten off to a blistering start as a freshman and made All-ACC, but he had struggled against more attentive defenses during the second half and shot only 62 percent from the foul line. Ademola Okulaja was a role player and would not fully blossom until his senior season. Vince Carter had been so disappointing as a freshman that unfounded rumors had him transferring to a school back in his native Florida. Senior center Serge Zwikker had been better than expected in his first starting role, but his single-digit scoring and rebounding averages were not making anyone forget Eric Montross.

The situation was so tenuous that a controversial transfer student who had yet to play a game for the Tar Heels—and began the season under suspension—was looked to as a savior by some desperate Carolina fans. Makhtar N'Diaye, Smith's first transfer from another four-year school, had been penalized for taking illegal travel expenses to a summer basketball camp from sneaker impresario Sonny Vaccaro. UNC and Smith maintained that N'Diaye had done nothing wrong, but the incident foreshadowed the continuation of a jaded career for the 6'9" Senegalese player.

When the Tar Heels lost their first three ACC games for the first time under Smith, blowing a 22-point lead to Maryland at home, critics again crowed that the game had passed the 65-year-old by. The rap was he hadn't recruited players to replace Jerry Stackhouse and Rasheed Wallace and could not coach the guys left in the program. Despite wide-spread criticism of Carter as "soft" and Williams as a selfish gunner and despite a players-only obscenity-laced shouting session after a 12-point loss at Virginia, Smith stayed poised and positive about his team in public.

Privately, he admonished the team to play harder but worried about the team's fragile confidence, Smith remained more even-handed than he might have in the past. Somehow, the Tar Heels

rallied from nine points down in the last two and a half minutes
to defeat N.C. State and avoid an 0–4 start, then managed a mild
upset with their best defensive game of the season against Clemson,
and finished the first half of the ACC schedule with a 3–5 record.
The turning point might have come in a seven-point loss at heavily
favored Duke. Almost winning in Cameron Indoor Stadium
seemed to give the players renewed confidence. "They had more
confidence in themselves than I had in them," Smith said.

In a remarkable turnaround, Carolina went undefeated over
the second half of the season and reached the ACC Tournament
finals by knocking off Tim Duncan and two-time defending champion Wake Forest for the second time in 17 days. And in defeating
N.C. State for Smith's 13th ACC Tournament title, he found
himself within one game of Rupp's record.

Smith had decided to bring Cota off the bench after a few
minutes of watching the game unfold and was flabbergasted by the
offensive efficiency of the team, which shot better than 50 percent
in 15 games of the 16 consecutive wins. But it had been Smith's
persistent planning and teaching that enabled Cota, the ACC
leader in assists, to get Jamison the ball at the low post, Zwikker on
the baseline, and Carter above the key for drives and dunks. When
opponents gave up and sagged inside to stop the easy baskets,
Williams nailed one big three-pointer after another.

A team that seemingly couldn't beat anybody good early in
the season, literally, couldn't be beat in February and March. The
Tar Heels were so into their own successful run that they easily
handled the pressure of their coach's impending milestone. They
defeated Fairfield and crushed Colorado in the first two rounds of
the NCAA Tournament in Winston-Salem, North Carolina, to
give Smith the most major college wins in history.

Smith notched wins No. 878 and 879 against California and
Louisville at the East Regional in Syracuse before the season—and
Smith's storied career—ended with a loss to Arizona in his 11th

Final Four at Indianapolis. The 1997 season solidified the myth of Dean Smith perhaps more than any other during a career that spanned four decades, eight presidents, and 35 opposing ACC coaches. Smith had scrapped his favorite plans in favor of what worked. He scrapped the pressure defense, stopped his incessant substituting, and—for the first time since Phil Ford—let a point guard dribble more than pass. Faced with his own increasing age, the attitude of fans with short memories, and the encroachment of pro basketball into the college game, he had the energy, patience, and resiliency to pull off yet another turnaround.

44 Championship Reunion

The 1957 and 1982 national champion Tar Heels lined up in the runway during the first half of the home game against Wake Forest on February 10, 2007, for the most moving halftime tribute in Carolina athletic history. Here were the players who had started it all with a fabled run to an undefeated season and the 1957 NCAA Championship and, as if ordained, the team that 25 years later won it all for a coach who built basketball at North Carolina into an elite sport. The late Frank McGuire had been gone for 13 years, but Dean Smith, aging gracefully, lined up with the other Tar Heel heroes.

The day was bigger than the game, a 104–67 blowout of Wake Forest. And it was even bigger than the American idols who were part of the 1982 national championship team—a freshman named Jordan, a role player that season and later the best-known athlete of his generation; a sweet, sensational sophomore named Sam, who will always be remembered for his wingspan and wider smile; and a junior named James—Big Game James—the heart and soul of Smith's first national champions.

The day was biggest for the 10 living members of the 1957 team and the deceased coach who came from New York to put basketball on the map in North Carolina and at its state university. Finally, and long overdue, a banner was hoisted among the others and the jerseys in the rafters, commemorating Frank McGuire and his perfect Tar Heels. "I don't think Coach McGuire gets enough credit for starting everything down here," said Lennie Rosenbluth, the 1957 Player of the Year. "And I don't think we get enough credit. Basketball was absolutely nothing at Carolina before McGuire came."

Without McGuire, none of this would have been there—Smith down on the floor, the man known worldwide as Michael who kissed his old coach on the head at the end of the ceremony, and the 22,000-seat stadium in which everyone stood at halftime while the current Carolina coach and his players were in the locker room.

Without McGuire, Smith might have coached at Kansas, and Roy Williams might be a successful high school coach in the mountains of North Carolina. Football at Carolina still might be bigger than basketball, which it was when McGuire arrived. The future stars who grew up in the state might have chosen other paths, such as baseball for Phil Ford, football for Worthy, and a career in the Air Force that late-blooming Jordan considered at one point.

The 2007 tribute to the two championship teams was all about amazing longevity. Carolina basketball blood brothers reached out across 50 years and were being honored by 22,000 people who had heard about them, read about them, and, in some lucky cases, *seen* all of them create this historic legacy.

Williams and his team had to miss the halftime ceremony, but in the closing seconds against Wake Forest, the head coach walked down the bench toward Section 119 where the honorees were all sitting. He looked up at them and begun applauding, and his players stood and clapped along with him. That evening, the 2007 Tar Heels were seated front and center at a private dinner at the Alumni Center on campus. Williams wanted them all to be aware and more appreciative than they might have been left to their own adolescent devices. "Don't be cool," he told them, which meant no headphones, no texting, and no nodding heads during the speeches. "We're a family," he reminded them. "Listen to what these retired Tar Heels say and try to relate it to your own careers. Imagine being their age because all of you will be some day."

Williams learned much of this from Smith, who used fewer words and imparted this tradition to his players more by example. He began each practice with a thought of the day, usually unrelated to basketball. He took them to faraway places, housed them in fancy hotels, and emphasized that the game of life was more important, but let's play hard and try to win anyway. "He was teaching us how to be coaches, businessmen, how to be successful, if we were listening," said Chuck Duckett, the head manager in 1982.

Smith respected his players as citizens first and athletes second. He never stopped teaching, trying to make his players better. He held individual meetings after the last game and gave out personalized practice plans for the offseason, following that up with letters during the summer. Even Jordan received a written regimen after he had been an All-American as a sophomore in 1983. Jordan was told to "shoot the same way" from different distances on the floor, refine his foul line routine, and play point guard in pickup games—the last counsel more for his pro basketball career than for his junior season at UNC. In asking Jordan to "visualize cutting down the nets in Seattle (site of the 1984 Final Four)," Smith obviously knew that Jordan's junior year would be his last in college. Smith was preparing him for his basketball life in the NBA.

During the reunion game in 2007, UNC ramped up security so Jordan would not be approached by fans, but on the court and later that night, he was just one of the guys, the freshman who had dreamt the night before of hitting the winning shot in the national championship game and then closed his eyes when he let it go with 17 seconds left against Georgetown. "The memories I have with the '82 team can never be replaced; it was like no other team I ever played on," said Jordan, who went on to lead the Chicago Bulls to six NBA titles.

Still, the most moving memories of the weekend came from the 1957 Tar Heels, who were almost all in their 70s. One of their starters, Bob Cunningham, had passed away in the previous year, and they seemed to know this was likely their last time together for such a ceremony in Chapel Hill. "It's mind-boggling that people still remember us after 50 years," Rosenbluth said. "We played for Coach McGuire, but it was Dean Smith and now Coach Williams who have kept everything going."

Jimmy Black, the only senior starter in 1982, was asked by Williams to speak on behalf of his team at the dinner Saturday night. He was reluctant at first because he wanted others to have their chance. "I spoke from the heart," Black said. "It was emotional because it wasn't just the players, coaches, and managers who were there, but also the secretaries, support group, and a few special fans who followed us all season. That was the beauty of it for me."

Black said he had no clue that his skip pass to Jordan on the left wing on the Monday night of March 29, 1982, would be part of history. He said they were just kids playing the game they had played all of their lives and doing what their coaches had taught them. "It never entered my mind what it would mean for the school and the basketball program," he said. "We were happy for Coach Smith, so everyone would stop talking about him not winning the big one."

After the game, Black and Smith shared a long, memorable moment in front of the bench. "He said, 'I love you, Jimmy,' and

I said, 'I love you, Coach,'" Black said. "Where in the world can a black kid from the Bronx and a Caucasian male from the Midwest hug each other and say that—except in sports?"

Black said he and his teammates had begun to develop the passion for each other and their unforgettable season during the past 25 years, similar to what they witnessed among the 1957 team. "I hope all of us are around for our 50th reunion," he said. "It will mean even more to our group than it does now because we'll still be here and, hopefully, telling our grandkids about it by then."

At the end of the ceremony on the court a few hours earlier, Black had led his teammates over to their 1957 counterparts. They took turns hugging each other. Jordan wrapped his arms around Tommy Kearns, the point guard who had jumped center against Wilt Chamberlain. Perkins embraced Pete Brennan, the smooth forward who saved the 1957 semifinal game against Michigan State with a last-second basket. Worthy hugged big man Joe Quigg, the center who hit the two winning free throws in the third overtime against Kansas. "They all thanked us," Rosenbluth recalled of the final moment under the Frank McGuire banner. "They said that, 'Without you, none of us would be here.'"

45 Dean Smith's Funeral

The service was open to family, close friends, and Tar Heel basketball letter winners.

One of those letter-winners was Pearce Landry of Greensboro, a minister, coach, and part-time financial adviser who played for Smith from 1992 to '95. Landry said the pastor told the packed church that Smith planned his own funeral, hand-picking scripture passages and hymns. "I know Coach Smith was smiling today," Landry said, "because he was still the teacher, and we were all the students. He probably had a lot of joy as we were sitting in the pews listening. He reminded us where true life is found: in a personal relationship with God and how we treat our fellow man. Even at his funeral, he was teaching us."

It was a lesson heard by a Who's Who of Carolina basketball. Among the former players attending the service were Michael Jordan, Phil Ford, James Worthy, Sam Perkins, Mitch Kupchak, Eric Montross, Rasheed Wallace, Hubert Davis, Jeff McInnis, Jerry Stackhouse, Donald Williams, Shammond Williams, Brad Daugherty, George Lynch, Derrick Phelps, Joe Wolf, and Warren Martin. The program from the funeral listed current UNC coach Roy Williams and Rev. Robert Seymour, Smith's pastor for 30 years, as speakers.

Also there were former Tar Heel coach Bill Guthridge; NBA executive Rod Thorn; and Larry Brown, Smith's former player and assistant coach and current coach at SMU and the only man to ever win an NCAA championship and NBA championship as head coach. Former Georgetown coach John Thompson, who was an

The Final Gift

Chances are, most of the $200 checks the late Dean Smith sent to about 180 former players will never be cashed.

Some of his lettermen over 36 years may take his advice and "enjoy dinner out compliments of Coach Dean Smith." But the great majority will never let that check—a final gift from their legendary coach—out of their sight. "Beautiful idea," said Jim Delany, Class of 1970 and current commissioner of the Big Ten Conference. "Waiting to receive my letter and check to frame and remember a pretty amazing guy, coach, and leader."

Similar sentiments poured in from around the country. Class move, Coach. Rest in Peace.

assistant coach on Smith's 1976 Olympics staff and whose Hoyas lost to Smith's Heels in the 1982 NCAA finals, also attended.

Williams, who played dozens of rounds of golf with Smith through the years, said his former boss is now in heaven with his favorite foursome—former UNC chancellor Christopher Fordham, local Chapel Hill psychiatrist Dr. Earl Somers, and former North Carolina High School Athletic Association executive director Simon Terrell, the husband of Smith's first basketball secretary, Betsy Terrell. Williams asked that the congregation all point to the heavens and give the foursome a big assist on getting back together. "I won't name names, but everybody was there," Landry said. "People came from near and far. People flew in from overseas. People drove from upstate New York or took a red-eye flight from California...John Thompson was there, and the bond they shared was really special. To see him there meant a lot to all us Carolina guys."

Two of Smith's children, Scott Smith and Kristen Smith, shared light-hearted memories of their father. "His oldest son and daughter spoke about their time with him, and they were funny," Bob McAdoo said. "[Kristen] said he used to tell them over and over that they were uncoachable."

Smith's friend Howard Lee, Chapel Hill's first and only black mayor, read 1 Corinthians 13. Mourners also heard Smith's selected scripture lesson from Matthew 25:31-46 and sang hymns "O God Our Help in Ages Past," "In the Bulb There is a Flower," "Now Thank We All Our God," and "Amazing Grace." "It was a phenomenal day of remembrance and celebration," Landry said. "The things that were so important to Coach Smith came through in the ceremony. There were moments of sadness, but most of us had said our good-byes over the last couple of years as we saw his health failing. For many of us it was a day to be sad, but also to celebrate what he had done for us. There were tears, but there was a lot of laughter, too."

Hundreds of parked cars filled the church's lot and overflowed onto the grass between the church and 15-501. More cars lined the road and were parked in nearby lots at University Mall.

Players tended to arrive in groups with old teammates gathering together to say good-bye to a legend. At times, players from different generations introduced themselves to one another, brought together on this day by the man they all called "Coach." "The man just meant so much to me and everybody there," McAdoo said. "He was ahead of his time. He was about civil rights. People thought his coaching career could be damaged by his political stances...but he didn't care. He stood by what he believed."

After the service many of the players gathered at a reception at the Carolina Club in the George Watts Hill Alumni Center on campus near Kenan Stadium. Landry said there were players from all of Smith's teams. "It was a day," Landry said, "that reminded us what Dean Smith lived for."

Smith's teams went 879–254 in 36 seasons at North Carolina. He won two national championships, took the Tar Heels to 11 Final Fours, and won 13 ACC Tournaments. He was voted ACC Coach of the Year eight times. And now, according to Town of Chapel Hill records, Dean E. Smith is buried on campus in the Old Chapel Hill Cemetery, in clear view of Carmichael Auditorium.

46 A Religious Draw

Frank McGuire claimed that before accepting the UNC job he never thought about how he would lure players from New York to North Carolina, a heavily Baptist state. Didn't most of his contacts run through the Catholic diocese, where every father, priest, and altar boy knew who he was? How was McGuire going to get kids to leave that environment and move to the South, where Catholic and Jewish people were scarce, and Protestant families ruled most churches, schools, and communities?

The answer would determine how long McGuire stayed in North Carolina and certainly how close he came to putting together a power like he had at St. John's. He began by bringing a local priest with him on every recruiting visit to apartments, brownstones, and homes in New York. McGuire assured parents that, indeed, there were Catholic folks in the South and that their boys would still be required to attend Mass on Sunday morning. "The people who recruited against me said to the Catholic families, 'Don't go to Carolina, they don't even have a Newman Club,'" McGuire recounted. "Eventually, I brought a Dominican father up from Raleigh to prove we had priests down there. It was tough breaking the ice, but once the boys saw for themselves and talked about it when they went back to New York we got it going."

Over the years McGuire's Catholic players rued the start of practice on Monday, when each had to state which Mass they had attended and have a damned good excuse if they missed one the day before. "They all believed Coach McGuire was at one of the services sitting in the back and Coach Freeman was at the other," former McGuire player Hugh Donohue said. "So if they lied about being in church, there was hell to pay."

McGuire had been part of the largest single influx of Catholic kids to Chapel Hill, where hundreds were sent for Navy pre-flight school in the 1940s. Mass was then celebrated at the Hill Hall auditorium on campus. Billy Carmichael, who had been one of only three Catholic students during his undergraduate days, led support for a Catholic church in town and began a building fund. Of course, McGuire was out front of the movement, in which W.D. Carmichael Sr. donated land on Gimghoul Road for a Gothic

Revival Church. It eventually became St. Thomas More and later moved to a larger tract outside of town for an adjoining school.

One early draw for kids considering Carolina turned out to be that freshmen were still eligible in the Southern Conference, and McGuire managed to have his scouts line up a couple of New York-area high school players to come with him. Unfortunately, Jewish star Lennie Rosenbluth wasn't one of them. He lacked the credits in math and foreign language for admission to UNC. So McGuire suggested he spend a year a Staunton Military Academy in Virginia, where Rosenbluth played a postgraduate season in 1953. By then McGuire was on the way to winning 17 games at UNC and establishing himself as somewhat of a miracle worker in the eyes of Tar Heel fans.

Another import, a 6'4" Czech named Jerry Vayda from Bayonne, New Jersey, hit a driving layup in the closing seconds of McGuire's first game against Everett Case, sealing an astonishing 70–69 upset against the eighth-ranked Wolfpack at a hushed Reynolds Coliseum. Although it would be two more years and six losses before McGuire beat State again, the first win was enough to convince Carolina fans they had found their man to truly make them big time in basketball.

In the spring of 1953, North Carolina and N.C. State were among seven schools that seceded from the Southern Conference to form the ACC. They joined Big Four rivals Duke and Wake Forest, plus Maryland, Clemson, and South Carolina in the new, smaller league created primarily to reap the rewards from football bowl games. (Virginia soon dropped its independent status to become the eighth member.) But the ACC instituted two rules that impacted its basketball teams: freshmen were declared ineligible for varsity competition, and the conference tournament champion—not the team finishing first in the regular season—would earn the lone bid to the NCAA championship playoffs. Case, so powerful that he had to approve N.C. State's participation in the new league, graciously offered use of his 12,400-seat Reynolds Coliseum for the ACC Tournament.

Rosenbluth, a 19-year-old freshman, arrived in the fall of '53 and soon preliminary games in Woollen Gym were out-drawing the varsity, which struggled to an 11–10 record in McGuire's second season. Students loved how Rosie shot from all angles and began backpedaling down the court on defense before the ball invariably went in. His scoring explosions, including 51 points against Chowan Junior College, gave the fans great hope for the future. State barely beat Carolina in their first two official ACC games that season as Case, dressed in his famous gray suit and sashaying the sideline like a ferret, worked the officials unmercifully to trigger a newspaper war of words that both coaches later called a publicity stunt. "Nobody ever dreamed it," McGuire said, "but Everett and I were really close friends until the night we played."

McGuire's put-on rivalry with Case always seemed to elevate Carolina's play, and the 1955 Tar Heels shocked State again in Reynolds Coliseum 84–80. But despite winning eight of their 14 ACC contests and Rosenbluth averaging over 25 points as a sophomore, the Heels' final record was still only 10–11. During an embarrassingly one-sided loss to Virginia in Greensboro, a few fans were booing when McGuire turned to his old coach and new assistant Buck Freeman, whom he had brought with him from New York, and asked what they should do. "Get better players!" Freeman snapped.

"I already got 'em," McGuire shot back, "on the freshman team."

The most important recruiting class in the history of Carolina basketball came down on what the *New York World Telegram & Sun* dubbed McGuire's Underground Railroad. (Willard Mullins' cartoon showed starry-eyed, suitcase-toting kids emerging from a subway station onto Franklin Street.) Four Catholic kids had been wooed by this irrepressible Irishman, who promised their families he would take care of them in the scary south.

Bobby Cunningham, a 6'4" guard from Harlem, won McGuire's loyalty after he slipped in his apartment, severely cutting his hand on a broken window his senior year in high school. Two surgeries, including one doctor's recommendation to amputate his thumb, scared off several coaches who had offered him a scholarship. With his hand heavily bandaged, Cunningham came home one day from school to find McGuire sitting in his living room holding papers to sign. Freshmen weren't eligible in 1954, so McGuire knew Cunningham would have plenty of time for the injury to heal.

Peter Brennan and Joe Quigg, a pair of rugged forwards from Brooklyn, could shoot lights out. And Tommy Kearns, a 5'11" pistol from Bergen County across the Hudson River, showed such wizardry with the ball that McGuire had a hard time getting him to give it up. Together with Rosenbluth, the Jewish player in the middle, these four Catholic players thought they could conquer the college basketball world when they committed to Carolina.

Meanwhile, McGuire smartly filled out his roster with Baptist players like Roy Searcy from Draper, North Carolina, and Methodist players like Ken Rosemond from Hillsborough. Most of those guys weren't expected to play, but it had far less to do with their religions than their basketball abilities. McGuire believed that kids from New York were more coachable and, as first-generation children of immigrants, had the pride and toughness to withstand the rancor of local rivalries.

47 Superstitions and Traditions

Roy Williams always wears a jacket and tie when he coaches (except during exhibition games and games in tropical places like Maui and the Bahamas). He says he does that because Coach Smith always dressed that way, and Smith learned that from his mentor, Frank McGuire. Williams adopted one more superstition from Smith: he never gets his hair cut on game days.

Superstition is probably more prevalent in organized athletics than any other walk of life. Coaches, athletes, and fans have superstitions ranging from the clothes they wear (and how they put them on the day of a game) to the food they eat (or don't eat) to the rituals they perform before games. When Walter Davis played with a broken index finger during the 1977 NCAA Tournament, the most cosmic Carolina fans wanted to share in Davis' pain. Like Davis, they tied their right index finger to their right middle finger with light blue ribbons and waved them hysterically as the Tar Heels marched all the way to the NCAA championship game against Marquette.

Before UNC played Houston in the 1982 Final Four in New Orleans, then assistant-coach Williams was told it was good luck to spit in the Mississippi River the morning of the game. Williams jogged the distance from the team hotel to the bank of the Mississippi and let fly. The Tar Heels whipped the Cougars. Two mornings later on the day of the national championship game against Georgetown, Williams went down to the river again. This time he was joined by Maureen Doherty, sister of UNC sophomore Matt Doherty.

The tradition stayed with Williams after he left Chapel Hill to become the head coach at Kansas in 1988. Anytime his Jayhawks played in New Orleans or anywhere within reasonable distance of the Mississippi, he made it a point to hack a loogie the morning of the game, often taking his entire team down to the river bank. Of course, it did not work in 1993 when the Jayhawks lost to North Carolina in the Final Four semis at the Superdome, but Williams went spitting two mornings later for the love of his alma mater, which wound up beating Michigan for the title. Williams continued the tradition in St. Louis in 2005 as UNC head coach when he won his first national championship after dropping a wet one in the ol' Mississip.

Spitting in the river wasn't Williams' lone superstition. Before the 1982 ACC Tournament, he bought a Mars candy bar and put it in his jacket pocket before the game to soothe his ulcer. He forgot it was there until after the game. For the rest of the season, he did the same thing, and the Tar Heels kept winning. Before the Georgetown game, he switched to a Zero candy bar because there were zero games left to win after that one.

Fellow assistant coach Eddie Fogler was almost as superstitious. He wore the same pair of rag-tag Carolina blue canvas sneakers to practice every day of the season. He used the same pen to keep team fouls and timeouts on the bench, vowing not to change pens as long as the Tar Heels kept winning. After their 16-point blowout loss at Virginia, Fogler tossed the pen in the garbage. He borrowed another pen before UNC's next game and kept it as a new winning streak began.

Longtime assistant coach Bill Guthridge had a superstitious tradition before road games. When he arrived at the visiting arena, he bought a box of popcorn and went up into the stands and finished the box before coming down and rejoining the team in the locker room. Guthridge started and maintained a tradition that he called the "blue team" handshake, which was using just the tips of his index and ring fingers and thumb to grab the same part of the recipient's hand. But it was generally for former players and coaches and people he trusted. If Coach Gut extended a full handshake to someone, it was either the first time he met the person or a sign he didn't like someone he already knew.

The way Carolina players dressed on the road was started by the dapper McGuire in the 1950s. The Tar Heels always traveled in coats and ties and carried fancy leather travel bags that McGuire had bought for the team. Smith continued that tradition, and, even as dress standards relaxed in the Roy Williams era, the Tar Heels always looked presentable on the road. They have to take out any earrings before meeting with the press and are never allowed to do interviews until they are fully dressed, no matter how long the media has to wait.

The thought of the day, another innovation Smith started to begin practice, has remained a part of Carolina basketball and is geared to not only make the players pay attention, but also to make them think about what the thought meant. Smith would often stop practice to test one of his players on what the thought of the day was. Many of those thoughts have stayed with players who have incorporated them into their careers in business, as well as coaching. "The biggest thing I took from Carolina Basketball was, 'You are only successful while you are succeeding,'" says Dick Grubar, a guard on UNC's three straight ACC championship and Final Four teams of the late 1960s. "That prepares you for the fact that you're not always going to be in the limelight. Things aren't going to always go your way, and you have to be ready to be successful every day."

While Carolina basketball is loaded with traditions, Williams has tried to open the program to outside organizations and charities that could benefit from the association. At Kansas he instituted a day to work with the local Special Olympics and has continued that at UNC. He also has one day a season when his team visits a local hospital and spends time visiting with and signing autographs for sick children. And before Christmas the Tar Heels always go shopping for needy families to make sure an extra gift or two is under their Christmas trees.

48 What's a Tar Heel?

The University of North Carolina's nickname, which also applies to North Carolina citizens, has at least two possible origins. One story hails back to the Revolutionary War and the troops of British General Cornwallis. After fording a river in eastern North Carolina, the British troops discovered their feet covered with tar, a product of North Carolina's abundant pine trees and one of the state's most important exports at the time. Some say the clever North Carolinians dumped it in the river to slow down the invading army. The British were said to have observed that if you waded in North Carolina rivers, you would get tar on your heels.

Another story comes from the Civil War. A group of North Carolina soldiers scolded their comrades for leaving the battlefield when things got tough. The soldiers threatened to stick tar on the heels of the retreating soldiers to help them stay in the battle. General Robert E. Lee is said to have commented "God bless the Tar Heel boys!" Whatever the reason for the moniker, our students and sports teams have long worn it with pride.

49 Rameses

For nearly 70 years the mascot of North Carolina's football team has been a ram. Since Carolina's nickname is the Tar Heels, it might seem strange to have a ram as a mascot, but there is a good explanation. "In 1924 school spirit was at a peak," said Vic Huggins, Carolina's head cheerleader back then. "But something seemed to be missing. One day it hit me. State had a wolf. What Carolina needed was a symbol."

Two years earlier the Tar Heels had posted a brilliant 9-1 record. The star of that 1922 team was a bruising fullback named Jack Merritt, who was nicknamed "the battering ram" for the way he plunged into lines. It seemed natural to Huggins to link a mascot with Merritt's unusual sobriquet. "Charlie Woollen, the athletic business manager at that time, agreed with the idea and gave us $25 to purchase a fitting mascot," Huggins said.

Rameses the First was shipped in from Texas, arriving just in time to be introduced at a pep rally before the VMI game. Complete with a monogram blanket on his back, Rameses helped make the pep rally one of the school's greatest. Then the ram was taken to Emerson Field where Carolina was an underdog to a strong VMI team. But for three quarters the Tar Heels battled the visitors to a scoreless tie. Late in the fourth period, Carolina's Bunn Hackney was called upon to attempt a field goal. Before taking the field he stopped to rub Rameses' head for good luck.

Seconds later Hackney's 30-yard dropkick sailed between the goalposts, giving the Tar Heels a 3–0 victory and a legendary mascot. Tar Heel rams have traveled everywhere from New York City (for the Carolina-Notre Dame game in 1949) to Jacksonville for Carolina's Gator Bowl appearances. There have been 19 different Ramses over the years, and in 2014 Rameses XIV gave birth to triplet lambs. They are all housed in a farm north of Chapel Hill and brought to the stadium on football game days and other special university events.

50 The Aycock Letter

Chancellor Bill Aycock and a young Dean Smith settled into cramped coach class seats on the first leg of their flight to San Francisco. It was 1960, and UNC's highest-ranking official and the school's 29-year-old assistant basketball coach were headed for a meeting with the NCAA to appeal accusations from the organization's infractions committee months earlier.

Head basketball coach Frank McGuire had been to the first hearing in Kansas City, and that one meeting had been enough for the dapper Irishman from New York City who seemed to play by his own set of rules. In Kansas City, McGuire had learned that the chairman of the infractions committee was the dean of the graduate school at Columbia University. Before arriving in Chapel Hill in 1952, McGuire coached St. John's teams that had regularly thumped Columbia and he concluded that the NCAA committee had it out for him and his UNC program.

Much to Aycock's embarrassment, McGuire refused to answer most of the questions asked of him that day, and the NCAA promptly cited Carolina basketball for excessive expenditures, specifically while entertaining recruits and their families. When the formal charges were mailed to Aycock, he gave McGuire a copy and asked him straight away, "Are they true?" McGuire said they were all a bunch of malarkey.

"I told him for his sake and the sake of the university, we've got to gather information to refute these charges," Aycock said.

However, McGuire had neither the time nor the paper trail Aycock needed. What he did have was his second-year assistant coach and he gave Smith to the chancellor. So this time it was Aycock and Smith going to meet with the NCAA. Since state budget rules of the day prohibited the chancellor from flying first class on university business, the two of them squeezed into the tourist cabin. Aycock remembered it was the only time he had ever heard Dean Smith utter a word about his boss. "You know, Coach McGuire would never ride tourist class," Smith said, smiling.

"I know that, but under the law, I have to," Aycock said.

Besides mapping out practice plans and running the practices when McGuire was off recruiting, Smith also had to piece together a history of McGuire's extravagant professional lifestyle, for which there were only piecemeal records. One of the incidents Smith had to retrace was the Tar Heels' road trip to Virginia and Maryland in 1958 while Smith was still coaching at the Air Force Academy. McGuire's style was to travel with an entourage, and along with the team, he loaded the bus to Charlottesville, Virginia, and College Park, Maryland, with alumni boosters and friends, players' families, and members of the press.

When they arrived at each stop, the bus unloaded to eat, and McGuire picked up the tab for everyone. This was not unusual behavior for the generous and free-wheeling head coach. Back at UNC, McGuire would turn in expense accounts to athletic director Chuck Erickson, who wanted receipts with every spending spree McGuire listed. McGuire always paid with the cash advance he received from Erickson and rarely kept any receipts, which Erickson called reckless and careless behavior.

Smith was left to untangle this Agatha Christie tale of entertainment gone awry. He first tried to find out every guest on that

1958 bus trip, taking affidavits from each one he could contact, testifying that McGuire had indeed picked up the check.

Why did the NCAA care so much about who ate what and where? The use of scouts to identify the best prospects in recruiting was under serious scrutiny, and McGuire's famed "Underground Railroad" had street-wise New Yorkers like Harry Gotkin locating city talent that someday might wind up in Carolina blue. The NCAA seemed convinced that unsubstantiated payments by scouts like Gotkin were really payoffs to prospects.

Smith's work and the presentation Aycock gave in San Francisco mitigated the charges to some degree, but on January 10, 1961, the NCAA placed Carolina's basketball program on a six-month probation for 15 violations that centered on their off-campus entertaining of recruits and their parents and, occasionally, their high school coaches. Gotkin was also cited for failing to document his expenses. That left the then sixth-ranked Tar Heels ineligible for the NCAA Tournament, and after they finished first in the ACC with a 12–2 record, their season was over because McGuire had pulled them out of the ACC Tournament as well.

They had played the rest of the regular season with a chip on their shoulder, which contributed to the nasty brawl at Duke Indoor Stadium on February 4, when the contentious game erupted and players and fans tangled on the court for 10 minutes before police could break it up. That turned out to be the beginning of the end for McGuire, who had won the 1957 national championship with the magical undefeated (32–0) team less than four years earlier.

After the season Aycock sent a letter to McGuire that basically said his days at UNC were numbered unless he could control his team's decorum during games. Aycock also noted that the NCAA would inspect the basketball program after the 1962 season and, based on its findings, could extend the probation. "The result of this inspection will be of great importance to me," Aycock wrote in the later dated April 28, 1961.

In addition, Aycock wrote that following the NCAA's review, he would recommend to president Bill Friday and the UNC board of trustees whether to terminate McGuire's contract when it expired in June of 1963. "The number of games won or lost during the next season will not be a material factor in my recommendation,"

The University of North Carolina
Chapel Hill

Office of The Chancellor

April 28, 1961

Mr. Frank McGuire
Head Basketball Coach
Woollen Gymnasium
UNC Campus

Dear Coach McGuire:

As you know, your contact with the University will expire on June 30, 1963. In keeping with University policy the question of renewal of the contract will be resolved one year prior to its expiration. This means that approximately a year from now I will decide on what to recommend to President Friday and to the Executive Committee of the Board of Trustees.

In an effort to be absolutely fair to you, I inform you now that my decision will rest largely on the unfolding events during the next twelve months. As you know, the NCAA will inspect our athletic program in connection with our current probation. The results of this inspection as it relates to basketball will be of great importance to me. Also I have been deeply concerned with the fact that our players have left the bench and entered the playing floor on two occasions in recent years. I shall look to you to maintain bench discipline to avoid re-occurrences. Although a coach has the same freedom to speak as any member of the University, I shall be concerned with the manner in which this freedom is exercised in the future.

The number of games won or lost during the next season will not be a material factor in my recommendation. All of us desire to help you in every way to avoid the many mistakes which have been made this year and to have a basketball season which will reflect the highest credit on the University. I am confident that you agree and that you join me in anticipation of a better year.

Sincerely yours,

W.B. Aycock

WBA: jp

bcc: Friday, Erickson and Hedgpeth
PERSONEL COPY FOR WBA

Aycock wrote. "All of us desire…to have a basketball season which will reflect the highest credit on the university."

McGuire resigned the following August and recommended Smith as his successor to Aycock in both words and his own letter. But by then Aycock already had Smith in mind from the time they had spent together trying to make its case to the NCAA. Of all the pictures and memorabilia Smith had in his office during his 36-year tenure as head coach, he was in only one of the photos. It was with Aycock, whose support he lauded in helping to rebuild the program, greeting him behind the Smith Center, which opened in 1986.

51 Brad Daugherty and the 1986 Class

Before Roy Williams had left Owen High School in Swannanoa, North Carolina, to join Dean Smith's staff in 1978, he had coached a pudgy 11-year-old named Brad Daugherty at his summer camp. On a subsequent visit home from Chapel Hill to see his mother, Williams learned that Daugherty had given up basketball for baseball and fishing. Williams went back to the mountains in the summer of 1980 and couldn't believe what he saw. That kid had sprouted to 6'8" and taken up basketball again. While he still needed to lose weight, Daugherty was dominating local pick-up games, some with small-college players. Because he had started school early, Daugherty was still only 14 and entering the 11th grade.

After learning that the young giant wanted to play college basketball, Williams laid down three options for him. Being blessed with size and talent, Daugherty could work as hard as he could and

Part of the 1986 class, Brad Daugherty, who would develop into the No. 1 overall draft pick, dunks against Virginia.

play at any level, maybe even all the way to the NBA; work a little and perhaps star at a small college; and not work at all and maybe still get a college offer somewhere. Williams then went back to tell his boss what he had seen.

After watching Daugherty shoot around the gym, Smith was amazed at the skill and dexterity for someone his size. Believing that Smith's teaching skill could improve his game more than any other coach, Daugherty turned down scholarship offers from Clemson and Maryland to sign with the Tar Heels in 1981. He watched them win the national championship on television the following March and eight months later he was forced into their starting lineup as a 6'10", 16-year-old freshman because James Worthy had turned pro following his junior year.

On Daugherty's official visit to Chapel Hill, he had sat on the front row with future Tar Heel teammate Steve Hale during Carolina's dramatic comeback win against Virginia in Carmichael Auditorium, when Worthy, Sam Perkins, and freshman Michael Jordan combined for 54 of UNC's 65 points.

From Jenks, Oklahoma, and a virtual unknown, Hale was a gifted student and hard-nosed competitor—Smith's kind of basketball player. The son of a coach at Oral Roberts in Tulsa, Hale relished the challenge of trying to play at Carolina when few people except Smith thought the herky-jerky lefty had a chance. "I had no idea how good I was," said Hale, who joined the freshman class with Daugherty and Durham's Curtis Hunter, the most highly recruited of the three. "I came in with no goals because I didn't know whether they would be too high or too low."

When Hale played and shot poorly as a freshman in 1983, Smith called him into the office and challenged him to apply the same hard work to his basketball as he did to his pre-med studies. Hale spent hours in the gym and by his junior year had turned into Carolina's best all-around player, setting the single-season record for free throw accuracy. He twice had nine assists in a game and once had 13, second to only Phil Ford's 14.

Hale started as a sophomore when freshmen Kenny Smith missed nine games with a broken wrist and moved over to start at shooting guard his junior and senior seasons, making All-ACC second team in 1986. Hale's sterling career ended in injury after suffering a collapsed lung against Maryland in his final home game and then returning for the NCAA Tournament with a heavily bandaged chest. He went on to med school and became a highly regarded pediatrician in Burlington, Vermont.

Daugherty took Roy Williams' first option to heart and turned into a two-time All-ACC first teamer and was the first player selected in the 1986 NBA Draft. He was a five-time NBA All-Star in his eight-year pro career with the Cleveland Cavaliers and then went into television broadcasting—first as a basketball analyst and then as a NASCAR commentator. Having developed an early love for dirt-track racing in the mountains, Daugherty also owned part of a NASCAR racing team.

The Unraveling

Frank McGuire's last Carolina team had gone 19–4 in 1961, placing first in the ACC standings with a 12–2 record, and, if not for the loss of several key players, successor Dean Smith might have enjoyed a much smoother transition as the Tar Heels' new head coach.

The unraveling began in January of 1961—the final, fractious season of McGuire's tenure—when the NCAA slapped UNC basketball with a probation that lasted until the summer. It banned

Carolina from the 1961 NCAA Tournament; McGuire and his team believed it could have won the national championship and played out that season with a collective chip on their shoulders. That sour attitude contributed to the wild melee in Durham on February 4, 1961, started by former Long Island high school antagonists Larry Brown of UNC and Duke's Art Heyman. Dozens of fans joined in the fighting between both teams, and 10 Durham policemen at the game could not restore order for more than 10 minutes. Heyman, who had originally signed with UNC before his stepfather and McGuire got into an argument the summer after his high school graduation, and Brown were suspended for the rest of the regular season, along with fellow Tar Heel guard Donnie Walsh.

That game was the beginning of the end for McGuire, who resigned under pressure the following August and was replaced by Smith, who was given a mandate by UNC chancellor Bill Aycock of decorum over won-lost record. The downward spiral continued when returning starters Yogi Poteet and Kenny "Moose" McComb flunked out of school in the spring, and the highly recruited Bill Galantai, who had been ineligible to play for the freshman team, was suspended for his sophomore season by the NCAA for having filed a false statement about his amateur status after playing for a semipro team during the summer. These were all part of the fallout from the flamboyant McGuire era over which Smith had little control as an assistant. In fact Smith had helped Aycock defend the charges against Carolina at the NCAA hearing in San Francisco in December of 1960.

When Smith's best sophomore, Bryan McSweeney, went down with a severely sprained ankle in the third game of the season and never fully recovered, the rookie head coach had lost four starters and fell further into the shadow of the heralded McGuire. Undaunted, Smith kept running his rigid practices and prepared for every game. He briefly suspended Brown, his starting point guard, for being spotted coming out of a Chapel Hill bar, though Brown contended that he only went in there to get other players out. To Smith appearances were now everything for Carolina basketball.

On the court Smith's attention to detail, such as waiting for the good shot and passing the basketball, was paying off in statistics, if not victories. Walsh, now a senior guard, was the first of many Smith players to set a single-season school record for field goal accuracy, hitting 56 percent of his shots. Practices, mostly loosey-goosey scrimmages with McGuire, became classrooms under his successor. The drills that Smith had implemented during practice—while McGuire sat in the stands and entertained sportswriters and his cronies—now became staples of a Smith team. As would become his inviolable custom through the years, Smith used practice performance to determine who would start and get most of the minutes during games. McGuire rarely used more than seven players, and his regulars were set early, changed only by a serious injury or, as his players joked, a "death in the family." McGuire's taunting ways turned into Smith's teaching methods.

Like McGuire, Smith began a practice by calling his players to the center circle with a shrill whistle. But that is where the similarities ended. Instead of McGuire trying to motivate his team with personal war stories or us-against-the-world tirades, Smith took that time to conduct a brief discussion of world news and later to implement the thought of the day. Smith occasionally doled out homework and sprung pop quizzes to his players the next afternoon. A teacher at heart, Smith wanted them thinking and alert at all times.

One final, highly visible difference was that Smith began closing some practices to the public and the press, leaving what appeared to be a void in the daily awareness of Carolina basketball. Going from the magnetic McGuire to the shy, far more private Smith seemed to many as a subtle de-emphasis of college athletics on the UNC campus. And Smith's first season did little to dispel those fears.

Besides the NCAA probation and the loss of several key returning players, the basketball schedule and its recruiting reach had been severely limited by UNC president Bill Friday, who was reacting to the point-shaving scandal that rocked N.C. State and touched UNC as well. Friday canceled the famed Dixie Classic over Christmas after reports that men with guns were roaming the concourse at Reynolds Coliseum in Raleigh. Friday did it for the protection of the players, some of whom were being approached by gamblers with money to shave points and alter the outcomes of games. It was the same scandal that had shocked New York City college basketball in the 1950s.

The unknown Smith also had a doubter in UNC athletic director Chuck Erickson, who wanted to conduct his own nationwide search for McGuire's successor. But as he did when replacing football coach Jim Tatum after he died suddenly in the summer of 1959 with assistant Jim Hickey, Aycock had made the quick decision to elevate Smith. Alumni and boosters remained in Erickson's ear about the young coach and his prospect to return Carolina basketball to national prominence. Erickson thought Smith had spent too much on new carpets in the basketball office and on long-distance phone calls. "Your phone bill is higher than the chancellor's and mine," Erickson told Smith one day.

"I should hope so," countered Smith, "you and the chancellor are not trying to recruit basketball players."

Despite the testy atmosphere that prevailed during and after Smith's first season and the 8–9 record, Smith, not yet 32 years old, pushed on, never doubting that he could eventually get the job done. With Poteet having regained his eligibility, McSweeney fully recovered, and pogo-sticking sophomore Billy Cunningham joining the UNC varsity, Smith expected a much improved team in

1963 and relished the challenge of seeing how the Tar Heels could compete with powerful Duke.

53 Five Championships in One Season

In 1971–72 UNC was the first college basketball team to ever win five tournament championships in the same season. This was because Dean Smith had a nationally ranked team that played deep into the NCAA Tournament and also because Smith liked to have his teams compete in as many tournaments as possible during the regular season—not only to get prepared for the postseason, but also to have his players see the world.

The Tar Heels, who had lost one starter (Lee Dedmon) off their 1971 NIT Championship team, had the first transfer in Smith's head-coaching career. His name was Robert McAdoo, a Greensboro, North Carolina, native whom Smith plucked from Vincennes Junior College to fill the void created when high school All-American forward Tom McMillen reneged on his commitment to UNC and instead signed with Maryland.

The 6'9" McAdoo was a deadly outside shooter who went on to be an NBA All-Star five times, was the league's MVP, and won two NBA titles. He was enshrined in the Naismith Basketball Hall of Fame in 2000. In other words he turned out to be more than an adequate replacement for McMillen, who enjoyed more success in politics as a senator than he did in pro basketball. He did play all three varsity years at Maryland, however, whereas McAdoo played only one at Carolina before turning pro. During that one season, though, the Tar Heels went 26–5 and won the ACC regular season with a 9–3 record. They also won those five tournaments, beginning with the championship of the old Big Four tourney played in Greensboro by scoring 99 points in both games and crushing Wake Forest by 23 and N.C. State by 31. McAdoo had 20 points and 13 rebounds in the title game win against State. Senior forward Dennis Wuycik added 20 points, junior point guard George Karl had 18 points, and unsung senior Steve Previs gave up the ball for 10 assists.

Over Christmas, the team flew to Madrid for a tournament hosted by the professional team Real Madrid that was basically two exhibition games. But two very tough exhibitions. In the 83–77 championship game win against Real Madrid, who had players in their 20s and 30s, Carolina's youngest—sophomore forward Bobby Jones—had 19 points and 12 rebounds. McAdoo had 14 and eight, Karl added 17 points, and junior forward Donn Johnston came off the bench to hit all five of his shots and score 10 points.

After returning home and spending Christmas with their families, the Tar Heels flew to New Orleans for the Sugar Bowl Tournament and drubbed St. Joe's 93–77 before holding off a tough Bradley team to win the championship 75–69. Four players finished in double figures, led again by Jones with 16 points and nine rebounds, Wuycik also with 16, McAdoo with 15, and Bill Chamberlain with 10. At that point, having already won three tournament titles, Carolina was 8–1 and No. 3 in the country. UNC's only loss was at Princeton in the third game of the season.

By the time the ACC Tournament began in March, the Tar Heels had already won 20 games but had played only four games against ranked teams (Virginia and McMillan's Maryland team). They easily defeated Duke in the ACC semifinals and then avenged a late-season loss at Maryland by beating the No. 13-ranked Terrapins 73–64 behind 24 points from Wuycik, 15 from Karl, 13 from McAdoo, and 11 from Previs. McAdoo, who had 17 points and nine rebounds in the semifinal win against Duke, was named MVP of the ACC Tournament, the second African American player to ever win the award after UNC's Charlie Scott in 1969. He joined Wuycik, Karl, and Previs on the All-Tournament team. Four tournament titles down.

On Carolina went to the NCAA East Regional in Morgantown, West Virginia, where the Tar Heels vied for a fifth trophy of the season and a berth in the tournament they most wanted to win—the Final Four in Los Angeles. Carolina crushed former ACC member and sixth-ranked South Carolina in the Sweet 16 game, sweet revenge for the heartbreaking loss they suffered to the Gamecocks in the 1971 ACC Tournament championship game, South Carolina's swan song from the ACC under former UNC coach Frank McGuire. Carolina blew out to an early lead and coasted to a 92–69 win against the "other" Carolina.

In the regional championship game, for the trip to L.A, the No. 2 Tar Heels battled third-ranked Ivy League champion Penn, coached by Chuck Daly, deep into the second half before pulling away for the 73–59 victory. McAdoo and Wuycik combined for 35 points and 13 rebounds as the UNC pep band struck up "California, Here We Come!" in the closing minutes of the game.

After winning their fifth tournament title of the season, Carolina was given a fighting chance to reach the national championship game against top-ranked UCLA and sophomore Bill Walton in the Los Angeles Sports Arena. But the Tar Heels were surprised by the quickness of 10th-ranked Florida State (long before the Seminoles joined the ACC), and their second-half comeback fell short in the 79–75 loss. FSU went on to lose to the Bruins for the national title two days later while Carolina finished the season with a meaningless 105–91 win against fourth-ranked Louisville in the Final Four third-place game that was abolished 10 years later.

54 The Matt Doherty Debate

The way Matt Doherty's Carolina basketball career ended was sad for both the former player and head coach, but almost tragic when you consider how it began. Doherty was the prototypical Tar Heel recruit and an honor student at Holy Trinity High School in Hicksville, Long Island, playing his first two seasons for coach Bob McKillop, who left to become an assistant and eventually the head coach at Davidson College.

The 6'7" Doherty was a scorer in high school but could do just about everything on the court. Dean Smith saw him as a versatile and vital member of future Tar Heel teams, whether scoring, rebounding, passing, or playing defense. Doherty was one of the earliest recruits to commit to UNC, telling Smith he wanted to come three days after his official visit to Chapel Hill in October of 1979. He cancelled his last scheduled visit to Notre Dame, where many people thought the Irish Catholic kid would go.

Doherty was the sixth man as a freshman but missed nine games with a broken thumb suffered when he tripped in a darkened movie theater while celebrating the end of final exams. But he returned to play a crucial role in the Tar Heels' run to the 1981 Final Four, scoring 28 combined points in West Regional wins over Utah and Kansas State and making the All-Tournament team. He was a starter for the next three seasons, during which Carolina won the 1982 National Championship and was ranked No. 1 for much of the time, and is perhaps best remembered for the short jumper he made to save his own Senior Day against Duke, which UNC won in double overtime.

But that's the good part of the story as it pertains to Matt Doherty and Carolina. After a brief stint in professional basketball and as a broker on Wall Street, he returned to the game he had played all his life as a radio broadcaster at Davidson and eventually as an assistant coach under McKillop. He moved on to serve seven seasons on Roy Williams' staff at Kansas before being named head coach at Notre Dame for the 1999–2000 season.

When Bill Guthridge retired and Williams turned down the UNC job in the summer of 2000, Doherty felt pressure to return to his alma mater and help out a program that seemed to have no Plan B after Williams decided to stay at Kansas. His coaching tenure actually began with great excitement. He drew a technical foul seven minutes into his first game at the Smith Center, exciting a usually lethargic crowd. Before each of his seasons, the first practice was called Midnight with Matt, during which Doherty and his assistant coaches played a half-court game against several of their players, all in good fun.

Despite compiling an 18-game winning streak, notching an epic upset of Duke in Durham in his first game against the archrival, and holding the No. 1 ranking for two weeks in February, Doherty's Tar Heels faded down the stretch of his initial season and went out in the second round of the NCAA Tournament to Penn State, finishing 26–7.

The infamous 8–20 season followed, a down year that Doherty had predicted when he took the job and realized he would lose most of his key players after his first season. He never recovered from that disastrous record that snapped several of UNC's sacred streaks in basketball and, despite rallying the Tar Heels to a 19–16 finish the next year, resigned under pressure in April of 2003 amidst reports of widespread player unrest.

Two unsuccessful coaching stints at Florida Atlantic and SMU followed, and Doherty wound up as a TV analyst with his basketball career pretty much over. He has since said he should have stayed at Notre Dame, which finished second in the NIT during his one season at South Bend, but took the Carolina job wholly unprepared because Williams assured him he could do it, and his old teammate Michael Jordan called and asked him to, saying if he didn't, the school was going "outside the family" to hire its next coach.

Doherty admitted he made mistakes when he returned to Chapel Hill, changing too many things too quickly as his intense coaching style belied the Midwestern-mannered Guthridge and Smith who preceded him. He was roundly criticized for bringing all four of his assistant coaches with him from Notre Dame, which meant longtime Tar Heel assistants Phil Ford and Dave Hanners were left without coaching jobs.

To this day, he considers himself largely a scapegoat for all that went wrong with a program that was lilting at the end of Guthridge's career. Clearly, he never received enough credit for signing five of the core players who went on to win the 2005 NCAA Championship after Williams finally returned in 2003. Normally, improving from eight wins to 19 would be enough to give a coach a fourth year, but the UNC administration put pressure on Doherty to walk away before it knew for sure that Williams would take the job the second time it was offered.

During Doherty's tenure the students were moved closer to the court in the Smith Center, in a riser section behind the home basket, which greatly improved the atmosphere in the much-maligned home of the Tar Heels. And he did beat Duke in his first and last regular-season games against the Blue Devils. As a player Doherty won eight of 10 games he played in against Duke. "I should have stayed at Notre Dame," Doherty insisted years later of the way his Carolina basketball connection ended.

Doherty was among the hundreds of former players and managers who attended the funeral of his two former coaches, Smith and Guthridge, in 2015.

55 Jerseys in the Rafters

Visitors to the Dean Smith Center are often awed by looking up and seeing the many banners and jerseys hanging from the girders of the massive dome. Obviously, UNC's six national championships—from 1924, 1957, 1982, 1993, 2005, and 2009—are celebrated by the biggest banners above the north end of the court. There are also banners signifying every Tar Heel team that won one of Carolina's 29 ACC regular season or 17 ACC Tournament titles, plus teams that won 18 NCAA regional championships and reached the Final Four, reached the Elite Eight, the Sweet 16, and the first two rounds of the NCAA Tournament.

The banners and jerseys hanging from the top of the Dean Dome make for an awe-inspiring sight. (Art Chansky)

Coaches Dean Smith, Frank McGuire (plus one for his undefeated 1957 national champions), and Bill Guthridge also have
their own banners, along with five banners for No. 1 ranked teams
(1957, 1994, 1998, 2005, and 2009). There is a banner listing nine
Naismith Hall of Famers from UNC, one with the Tar Heels' six
appearances in the NIT (1971 champions), and even one that lists
UNC's eight Southern Conference championships before the ACC
was founded.

The 50 jerseys hanging from the south end of the building
elicit the most of the questions from fans who crane their necks
to look upward. There is a front row of white jerseys and blue
backgrounds with names and numbers. And behind them are 42
all-white jerseys with names and numbers. Here are the criteria for
players having their jerseys hung in the rafters and on which row.

The front row (white and blue) jerseys are the retired numbers,
meaning those numbers will never be worn again by a Carolina
player. For example, 14 UNC players wore the No. 12 before Phil
Ford put it on in 1974 and took it off in 1978. But No. 12 has been
retired because Ford was the 1978 Player of the Year (recognized by
the Associated Press, National Association of Basketball Coaches,
U.S. Basketball Writers, *The Sporting News*, Wooden Award, and
Naismith Award), the single and automatic criteria for having a
jersey number retired at Carolina. The complete list of players who
have had their jerseys retired are:

- Jack Cobb, 1926 (Cobb's jersey has his name and an inter-
  locking "NC" on it because he played before uniforms had
  numbers.)
- No. 20—George Glamack, 1940 and 1941
- No. 10—Lennie Rosenbluth, 1957
- No. 12—Phil Ford, 1978
- No. 52—James Worthy, 1982
- No. 23—Michael Jordan, 1983 and 1984

Honored Jerseys

Number	Name	Year	Criteria
*	Cartwright Carmichael	1924	2
00	Eric Montross	1994	2
00	Brendan Haywood	2001	2
2	Raymond Felton	2005	2
5	Ty Lawson	2009	1, 2
5	Marcus Paige	2016	2
8	Jim Jordan	1946	2
11	Larry Brown	1963	5
12	Lee Shaffer	1960	1, 2
13	John "Hook" Dillon	1948	2
15	Vince Carter	1998	2
21	Mitch Kupchak	1976	1, 2, 5
21	Donald Williams	1995	4
22	York Larese	1961	2
22	Bob Lewis	1967	2
22	Wayne Ellington	2009	4
24	Walter Davis	1977	2, 5
30	Al Wood	1981	2
30	Kenny Smith	1987	2
30	Rasheed Wallace	1995	2
31	Bill Chamberlain	1972	2
31	Mike O'Koren	1980	2
32	Billy Cunningham	1965	1, 2
32	Rashad McCants	2005	2
33	Charles Scott	1970	2, 5
34	Bobby Jones	1974	2
34	J.R. Reid	1989	2
34	George Lynch	1993	3
35	Pete Brennan	1958	2
35	Doug Moe	1961	2
35	Robert McAdoo	1972	2
40	Tommy Kearns	1958	2
40	Joseph Forte	2001	1, 2
40	Harrison Barnes	2012	2
41	Sam Perkins	1984	2

42	Brad Daugherty	1986	2
42	Jerry Stackhouse	1995	2
42	Sean May	2005	3, 4
44	Larry Miller	1968	1, 2
44	Tyler Zeller	2012	1, 2
44	Dennis Wuycik	1972	2
45	Tom LaGarde	1977	2, 5

* Uniform did not have number back then

- No. 33—Antawn Jamison, 1998
- No. 50—Tyler Hansbrough, 2009

Of course, the players whose jerseys are retired accomplished many other accolades at UNC (ACC Player of the Year, All-American teams, Olympic gold medals), but only becoming a recognized Player of the Year will get your jersey and number retired in Chapel Hill.

The three rows of all-white jerseys behind are the "Honored Jerseys" at UNC. These are numbers that continue to be worn by Tar Heels, but the names of these players met certain criteria for being up in the rafters. Those criteria are as follows:

1. ACC Player of the Year
2. First or second-team All-American
3. Most Valuable Player of an NCAA Tournament championship team (as voted by their coaches and teammates)
4. Most Outstanding Player of the Final Four
5. Olympic gold medalist

56 Elston, Jones, and the 1974 Season

The 1974 season is remembered best for Carolina's dramatic comeback victory against Duke in which the Tar Heels rallied from eight points down with 17 seconds left in regulation to win in overtime. The Tar Heels finished 22–6 and 9–3 in the ACC, were ranked as high as No. 4 in the country, and finished at No. 8.

Of course, that was the season that N.C. State won the national championship behind David Thompson and Tommy Burleson and extended its winning streak over the Tar Heels to seven in a row. (That would be nine before it was snapped in February of 1975.) But Carolina, which had 12 players that appeared in at least 25 of the Tar Heels' 28 games, had an excellent team in 1974 that did not receive its just do. Its three conference losses were to Maryland and to State (twice).

The leader of that team was senior forward Bobby Jones, who had developed into one of the best players in the country and wound up going in the first round of the NBA draft to the Houston Rockets but signed with the ABA's Denver Nuggets and then later played for the Philadelphia 76ers. Jones averaged 16 points and 10 rebounds, shot 58 percent, and, amazingly, was third on the team in assists.

The unsung hero of that team, however, was Darrell Elston, a lightly recruited basketball player from Indiana who had been a football star in the Hoosier state. Elston broke into the starting lineup as a junior in 1973 and started every game his senior season, averaging 15.3 points and leading the team in assists with 158, which was 5.6 per game. Elston was also deadly from the foul line, hitting better than 87 percent of his free throws. He made second team All-ACC that season after being a benchwarmer for most of his college career. In Dean Smith's overall score system that season, Elson led the team with an 81.5 score compared to Jones' 81.

Freshman Walter Davis, who made the 35-foot bank shot against Duke that sent the game into overtime, where the Tar Heels won 96–92, became a starter midway through the season and wound up averaging 14.3 points a game. Davis was on his way to becoming an All-ACC player and NBA first-round draft pick in 1977. Sophomore Mitch Kupchak missed playing in only one game (as did Davis), and Dean Smith also used seniors Ray Hite and John O'Donnell, juniors Ray Harrison and Ed Stahl, and freshman John Kuester in all 28 games. Junior Brad Hoffman played in 27, sophomore Bill Chambers in 26, junior Mickey Bell in 25, and freshman Tommy LaGarde in 22. Also on that 20-man roster were junior UNC three-sport star Charles Waddell, sophomore Tony Shaver (now the coach at William & Mary), and freshman Bruce Buckley.

The 1974 Tar Heels were 22–4 and ranked sixth in the nation after beating Wake Forest in the first round of the ACC Tournament in Greensboro. In the semifinals against Maryland, the rubber match on the season, the fourth-ranked Terrapins of coach Lefty Driesell clobbered Carolina by 20 points and went on to lose the epic overtime championship game to N.C. State, which returned to the Greensboro Coliseum two weeks later to dethrone UCLA in the Final Four and defeat Marquette to win the Wolfpack's first of two national championships.

Since only one school from each conference was still allowed in the NCAA Tournament, Carolina went back to the NIT for the second straight season and lost to Purdue in Madison Square Garden. The Boilermakers went on to win the NIT title game against Utah, whose coach Bill Foster took the Duke job the following week. UNC had gone 47–14 and remained nationally ranked during the 1973 and 1974 seasons but was completely overshadowed by an N.C. State team that had lost one game in two years and won the national championship. It was considered one of the "forgotten" teams of Carolina basketball, and the most forgotten star was Darrell Elston.

UNC's 20-man roster in 1973–74 represents the most players Dean Smith carried in his 36 years as head coach.

57 Ol' Roy's Luck with Iowa

Roy Williams had already had great success recruiting the state of Iowa before he was named head coach at North Carolina in 2003. In his 15 years at Kansas, he recruited three All-Americans from the Hawkeye State—Raef LaFrentz in the 1990s and Kirk Hinrich and Nick Collison, who played on the Jayhawks' 2002 and 2003 Final Four teams. All three players went on to NBA careers.

When the No. 1 high school player in the country turned out to be Harrison Barnes from Ames, Iowa, all Williams needed was access to a UNC jet to make as many trips to see Barnes as was necessary to get his commitment. Early on, all the recruiting experts had Barnes pegged for Duke, but that did not deter Williams. He confided that he took 11 trips to Ames to either visit Barnes or watch him play, while he believed Duke's Mike Krzyzewski was only out there three times. Barnes made official visits to both campuses, and, reportedly, his trip to Durham actually helped him decide on Carolina.

Duke put Barnes and his mother behind the home bench, where they could see into the Blue Devils' huddle and hear what was being said. In that particular game, as with others, Coach K used plenty of foul language to motivate his team. Krzyzewski's

Marcus Paige from Marion, Iowa, calls for Four Corners against Georgia Tech in 2015 to honor Dean Smith, following the passing of the legendary coach.

cursing was already well known around the ACC, but apparently it was news to Sylvia Barnes. After they left Cameron Indoor Stadium, she supposedly said to her son, "You can go anywhere you want, but I am against my son going anywhere the coach talks to his players like that."

When in the fall of 2009, Barnes was going to announce his decision, he asked the coaches from all the schools that were on his final list—Carolina, Duke, Iowa State, and UCLA—to set up computers so Barnes could make his decision over Skype. All of them abided, and after Barnes thanked all of the schools that recruited him, he said, "Coach Williams..." At that point, the world knew that Roy Williams had hauled in another Iowan.

Two years later, after Barnes left early to be drafted by the Golden State Warriors, UNC signed Marcus Paige out of Marion, Iowa, and Paige became the fifth All-American from Iowa to play for Williams. The eighth freshman point guard to start his first game at North Carolina, Paige developed into the star player on both the 2013–14 and 2014–15 teams, leading both squads in scoring. He looked forward to a steller senior season in 2015–16.

White Phantoms

The 1926 season saw the Tar Heels receive a new team nickname. In 1924, while watching Carolina defeat Alabama for the "Championship of the South," *Atlanta Journal* sportswriter O.B. Keeler wrote, "they [Carolina] elected to play the Tuscaloosans man to man, as basketball was played in the good old days when 'every man had a shadow.' And all through the rush and hurry of that eventful first half, every Crimson athlete carried with him a white shadow; a shadow from which he could not step away. Carolina was on guard and it was man-to-man—a white shadow moving like a ghost across the floor, by every Crimson player."

Keeler would paint a similar picture of the Tar Heel defense during the 1925 Southern Conference Tournament. Keeler's description led Luther Byrd, the 1925–26 sports editor for *The Daily Tar Heel*, to start referring to the team as the "Flying Phantoms" or "White Phantoms." On January 12, 1926, Byrd used the name for the first time when he wrote, "Five 'Flying Phantoms,' sporting new and spotless uniforms, flashed out on the polished court." A week later on January 19, 1926, Byrd referred to the team as the "White Phantoms" for the first time in describing Carolina's 50–20 win against Clemson. From there, the name took off as newspapers across the state came to refer to the Tar Heel basketball team as the White Phantoms for the next 24 years. Contrary to popular opinion, the name "Tar Heels" was not abandoned during that time but instead was used interchangeably with "White Phantoms."

At the beginning of the 1949 school year, *The Daily Tar Heel* opined that the name "White Phantoms" should come to an end. It seems *The Daily Tar Heel* sports editor Billy Carmichael III had had enough of the various nicknames used to describe Carolina's athletic teams. He believed that there should be just one nickname and that all of Carolina's athletic teams should simply be called the "Tar Heels." He later told people that he did not like the racial overtones of the White Phantoms nickname.

So, as the school year opened in September, his first goal was to set the record straight and get everyone on the same page. No more White Phantoms for the basketball team and no more Blue Dolphins for the swim team. In his first column of the new school year, Carmichael wrote that *The Daily Tar Heel* would "abolish the galaxy of nicknames that are used for Carolina athletic teams and return to exclusive use of 'Tar Heels,' the official nickname of the school."

Traditions, however, die hard. It took two years for the UNC athletic department and the media to follow Carmichael's lead, but *The DTH* never again intentionally (though there was the occasional slip-up) referred to the basketball team as the White Phantoms.

59 Academic Scandal

During the UNC athletics academic scandal that began in 2010, the biggest angst was over whether the 2005 and/or 2009 NCAA Championship banners hanging from the rafters of the Dean Smith Center would have to come down because of NCAA violations committed by any of the players on either of those two teams. It appeared a long shot with the NCAA scheduled to give UNC its second notice of allegations in four years and rule sometime in 2015 or early 2016.

The scandal involved mostly athletes who were enrolled in classes offered by what was then called the Department of African and Afro-American Studies (AFAM) stretching back almost 18 years. While every class under investigation was legitimately offered by UNC, the university deemed them "irregular" because of the easy assignments given to both athletes and non-athletes enrolled and the liberal grades handed out for independent study papers by Deborah Crowder, who was the assistant to since-deposed department chairman Julius Nyang'oro.

The scandal was first exposed in the football program under coach Butch Davis in 2010, and it later stretched to an estimated

3,100 enrollments in what the media termed "paper" or "no-show" classes. UNC basketball became involved when it was revealed that most of the players Roy Williams inherited when he returned to Carolina in 2003 were designated as AFAM majors and taking heavy loads of AFAM courses. The faculty added a loud voice to the scandal, even though some professors had been complicit with what they knew or suspected was going on.

French history professor Jay Smith went on national television in 2014 and said that UNC should take down the 2005 and 2009 NCAA banners as a gesture of good faith for basketball's involvement in the scandal. Smith later released a book entitled *Cheated* with Mary Willingham, the fired former learning specialist at UNC who made sweeping claims that some of the basketball players she tutored had reading skills at the elementary school level. Willingham's claims were later refuted by studies that showed she used incomplete data to make her determinations.

Another faculty member, associate professor Lew Margolis, did local radio commentaries during the 2015 basketball season, saying head coach Roy Williams should resign because he knew—or should have known—how many of the AFAM classes in question his players were taking. Margolis claimed it was the responsibility of the coaches to know their players' majors, in which classes they were enrolled, and the legitimacy of those classes.

The academic scandal at UNC got a second life after new chancellor Carol Folt and Board of Governors president Tom Ross decided to commission a third investigation into the scandal (after the first two done internally and by former North Carolina Governor Jim Martin) and hired former federal prosecutor Kenneth Wainstein to review all documents and interview any and all individuals who would speak to him. Since UNC and the NCAA do not have subpoena power and could not force Crowder and Nyang'oro to talk, Orange County district attorney Jim Woodall granted them immunity from prosecution if they would agree to be interviewed by Wainstein and his staff.

Although the prior investigations had given UNC enough information on what went wrong to implement more than 70 reforms in how classes were assigned, taught, and monitored, the 131-page Wainstein Report released on October 22, 2014, did the opposite of providing the answers that would end media and public interest in the scandal. While connecting the dots between how Crowder and Nyang'oro perpetrated and executed the irregular classes, it raised many more questions about which athletes were enrolled and whether they did their own work on the papers that were assigned to them.

The Wainstein Report was also handed over to the NCAA, which reopened its investigation into UNC athletics with the possibility of additional penalties being tacked onto the three-year probation, scholarship reductions, and one-year bowl ban already handed to the university's football program in 2012. Since at least one athlete from many of the 28 varsity sports offered at UNC was enrolled in the questionable classes, plus hundreds of non-athletes, it seemed unlikely that either the football or men's basketball programs would be sanctioned. The university receiving a stiff fine from the NCAA for lack of institutional control during the entire period in question seemed more likely.

Nevertheless, great angst continued among alumni and fans that those hard-earned national championships would have to be vacated and the banners removed from the Smith Center. Although teams that had reached previous Final Fours (Villanova in 1971, Michigan in 1992 and '93, and Memphis in 2008) had those accomplishments vacated by the NCAA, no national championship had ever been nullified in men's basketball. UNC fans were relieved when the NCAA did not charge violations to any player on those 2005 and 2009 teams.

60 From Converse to Nike

After graduating from UNC in 1975, one-time walk-on player Mickey Bell thought he wanted to be a coach. Dean Smith told Bell he thought he could help him get an assistant's job at East Tennessee State. Bell told Smith he did not want to live in Johnson City, Tennessee. "My coaching career ended right there," Bell said. "Coach Smith said, 'If you want to coach, you go anywhere your chance is to get into the business.'"

Instead, Smith helped Bell land an entry-level position with the Converse shoe company in 1976. Bell moved from the Converse office in Charlotte to corporate headquarters in Boston 10 years later. In 1993 he was promoted to president. Most people thought that would only strengthen the company's relationship with Carolina, which had worn Converse shoes for 32 years.

But then the Tar Heels were approached by Nike, which the current Tar Heel players favored, and the company was willing to not only provide free shoes and apparel to UNC, but also to pay Smith and his coaching staff a stipend. "With the loyalty and consistency Coach Smith had exhibited," Bell said, "it was always assumed he would not change. But Carolina's national prominence attracted other companies with much larger war chests than Converse."

Nike offered six figures to Smith personally and $2.3 million worth of shoes and apparel to the UNC athletic department for its other 26 varsity sports at that time. The deal looked good enough to consider. Smith gave each of his returning players a pair of Nike shoes to wear during the summer of 1993, immediately following the Tar Heels' national championship win against Michigan in New Orleans. They all approved the change, and Carolina began wearing Nikes for the 1993–94 season. "I think the numbers some companies were offering were getting to the point where Coach Smith was almost embarrassed by them," Bell said of what became known as the Shoe Wars. "That's a good example of the way he is. If he were going to participate, he wanted to make sure that other people in the athletic department and university itself would also benefit."

That move erased a line item in the athletic budget for shoes and apparel for most sports, which saved UNC about $3 million at the time. The relationship with Nike grew over the next 20 years to the point where Carolina remains one of Nike's signature schools, and the shoe company provides Tar Heel basketball with special uniforms for special occasions. In the process Nike has earned far and away the dominant market share in the college athletic shoe and apparel business.

How did the change from Converse to Nike affect Bell's relationship with his old coach? "He taught me long ago that you're not going to get every call," said Bell, who eventually left Converse for other business opportunities. "Sometimes you are going to face adversity, and the key is how you recover from it. He called me and said because it was good for the university they were going to make a change and he hoped I understood. Afterward, I wrote him a letter saying that nothing will ever affect my opinion of what he did for me and what Carolina basketball means to me. From that point on until I left Converse, every time I wrote him a letter or note, I told him I would always pull for the Tar Heels—except now it was from the ankles up!"

61 Baddour Was Smith's Pick

In the summer of 1997, Dean Smith was arguably the most powerful man on the UNC campus. Michael Hooker was the new chancellor, a Carolina grad who admittedly idolized Smith since his days as a student. But when it came down to selecting the successor to athletic director John Swofford, who left to be the new commissioner of the Atlantic Coast Conference, the questioned loomed, "Who really ran the University of North Carolina?"

Nearing retirement, Smith was a control freak when it came to the basketball program he had built into the nation's best over the past 30 years. He wanted to insure its continued success and believed the way to do it was by leaving it inside the fabled "Carolina family." Fiercely loyal, Smith also favored promoting from within to reward longtime lieutenants. Thus, he supported senior associate athletic director Dick Baddour, Swofford's second in command, for the position.

If Baddour got the job, Smith figured, he would have to let the iconic head coach execute his own succession plan. That would likely mean Smith's own right-hand man, Bill Guthridge, coaching the Tar Heels for as long as he wanted and then someone within the family taking over long term, such as Smith's former assistant and then-Kansas coach Roy Williams.

The brilliant Hooker was considered a maverick who had his own ideas about a lot of things, particularly the UNC athletic department. Hooker contracted lymphoma and died only three years into his chancellorship, but he correctly foresaw the biggest need for UNC athletics in the future as fiscal. Thus, he wanted the university's chief development offer, former Tar Heel quarterback Matt Kupec, to take over for Swofford. Kupec had led a record-breaking university capital campaign, started by Hooker's predecessor Paul Hardin, which easily passed the goal of $400 million. Since Kupec's fund-raising staff had brought in another $100 million or so for five years after the Bicentennial Campaign ended, he was referred to as the "billion dollar boy" by many fat cat alumni who socialized with Kupec on home football weekends, at bowl games, and Final Fours.

When he found out Kupec was also seeking the job, Smith was not confident Hooker would agree to his future plan for the basketball program. In alumni meetings all over the country, Hooker answered fretting fans who asked what would happen when Smith retired. He would respond, "Like you, I hope Dean Smith coaches forever, but when he retires, it may be the easiest hire I will ever have at the university. Look what kind of program he will be leaving. We will have our pick of almost any coach, college or pro, to take over. Who wouldn't want to be the Carolina basketball coach?"

While that calmed the alumni and fans, it scared Smith. If Hooker was successful in making Kupec the athletic director, the next basketball coach could be anyone. So Smith asked to be put on the search committee for the new AD, along with football coach Mack Brown.

Baddour's interview went smoothly in front of the 14-person committee because he had worked with almost all of them for years. Besides Smith and Brown, there were UNC Olympic sports coaches, faculty members, alumni, and one student-athlete at the meeting. Baddour had prepared by filling up almost three legal pads with notes that covered his plan for UNC athletics over the next 10 years. Smith, who had turned down the chance to be athletic director several times, didn't much care about that. He considered himself the "athletic director for basketball" and did not want any help from outside his program unless he asked for it.

Kupec's interview was far different after he greeted the committee and passed around copies of a neatly bound booklet that outlined his "Twenty-Point Plan" for the future of UNC athletics. He never got to discuss that plan with the committee after he was grilled—some say harshly—by Smith about his lack of experience as an athletic director. Following the uncomfortable interview, Kupec felt like he would have a hard time working with the people in that room and their colleagues. He withdrew his name the next day and remained as head of UNC development until he resigned in 2012 over allegations that he had used university aircraft for personal reasons. Smith retired in October of 1997, and, as planned, Guthridge was promoted to head coach and led the Tar Heels to two Final Fours in his three years as head coach.

Baddour stayed 14 years as athletic director until he, too, stepped down amidst the growing UNC football and academic scandal. Football coach Butch Davis had been fired, and chancellor Holden Thorp knew Baddour was close to retirement himself and that he wanted a new athletic director to hire a new football coach. That happened when Bubba Cunningham was named AD in 2011, and Cunningham then hired Larry Fedora to coach the football team.

Ironically, during Baddour's tenure, he actually broke with Smith after Roy Williams turned down an offer to succeed Guthridge in the summer of 2000. Smith wanted to hire former player and assistant coach Larry Brown, who was prepared to leave the NBA Philadelphia 76ers, to coach his alma mater. But Baddour and new chancellor James Moeser (who succeeded the deceased Hooker) decided the then 59-year-old Brown was not a good fit after having left two programs, Kansas and UCLA, on NCAA probation. UNC instead hired Matt Doherty, who lasted three years before Williams accepted the job the second time it was offered in 2003. Among the reasons Williams left Kansas after 15 years and returned to his native state, he said, "I could not turn down Coach Smith a second time."

62 Great Scott

Charlie Scott was not supposed to be the first African American scholarship athlete at UNC. He became that only after Dean Smith failed to find a qualified or accepting candidate to break that important racial barrier and then discovered Scott was wavering on his commitment to attend Davidson and player for coach Lefty Driesell.

Even before Smith took over for Frank McGuire in the summer of 1961, his goal was to integrate the Carolina basketball program. After all, his father, Alfred Smith, did the same with high school basketball at Emporia High School in Kansas, despite the objections of his high school principal, threats from opponents, and his own banishment from the Kansas High School Athletic Association.

McGuire had tried to do that at UNC in the early 1950s when he offered a scholarship to Philadelphia seven-footer Wilt Chamberlain. But "Wilt the Stilt" did not have the SAT score or high school class rank to be admitted and he eventually played against McGuire and the undefeated Tar Heels in a losing effort for Kansas in the 1957 title game.

During his first season as head coach, Smith went after Lou Hudson, a 6'5" star for Greensboro Dudley High School in North Carolina. Hudson was graduating third in his senior class and was very close to the required SAT score for in-state students. But there would be only 62 African American undergraduates enrolled in the fall of 1962. Hudson was not accepted and went instead to Minnesota, where he became an All-American and first-round NBA draft choice.

The following year, Smith had his eye on in-state and 6'3" Willie Cooper from Elm City High School who did have the academic chops to get into Carolina. Cooper played on the 1964 freshman team and was invited to walk on to the varsity as a sophomore. During the first week of practice, Cooper informed Smith he was dropping basketball to concentrate on his studies after failing an economics test. Smith regretted that he had not visited every black high school in North Carolina to personally find the right student and basketball player.

In the fall of 1965, UNC radio broadcaster Bill "Mouth of the South" Currie told Smith about Scott backing off his commitment to Davidson because of at least one racist incident the youngster from Harlem had experienced while visiting the school. Scott was completing his senior season at Laurinburg Institute about two hours from Davidson and had committed to Driesell after working at his summer camp in 1965. When Smith contacted Laurinburg headmaster and coach Frank McDuffie, he was told that Scott might not be going to Davidson and, in fact, was in the process of visiting other schools. McDuffie also told Smith that Scott was on track to be the valedictorian of his graduating class and already made higher than 1200 on his SATs.

Smith dispatched assistant coach Larry Brown to watch Scott play, and Brown said he was more talented than high school All-American Rick Mount, who appeared on the cover of *Sports Illustrated* during his senior year at Lebanon High School in Indiana. Mount was on his way to Purdue and would eventually get to play against UNC and Scott in the 1969 Final Four.

Smith and second assistant John Lotz went to see Scott play for themselves and came away impressed with his tremendous speed and leaping ability. Through McDuffie, Smith invited Scott to make an official visit to Chapel Hill over Jubilee Weekend that spring, when the Temptations and Smokey Robinson and the Miracles were performing for the Carolina student body. McDuffie drove Scott up on Friday, and after spending the weekend with members of the 1966 Carolina freshman team and a black cheerleader plus attending Sunday morning service at Smith's integrated Baptist church, Scott was driven back to Laurinburg by Brown and Lotz.

The two coaches were from New York and clicked right away with Scott. They asked him if he had a good weekend, enjoyed Chapel Hill, and wanted to play basketball at Carolina, and Scott answered yes to all three questions. Upon arriving in Laurinburg, McDuffie said it was okay to sign with the Tar Heels and later acknowledged that Scott was the perfect player to pave the way for other African American athletes at the state university. Scott enrolled the following autumn and played for Brown on the 1967 freshman team, though he did miss 10 games with a broken foot. But it was clear that the 6'5" Scott would step into the starting spot on the varsity left vacant when All-ACC guard Bobby Lewis graduated.

Sophomore Scott took the court on December 2, 1967, against Virginia Tech in Carmichael Auditorium, finally breaking the color barrier at Carolina. He scored 18 points with four assists and no turnovers in the fourth-ranked Tar Heels' 89–76 win over the Gobblers. He went on to average 17.6 points a game, second only to All-American senior Larry Miller's 22.4 and joined Miller on first team All-ACC. After the season, Scott rejected the boycott by black athletes of the 1968 Olympic Games in Mexico City and made the team at the tryouts in Albuquerque, New Mexico, leading the trials in scoring and assists. He then was one of the stars who won the gold medal in early fall.

Scott's great start at UNC helped Bill Chamberlain become the second African American basketball player in Smith's program. Chamberlain, from Long Island, and Scott played together on the 1970 Carolina team. Scott graduated in 1970, and Chamberlain graduated in 1972. After that followed a hit parade of black athletes from Walter Davis to Phil Ford to Dudley Bradley to James Worthy to Michael Jordan, all of whom eventually joined Scott as first-round NBA draft choices.

Scott finished at UNC with a career average of better than 22 points a game and left Chapel Hill as the second all-time leading scorer behind Lennie Rosenbluth of the undefeated 1957 NCAA champions. He may be best remembered for two games at the end of his junior season, when he scored 28 points in the second half (40 for the game) to rally Carolina from a second-half deficit against Duke and win a third straight ACC championship. A week later Scott scored 32 points, including the buzzer-beater to defeat Davidson and the coach he almost played for, Driesell, in the East Regional, sending the Tar Heels to their third NCAA Final Four in a row.

The Great Scott was a first-round pick of the Virginia Squires of the old American Basketball Association, where he won Rookie of the Year in 1971 and league MVP in '72. He later won an NBA championship with the 1976 Boston Celtics.

63 UNC and the Olympics

When Dean Smith took over as the USA Olympic basketball coach from retired Oklahoma State coach Hank Iba, he advised the selection committee to put a squad together of players he knew and would form a cohesive and talented team in the six weeks of practice time they all had before the 1976 Olympic Games in Montreal. Smith had been named Olympic coach in 1975 by a committee that included three-time Olympic coach Iba (1964, '68, and '72), Red Auerbach, and Dave Gavitt, among others. "It was a great honor," Smith said in his 1999 autobiography *A Coach's Life*. "I felt, however, that a different coach should be selected for each Olympiad so others could share in this great experience. This was my feeling and still is."

The controversial ending to the 1972 Olympic basketball tournament in Munich, in which the U.S. lost the gold medal for the first time ever to the Soviet Union on what Smith termed "a series of horrendous officiating calls," put great pressure on the Americans to win back the gold in Montreal. The 1972 Olympic team members, who included UNC star Bobby Jones, had refused to accept their silver medals in Munich. "At Carolina we never talked to our players about winning," Smith said. "With the Olympics it was all about winning. We had one goal and one goal only: to win the gold medal."

The team had four UNC players—Walter Davis, Phil Ford, Mitch Kupchak, and Tom LaGarde—and three more from the ACC: Duke's Tate Armstrong, N.C. State's Kenny Carr, and Maryland's Steve Sheppard. In addition, there were two stars from Indiana's undefeated 1976 national champions: guard Quinn Buckner and forward Scott May. Smith knew that Bob Knight's players were talented, disciplined, and hard-working. The squad also had Notre Dame All-American Adrian Dantley, Michigan's Phil Hubbard, and Tennessee's Ernie Grunfeld.

This was long before the U.S. and International Olympic Committees approved the participation of American professional players from the NBA in 1992, the so-called Dream Team that was led by Michael Jordan. Smith and his assistant coaches—Bill Guthridge from UNC and John Thompson, coach at St. Anthony High School in Washington, D.C.—had about six weeks to put together the team for what would be a difficult challenge against professional players from most of the other countries competing.

Smith had also been married to Dr. Linnea Weblemoe shortly after her graduation from the UNC Medical School. The wedding was the day before he had to leave for Las Vegas and the annual National Association of Basketball Coaches (NABC) meetings. So their honeymoon consisted of Smith attending the meetings and then coaching the Olympic team through its exhibition schedule before departing for Montreal. The traveling party also consisted of Smith's son, Scott; Dean's parents; and Dean's sister, Joan, who all got to attend the Opening Ceremonies and other Olympic events while Smith, Guthridge, and Thompson were preparing the team for the men's basketball tournament. They had to get ready to play against older European teams that had been together for years under international rules, which included a wider lane and allowed much rougher play.

Some of the best college seniors of that year, including John Lucas, Leon Douglas, and Robert Parish, declined to try out and preferred to get ready for their rookie years in the NBA. But it did leave Smith with a squad of familiar players that he termed easy to coach. Smith also had the advantage of his longtime assistant Guthridge, an organizational master who could anticipate every move Smith made, and Thompson, the great motivator and future Georgetown coach who had met Smith when he sent his adopted son, Donald Washington, to play for Carolina in the early 1970s.

Smith said he did not want any inflated egos on the Olympic team—just unselfish players who were good defenders. Smith got three players he wanted, but several others did not make it. Still, he was criticized by the media and other coaches for having four Tar Heels and seven from the ACC on the squad. Rival coaches thought Smith was favoring his own players and would use it as a recruiting advantage, which seems humorous 40 years later as Duke's Mike Krzyzewski is in his 11th year as head coach of USA Basketball and is going for his third gold medal in 2016 in Rio. Krzyzewski has received far more criticism than Smith for using his USA Basketball position as a recruiting advantage for his program at Duke.

Ford, Davis, and Kupchak were no-brainers; all three made All-ACC and All-American teams and knew exactly what Smith wanted in putting the team together. LaGarde was a controversial fourth pick from UNC because he was not as heralded as the other three but had made the Pan-American Team in 1975 and was badly needed on an Olympic team devoid of quality big men. Armstrong, Carr, and Sheppard were All-ACC players against whom Smith had competed. Armstrong and Sheppard were the last two men off the bench because neither was great defensively.

The USA team opened play in Montreal by blowing out Italy after leading by 30 in the second half. Puerto Rico led by Marquette guard and Puerto Rican native Butch Lee was the next opponent, and the Americans were overconfident because they had seen Puerto Rico lose by 21 points to Yugoslavia. But Puerto Rico shot 64 percent against the U.S. and nearly pulled the upset before losing 95–94. The U.S. won Pool A by defeating Yugoslavia and Czechoslovakia and reached the gold medal game by easily defeating Canada in the semifinals.

Many Americans wanted to see a gold medal grudge rematch against the Soviet Union, but the Soviets lost to Yugoslavia by five points. The USA team thus was heavily favored to beat the Yugoslavians again and bring the gold medal back to America. After a stirring patriotic pep talk from the 6'10" Thompson, the team went out and built a 44–22 after just 14 minutes. The margin was never closer than 10, and the U.S. players literally danced away the final 10 seconds.

Since coaches do not receive medals in the Olympics, Smith, Guthridge, and Thompson stood off to the side as each U.S. player received his gold medal. Smith gathered his family, and they all headed back to North Carolina the following morning.

Jimmy Black

Dean Smith and assistants Bill Guthridge and Eddie Fogler had to get themselves back up after what seemed like a devastating loss at Providence on February 12, 1978. Their seventh-ranked Tar Heels had let one slip away at the No. 20 Friars—a game that was almost cancelled due to a blizzard that had blanketed the state of Rhode Island.

They not only had lost the game, but their star sophomore forward Mike O'Koren also had left the floor in the second half with an injured ankle that the coaches and trainers believed to be broken, which would have cost O'Koren the rest of his season. (It turned out to be severely sprained.) As the team trudged out of Providence, the coaches piled into a rental car for an appointment in the Bronx that had been made weeks earlier. And because this was a recruit they had to have, Smith, Guthridge, and Fogler decided not to reschedule the home visit with 6'2" point guard James Frederick Black.

If it hadn't been for the loose lips of a couple of other coaches, the UNC staff might have flown back to North Carolina with the team. And the Tar Heels probably wouldn't have won the 1982 national championship four years later. Earlier that 1978 season, Fogler was in Greenville, North Carolina, watching a high school game. Larry Gillman, then the coach at East Carolina, sat down next to Fogler. Gillman's team had just returned from playing at Iona College in New Rochelle, New York. Gillman told Fogler that then-Iona coach Jim Valvano was boasting about having the best point guard in New York City locked up. "What's his name?" Fogler asked.

"James Black," Gillman responded.

"Never heard of him," Fogler said, smiling slightly.

Actually, Smith had heard of Black through a letter from Jack Curran, the coach at Archbishop Molloy High School in Queens. Curran recommended Black to Smith and suggested the Tar Heels take a look. About a week later, Guthridge was recruiting in New York and went to Cardinal Hayes High School to see the guard who was supposedly going to Iona. As the 30-year assistant to Smith and later head coach of the Tar Heels, Guthridge was not the excitable sort, generally conservative in his evaluation of high school talent. Guthridge's notes in Black's recruiting file read: "explosive, quickness, defensive potential, good hands, unselfish, savvy...*the motor we need.*"

All three Carolina coaches watched Black lead Cardinal Hayes into the New York Catholic semifinals during his senior season. For Black—known as James to his coach and "Freddy" to his parents—the switch from Iona to Carolina was swift. Black knew a lot about the Tar Heels, who did not know he had family living in Raleigh who could provide a home away from home.

The Carolina coaches loved his quickness and extraordinary ball handling, recognized he wasn't a great outside shooter but were impressed with his clutch foul shooting. A year later Black would sink three critical free throws to seal a victory over seventh-ranked Duke in Chapel Hill. But it was Black's defensive potential that really turned on the UNC coaching staff. As he would continue doing in college, Black regularly blocked opponents' shots from behind. His cat-quick hands were reminiscent of Dudley Bradley, already dubbed the "Secretary of Defense" at Carolina.

Following the visit in the living room of Black's Bronx apartment in the projects that snowy Sunday in February, Smith invited Black for a weekend in Chapel Hill. Loyal to his original leanings toward Iona, Black asked Valvano's permission to go. Upon his return from the trip that spring, Black told Valvano that Carolina was his school. Valvano wished him luck and, even though he predicted UNC's talent glut would make it hard for Black to get playing time, they remained friends even after Jimmy V was named head coach at N.C. State and lost six games to Black and the Tar Heels in his first two seasons with the Wolfpack. Valvano wasn't all wrong because it took until Black's senior year for him to be fully appreciated by his own fans.

Other than scoring, Black's career statistics rival Phil Ford's as the top point guard in UNC history. Black played in what was then an ACC-record 105 victories; his class was the first since the Bill Bunting-Rusty Clark-Dick Grubar class to win three ACC Tournament titles. He played in two Final Fours and quarter-backed the school's first national championship team in 25 years. Black finished as Carolina's second all-time assist leader behind Ford despite being a starter only his last two seasons. (They were later surpassed by Kenny Smith and Ed Cota, the NCAA's third all-time assistant maker with 1,030.)

By his senior year, Black received the ultimate honor of being called a "coach on the floor" by Smith, who rarely overruled his offensive and defensive calls during the second half of the championship season. Against Alabama in the Sweet 16 in Raleigh, Black recognized instantly when the Crimson Tide switched defenses late in the game and whipped a pass underneath to James Worthy, who drew the fifth foul on Alabama big man Eddie Phillips.

But Black's story is even more personal. As a sophomore he lost his 39-year-old mother to congenital heart disease. Before his junior year, Black survived a frightening auto accident that left him with a badly sprained neck. It could have been far worse.

He came back from the wreck a different player, lifting weights and running with a neck brace during preseason conditioning. When the brace came off the day before practice started, Black turned into one of the team's hardest workers after, admittedly, not liking to practice very much during his first two seasons.

By the time Carolina won the ACC championship and reached the 1981 Final Four in Philadelphia, Black had become an extension of Smith on the floor. He took the loss to Indiana in the NCAA championship game as hard as any Tar Heel, shouldering the burden for the team's poor performance against the Hoosiers' aggressive defense led by sophomore Isiah Thomas.

As a senior Black was determined to take his team back to the title game and win it this time. He candidly told the press during the Final Four in New Orleans that this one was for his coach. And when it was all over against Georgetown in the Superdome, Smith and Black were the first two Tar Heels to embrace. "We got it for you, Coach," Black said, tears streaming down his face.

"I love you, Jimmy," Smith said.

65 Losing Anderson and Hurley

In the spring of 1988, Kenny Anderson and Bobby Hurley were the rich man/poor man of high school point guards.

Anderson was the thoroughbred, a lithe lefty who had been a legend since his days on the playgrounds of New York City. He was the first Stephon Marbury and Sebastian Telfair, the boy who played with men and could only avoid college stardom if he didn't do the right thing on the street corner and classroom. The college coach who got him might only have him for two years, but those two would make someone's program. That's how good Anderson was.

Hurley was Seabiscuit from across the sea—or at least the Hudson River. Smaller and slower than Anderson, his pedigree was more impressive than his performance on some nights. He had game, taught to him by a strict coaching father in a hardscrabble New Jersey neighborhood, but he also had a funny-looking jump shot that he sort of spun off his hands from in front of his forehead. Where Anderson was a can't miss, recruiting analysts debated whether Hurley was good enough to star for a major college.

Anderson was the No. 1 prospect on Dean Smith's list. Smith didn't rule New York recruiting like his predecessor Frank McGuire once had, but Carolina's connections with high school coaches such as Jack Curran of Archbishop Molloy in Queens still made the Tar Heels the favorite for almost any player they wanted.

Smith had swooped in at virtually the last minute in 1983 and stolen Kenny Smith away from Virginia. And Kenny Smith was related to Anderson, truly the next great guard out of the City.

Hurley had followed the Tar Heels since attending Smith's summer camp after the seventh grade. His father, Bob Hurley, was the coach at dirt-poor St. Anthony in Jersey City, which he had turned into a high school powerhouse with basically smoke and mirrors and a lot of elbow grease. Since Jim Spanarkel and Mike O'Koren from rival Hudson Catholic had played for the Blue Devils and Tar Heels, respectively, in the late 1970s, Bob Hurley had followed both teams closely.

Although Smith coveted Anderson, who early on was considered a lock to follow in his cousin Kenny's footsteps, he recruited other point guards. He informed the Hurley family that Anderson was his priority, which had been Smith's longtime policy; generally, he was able to get his second choice to wait to see what No. 1 would do. That's how big playing for Smith and the Tar Heels had become.

But recruiting was changing along with college basketball. High school players received much more publicity, thanks to an increase of All-Star games and AAU summer teams and the influx of recruiting services that were now ranking players all the way down to the 10th grade. And, as Duke had proven, Carolina was no longer the most followed college team. For high school players who didn't much care about yesterday, today's superstar was Michael Jordan of the Bulls, not the erstwhile Tar Heel.

During the summer of 1988, Hurley and his father told Smith they couldn't wait for Anderson's decision. By that time Duke was already in there solid. Krzyzewski played off Smith's system. He forgot Anderson, told Hurley he was Duke's top choice, that they weren't recruiting any other point guards, and that he would get to play alongside Billy McCaffery, a shooting guard Duke was also recruiting.

That wasn't going to work at Carolina because Anderson and Hurley were both playmakers who needed to have the basketball. "They had a really good chance at Kenny Anderson, and he was a great player," Hurley said years later. "It looked like he was going to end up there. They suggested us playing together and tried what they could to keep me interested. But I realized I should move on to other schools."

So Hurley committed to Duke and said he would sign with the Blue Devils before the 1989 season, his senior year at St. Anthony. Smith continued recruiting Anderson and didn't realize he was losing ground with him. UNC no longer had assistant coach Eddie Fogler, who always had his ear to the ground when it came to recruiting kids in his native New York City. Carolina missed some obvious signs on Anderson.

Georgia Tech coach Bobby Cremins, another New Yorker, had moved in and was chasing Anderson, calling him almost every day and writing him what he eventually estimated as 200 letters. Plus, Syracuse and coach Jim Boeheim were closing hard. Among coaches, it was common knowledge that Boeheim thought Cremins was going way over the NCAA limit on contacts and visits with Anderson, but coaches rarely blew the whistle on each other.

Anderson, caught up in the hype and with no one from North Carolina to babysit him, told Cremins he didn't think he was going to UNC after all. Rather than joining Dean Smith's stable of stars, he liked the idea of making a new name for himself at Georgia Tech. During the fall signing period of 1988 after Hurley had signed with Duke, Anderson sent his letter of intent to Atlanta instead of Chapel Hill. Cremins welcomed Anderson with the clear understanding that he would stay only until he was a high NBA draft pick.

Smith insisted honesty was still the best policy, but gambling on Anderson left the Tar Heels almost as thin in the backcourt as Duke had been. They had no qualified substitute behind sophomore King Rice, leading to Smith's political joke about the beleaguered vice president at the time: "Rice has to remain healthy like [President] Bush has to remain healthy, although I don't know who our [Dan] Quayle is."

In retrospect, Hurley was the better choice for Carolina because, regardless of how he turned out, his father's vast connections with high school coaches across the country was going to help whichever program signed his son. Bob Hurley, the longtime UNC fan, turned into a Duke advocate and his son a central figure in the escalating game of one-upsmanship between the two schools that continued for decades.

66 Eat at Sutton's and Get Your Gear at Shrunken Head

East Franklin Street has landmarks that Tar Heel fans must visit on any trip to Chapel Hill. Of course, there is Four Corners Grille on 175 East Franklin at the corner near the old post office. Right next to it is Ye Olde Waffle Shoppe, the oldest and still most popular breakfast eatery in the downtown area. Two others can't-miss destinations are Sutton's Drug Store and the Shrunken Head.

Sutton's was established in 1923 when, believe it or not, there were four drugstores on East Franklin Street. The others are gone, and only Sutton's remains, though it closed its actual pharmacy in 2014, and veteran pharmacist John Woodard sold his inventory and list of customers to the sprawling CVS that opened in the space where Bank of North Carolina used to be just down the street.

Sutton's has survived all these years not as a drug store but a place to see and be seen when it comes to Carolina athletics, particularly basketball. The breakfast and luncheon counter is a popular stop for a quick egg sandwich or hot dog, and booths have been added to accommodate the large lunch crowd that wanders in to see if any Tar Heel hoopsters are hanging around. Manager Don Pinney has continued the 20-plus year tradition of taking color photos of any and all celebrities that eat at Sutton's, and they are not just athletes. Recently, actor Rob Lowe and his wife came in for lunch with their son, who goes to Duke.

The photos are literally wall to wall with almost every basketball player who has put on a Tar Heel uniform over the last 40 years. Some you will recognize right away; others you and your friends will debate who they are. And, of course, the current Carolina players are always pictured with five or six jammed into a booth. Sutton's offers what you would call gourmet greasy food—delicious french fries served piping hot with your burger, hot dog, or sandwich; and any kind of breakfast biscuits, eggs, or omelets with bacon, sausage, or ham and home fries or grits. Where else can you find a two-egg omelet for under four bucks? Don and his longtime cook, Dimas, will make it to order.

Two doors down from Sutton's is the Shrunken Head Boutique, one of the smallest shops on Franklin Street with one of the longest histories. The late Shelton Henderson started the family business in 1969, and his wife and daughters have kept it going after Shelton passed away in 2014. Besides its famous motto "How Sweet it is to be a Tar Heel," the charm of the Shrunken Head is how crowded it can get on any day, especially gamedays, when dozens of people squeeze into the small aisle that separates the UNC-logoed clothing items and the specialty trinkets—from can openers that play the Tar Heel Fight Song to that week's blue-and-white buttons that implore fans to "BEAT" the upcoming opponent. Most of the screen printing is done in the back room of the Shrunken Head, which can produce custom T-shirts with any saying the customer desires.

The Shrunken Head has had plenty of competition on Franklin Street, and some of them have not been able to keep up. There are two other staples of the "100 block." Chapel Hill Sportswear, the largest apparel store in downtown, opened in 1989 and was in part financed by former 5'11" Tar Heel point guard Tommy Kearns, who jumped center against Wilt "the Stilt" Chamberlain in UNC's 1957 triple-overtime NCAA championship game victory against Kansas. Kearns went on to be a millionaire stockbroker in New York City and signed Chamberlain as one of his first clients. Chapel Hill Sportswear is now owned by former Tar Heel athlete and longtime supporter Kathy Sapp. She recently moved Chapel Hill Sportswear to a larger space in the building that once housed the famous Intimate Bookshop. Underground Printing, another new custom shirt and apparel maker, moved into the old Chapel Hill Sportswear space in 2012.

Across the street is Johnny T-Shirt, which opened in 1983 and has given the competition across the main drag headaches ever since. The original owner, Chuck Helpingstine, died tragically in 2014 from a still-unexplained accident or suicide when he fell from an overpass outside of town. Johnny T-Shirt continues to flourish and is now run by the Helpingstine family and its loyal managerial staff. Still, Sutton's Drugstore and the Shrunken Head remain the longest standing and most popular stops for regular Tar Heel fans and first time visitors.

67 Dean Smith's Letters

When Dean Smith passed away in February of 2015, so many stories about his relationship with players off the basketball court surfaced. Former players, coaches, managers who were part of

Carolina basketball, plus some of Smith's favorite recruits who went elsewhere, told stories about the cards and letters—with personalized handwritten notes at the bottom—that they continued to receive from Smith long after their playing days were over.

In 1995 Mike Cooke, who was on Smith's first Tar Heel team in 1962, said, "After 33 years and now with lettermen numbering almost 200, it is still amazing that Coach Smith could find the time to correspond with all of us, take our calls, help us with our problems, and be there to listen."

Even after he retired, until he began to suffer from the cognitive progressive dementia that eventually ended his life, Smith sent handwritten Christmas cards to all of his former players, plus to some players who never wore a Carolina uniform. After Smith grew ill, his longtime secretary Linda Woods kept up the policy, using the Christmas cards as a way for the stricken coach to still connect with his players. It was a habit Smith developed very early in his coaching career, something he picked up from former Duke coach Vic Bubas.

Woody Durham, voice of the Tar Heels for 40 years, remembers wandering to the back of the plane on Carolina's red-eye flight to Madrid in December of 1974. "Pretty much everyone was sleeping, but I noticed a light on toward the back of the plane," Durham recalled. "It was Coach Smith, and he was writing Christmas cards. The one he was writing when I stopped by was to Tom Riker, who played for South Carolina [after Smith had recruited and failed to sign him]."

Smith wrote to many opposing players after they graduated, congratulating them on their careers and wishing them luck in the future. He wrote to Bobby Hurley, a longtime Tar Heel fan who went to Duke after Smith told him Kenny Anderson was his top recruiting prospect at point guard. (It turned out Smith got neither Hurley nor Anderson, who went to Georgia Tech.)

While at Virginia Marc Iavaroni had played in several heated games against Carolina. In fact, Virginia coach Terry Holland had publically criticized Smith for what he characterized as a "shoving match" between Smith and Iavaroni while leaving the court at halftime of an ACC Tournament game. "He wrote me a very classy letter, basically saying he had made a mistake not recruiting me and that I had made myself into a good college player," Iavaroni recalled. "That [letter] meant a lot because part of me was jealous that I never got to play for such a dynasty."

In 1987 Smith passed over Sean Miller of Beaver Falls, Pennsylvania, and signed King Rice as a point guard. Miller (the head coach at Arizona) went on to have an excellent career at Pitt, and Smith later admitted his error in judgment to Miller's father and coach, John. "Sean had been at Pitt one year and played on television several times," John Miller said. "That summer I was at a camp where Coach Smith was giving a clinic. He came over, shook my hand, and right in front of several other coaches, said, 'I was wrong. I love King Rice, but Sean could have helped us last season.'" Like all those who played at UNC, the Miller family got a Christmas card every year from Smith until he grew ill.

68 Park and Ride to the Games

Because of the Dean Dome's tucked-away location at the bottom of a ravine on South Campus, parking has always been a problem for UNC basketball games since the Smith Center opened in 1986. There is really no getting around it, unless you act like one of those fans who attended James Worthy's Lakers games at The Forum—come fashionably late and leave early to beat the traffic.

(But whoever is coaching the Tar Heels notices that, and it usually makes him mad.) And you still need to find a place to park.

Only the VIPs, like the big donors and the media, get parking passes anywhere near the building. And even if you come very early, that still won't avoid the traffic heading to the Smith Center inching along Manning Drive and down Skipper Bowles Drive to the lots next to the arena. While leaving, there is about a five-minute window to get to your car and get out of the lots before the lines form. If you miss that five-minute window, it could mean an extra half hour getting home.

The best way to go to Carolina basketball games is to join the masses that use the Tar Heel Express—park-and-ride buses that run from five locations: University Mall on Estes Drive, The Friday Center on Route 54 across from Meadowmont Village, Southern Village on 15-501 South, Jones Ferry Road, or from Franklin Street in front of the Carolina Coffee Shop. (The latter is my favorite because you can park cheaply downtown, have time to eat lunch or dinner, and then ride the bus to the game.)

The buses are often packed, and some patrons must stand during the short ride to the Dean Dome, but the Tar Heel Express definitely has priority on the roadways that lead to the Smith Center. The cost is cheap, too; it's just $5 for a round-trip ticket. The buses begin running 90 minutes before the scheduled tip-off and about 30 minutes before the games end. If you stay for the entire game, many of which go down to the wire, expect to wait in long lines to get on a bus back to your designated park-and-ride lot. But at least you will have a lot of people to talk to about the game.

69 The Point-Shaving Scandal

After the 1961 season, the second point-shaving scandal in 10 years exploded. Two UNC players were eventually implicated. Tar Heel reserve Lou Brown (no relation to Larry Brown) was the gamblers' go-between and testified against Aaron "the Bagman" Wagman, a New Yorker charged with 37 counts of corruption and one charge of conspiracy, under immunity. Over the next year, dozens of players were busted, but most made similar deals to help nail Wagman and his cohorts.

Four N.C. State players were accused of shaving points against Wake Forest, Duke, Georgia Tech, Maryland, and South Carolina. Anton Muehlbauer, Stan Niewierowski, Terry Litchfield, and Don Gallagher were charged with accepting money to influence the final scores of games, though they also cooperated, and the charges were later dropped. They testified that players who took bribes in fixed contests made at least $1,000 a game. The gamblers and bookies stood to make a lot more by laying bets on teams to either lose games or win by less than they were favored.

Culminating an investigation that had lasted three years, New York district attorney Frank Hogan indicted Wagman and three others for hiring players to shave the points. Wagman went to jail for doling out bribes of almost $30,000 in two years. Brown's first-person account in *LOOK* magazine, told to Raleigh sportswriter Dick Herbert, pointed the finger at himself and another Tar Heel, the four State players, and several from other schools in the East. Brown said the police had a tapped phone conversation, in which Wagman offered him $1,000 and UNC teammate Doug Moe $1,500 to fix the UNC-Clemson game in Charlotte in 1960. Heavily favored and ranked 19th, Carolina won it by only five points. Moe admitted accepting $75 from one of the fixers but denied shaving points in any game and was never convicted. He was still banned from playing in the NBA for his involvement in the scandal. "I didn't see anything wrong in taking the money from Wagman for doing nothing," Moe told *LOOK* magazine. "But I guess I was involved, wasn't I?"

Most of the players involved went on to become law-abiding adults, remorseful for their wrongdoings. They were all impressionable kids at the time who made poor judgments, persuaded by the fixers that they weren't actually "dumping" games, only affecting final scores. Brown said when coach Frank McGuire found out "he was furious, but he tried to help me, even offered to get me a lawyer. And he said something that helped me keep going: 'It isn't the end of the world. What you've got to think about now is doing right the rest of your life.'"

Brown took McGuire's advice, went back to school, and eventually became a college professor. Moe went overseas and turned into a pro basketball hero in Italy; he later starred in the old ABA and coached three NBA teams. Eventually, Bill Friday, president of the University of North Carolina system, banished the Dixie Classic that, while not directly linked to the gambling scandals, was seen as an unnecessary breeding ground for fights and fixes. Friday blamed the growth of big-time college athletics for problems at the Dixie Classic, which drew more than 70,000 fans in 1960. He also announced a recruiting and scheduling de-emphasis at State and Carolina to "eliminate or correct conditions that have discredited the sport." That's how dirty the game had become.

70 Recruiting Styles

For years the *coaching* of Carolina's head coach has been open to debate. After all, second-guessing is considered a God-given right among most basketball fans. Frank McGuire admittedly wasn't much of an X-and-O guy; in fact, he did not bother with many details. He left most of that to assistants Buck Freeman at first and then Dean Smith while he went recruiting.

Smith, some said, tinkered too much with the game and its nuances. But once he got his program rolling, he had the players to experiment all he wanted. Former N.C. State coach Norman Sloan put it bluntly one day when asked about his adversary 25 miles down Tobacco Road. "Dean Smith is a great recruiter," he said, period.

Roy Williams fuels his own argument by saying he'll never be another Dean Smith. He owes "95 percent" of what he knows to Smith, but Williams admits he's too stubborn to try a lot that hasn't already worked for one of his own teams. There was no doubt, however, that Williams could bring in the players—with even more success than Smith and perhaps more than McGuire, one of the game's greatest recruiters. Having talent remains the single strongest plank in the Carolina foundation.

McGuire taught Smith, who in turn showed Williams how to recruit strategically and eventually more effectively than his mentor. All three devoted themselves to a system of scouting good high school players and targeting those they wanted. Some people called it a selection process, rather than recruiting, in deference to UNC's national reputation. Long before recruiting received much publicity, McGuire was the most masterful salesman the college game had ever known, using the power of his persuasion and guile.

He had scouts all over New York, identifying the best players. When McGuire walked into a high school gym, he couldn't care less about the game that was going on. He was there to see if a certain young man measured up to his two standards: talent and toughness.

After he left St. John's, McGuire's special brand of magic lured Catholic kids from New York to the South in the 1950s, and he did it by winning over parents of the teenagers. Sometimes, he brought along a parish priest when he visited Catholic families to assure them that attending Sunday Mass would be required, even 500 miles away from home. McGuire's main talent turf was New York because he had grown up there and was so well connected. He also favored the style of freelance offense and zone defense New York high schools liked to play.

When McGuire zeroed in on a youngster, he had little trouble finding someone familiar with the targeted family, and certainly they all knew of *his* name and reputation. "McGuire was a giant figure in New York," Lennie Rosenbluth said. "He either liked you or you were the enemy. If he liked you, he'd do anything in the world for you. If he didn't like you, forget about it."

When he decided which players he wanted to recruit, McGuire made visits to their homes that were like royalty. He treated the parents with utmost respect and expected them to have complete faith that he would take care of their sons because that is what he promised. Paying homage for raising such a fine young man, McGuire often spent more time with the mother in the kitchen or the father on the porch.

When he first arrived at UNC from the Air Force Academy, Smith had almost no recruiting experience. McGuire did most of that in person or through his people in New York. Smith sometimes accompanied his boss to observe players. When he took over at UNC, Smith drew from McGuire's lessons and also watched

Roy Williams is known for his intensity and work ethic on the court and on the recruiting trail.

how young Duke coach Vic Bubas, who had been Everett Case's chief recruiter at N.C. State for years, went after high school stars.

Smith inherited McGuire's longtime friends from New York and made them his contacts, though he adopted a slightly different method, too. Unlike McGuire, he thought he needed some North Carolina stars on his roster. "Coach Smith and Coach McGuire had different approaches, but they had a lot of similarities as well, which is why Carolina has been so successful," said Larry Brown, who played for both men.

Smith decided to go after a mix of the best players anywhere who were good students and he later presided over one of the great national recruiting machines in college sports. He embraced the McGuire way, began recruiting regionally, and added academics to the sales pitch. Phil Ford always remembered that during Smith's first visit to his home there was virtually no talk of basketball. While other coaches guaranteed Ford a starting position as a freshman, Smith's only promise to Phil Sr. and Mabel Ford was that their son would be the first from their family to graduate from college. That set Smith apart from the other coaches and made Carolina the winner.

Smith ranked the players he recruited by position and told them all where they stood, hoping those rated second and third would still come if Smith lost out on his top choice. He disdained how other coaches told all of their recruits the same story, trying to get away with it.

His candor worked most often, especially before scouting services and ratings popped up in newspapers and on the Internet.

Eventually, Smith relied more on assistant coaches Bill Guthridge and Eddie Fogler, who were savvy talent evaluators, as his lead scouts. He saw fewer high school games and, once he decided on his top targets, used the entire UNC experience to close the deal. A recruit spent most of his campus visit with the Carolina team, which had to sign off before Smith offered him a scholarship.

Smith usually made his final pitch at a home visit with his two assistant coaches, strategically scheduling it a few days after the recruit had been to another school he was seriously considering.

Like Smith, Williams has fixated on the character of young men and he has either cut recruiting visits short or never scheduled them if he thought there was as much bad temperament as talent in the offing. He once visited a recruit who showed up late for the appointment, walked right past Williams, and grabbed something from the fridge, then came back to chow down in front of the bemused coach. When the mother tried to intervene, and the youngster treated her rudely, Williams told the onetime recruit two things as he got up to leave: don't treat your mom that way and pick another school.

Being clear about character became so important to Williams that he logged thousands of miles to see a prospect play a second and third time—often as the only college coach left at a high school tournament game that went on until midnight. He kept going even after the recruit signed because he wanted to demonstrate that the relationship was just beginning as the courtship was ending. Williams has had capable assistants at both Kansas and Carolina and relied on them for many recruiting duties, but he has done more in-person visiting and phone calling than most head coaches.

Like McGuire and Smith, who didn't use the typewriter or email, Williams is surprisingly low tech but remains remarkably relevant to the younger set. He uses his cell phone for convenience on the road but does not carry it everywhere he goes. He does not text or tweet and has barely heard of Facebook. His secretary prints out emails to him and responds after showing them to the coach. Williams' biggest need is to have private planes at his disposal so he can recruit more efficiently. At Carolina, one of three small jets can be ready within an hour.

Williams has cast a wider net than either McGuire or Smith, sometimes recruiting as many as seven or eight players from one high school class and ranking them by position similar to the way Smith did it. He will never lie to a player from the moment he meets him. A perfect example was a recent one. Unsure whether Sean May and Marvin Williams would be back for the 2006 season, he assured Tyler Hansbrough and the other five players he was recruiting only that they could "help the team in some way" their first year in school. He is plain honest and has seen other coaches burned by making promises they could not keep.

71 Reese Got His Chance

It was a long haul for Brian Reese, the player UNC signed after Grant Hill shocked both Duke and Carolina by choosing the Blue Devils despite having been a Tar Heel fan for most of his life. Reese never was a star like Hill, but Reese was no slouch. The 1992–93 season was when his acrobatic athletic skills merged with good health and two years of collegiate experience to produce a key element of the Tar Heels' national championship drive.

Reese's raw ability was evident when he arrived in Chapel Hill two years earlier. The challenge was to fit that to the Tar Heels' highly structured playbook. It all meshed in 1993, when Reese averaged 11.4 points a game, was third on the team in assists, and shot 51 percent from the floor. He personified an NCAA title team where the sum of the parts proved stronger than the individual parts. "Growing up in New York, it was one-on-one," the Bronx native said during that season. "You can see the moves I make. They come from the playground. Someone always wants to try something new on you. Then becoming an All-American in high school, you have to take shots. It's you, you, you. That is the way they put it on you. You have to be the Man every game. But at Carolina it's different. Everybody's an All-American. Coming to Carolina was a big change for me, mentally and physically. I'm from New York. I never ran a day in my life. Running track? Get in shape? I didn't know what that was. I rode buses, trains, cabs everywhere. Running? I didn't know what that was."

His first two seasons were all about that—getting in shape and learning the system. But he had his moments. As a freshman he got hot at the end and made 30 of his last 49 field goal attempts to shoot 53 percent for the season. As a sophomore he picked up his own missed shot and drained a 12-footer to beat Wake Forest at the buzzer. And as a junior, Reese starred in UNC's biggest win of the season at sixth-ranked Florida State, scoring 18 of his 25 points in the second half, including six straight at crunch time, and was featured on the cover of *Sports Illustrated* the next week as Carolina ascended to the No. 1 ranking. He also had 13 points and eight rebounds against Arkansas in the East Regional semifinal at the Meadowlands.

Carolina fans remember Reese for missing the dunk at the end of regulation against Cincinnati in the regional final on an expert play drawn up by Dean Smith. But that is now an affectionate memory since the Tar Heels went on to win in overtime. "It takes some time before you grasp things, but you eventually realize that this approach to basketball has been winning games for a long time," Reese said.

Reese was the only starter in 1993 who could recall watching the Tar Heels' first national championship in New Orleans in 1982, when they edged Georgetown 63–62 in a game just as tense and exciting as their 77–71 win against Michigan Fab Five 11 years later in the Superdome. "I was more of a baseball fan back then," Reese recalled, "but I watched the game because [Georgetown's] Fred Brown was from my neighborhood. He went to school with my older brother. Then I started noticing how North Carolina played, the way they played together. I'd never seen anything like that. Then I got into basketball, and North Carolina was my team from then on. I started wearing North Carolina things, wearing their colors."

And he finally got to wear them officially when Hill chose Duke and the scholarship opened up for Reese, who today is an assistant coach for fellow UNC alum King Rice at Monmouth University.

72 Roy and the KU Sticker

San Antonio, the southern Texas cow town famous as the home of Davy Crockett's last stand, might be the best site of all for the Final Four. The great weather, raucously fun Riverwalk, and relatively good sight lines for a football stadium at the Alamodome could make the city favored if the NCAA ever held a vote about where to permanently stage college basketball's crown jewel. The Carolina contingent, however, might give it a thunderous thumbs down.

The Tar Heels were easily the best team in the field on their first trip to San Antonio and endured one of the most embarrassing weekends in their glorious history. The dismal dome shooting that had plagued them twice in Indianapolis (1991 and 1997) and Seattle (1995) followed them to Texas in the 1998 national semis against third-seeded Utah. Bill Guthridge's powerhouse team fell way behind in the first few minutes and, despite an admirable comeback in the second half, went down to the Utes coached by the rotund Rick Majerus.

The second time UNC made the Final Four in San Antonio, Roy Williams was Carolina's coach, and his team was *playing* Kansas in a game he would never schedule. Although the athletic director and much of his staff, plus the players and most of the people Williams worked with at Kansas, were all gone, the game remained a little too close for comfort. From the first press conference in Chapel Hill through the mandatory media sessions that began on the phone and continued once the teams arrived in San Antonio, Williams was peppered with questions about his 15 seasons in Lawrence, Kansas.

Williams caught the flu two days before the game and woke up on the morning of the Saturday semifinals feeling terrible. But the shootaround and team meetings went well, and Williams has since insisted that when his team left the locker room after the UCLA-Memphis semifinal he thought the Tar Heels would play great. "We prepared exactly the same way we had for the ACC Tournament and the first four NCAA games," he said later. "The team showed me so much confidence looking me in my eye…I was shocked we didn't play great."

Carolina was ranked No. 1 for all but six weeks of the 2008 season and was favored to win the national championship, even though all the No. 1 seeds had reached the Final Four for the first time, and it was more of a crapshoot. The Jayhawks were more focused than the Tar Heels, whom Williams characterized in retrospect as "so excited to be there we were looking around when Kansas hit us in the mouth…like a boxer who gets hit and takes two or three rounds to clear his head."

Indeed, the game was lost early when Kansas leapfrogged its lead from five points to 13 before a media break and then all the way to 38–12 before Williams called a timeout with 7:32 left in the first half. Much has been made of the way Carolina cut the deficit to 17 at halftime and all the way down to four points midway through the second half, and if Danny Green's long shot that went halfway in had stayed down, the Tar Heels might have pulled off the greatest comeback in NCAA history. But they expended so much energy getting back into the game, they could not stop the next Kansas run. "We'd played so well, sometimes you fail to see the other team is pretty damned good," Williams said. "The last month of the season, Kansas was playing better basketball than anybody, and I thought they were the best team. But people failed to give them the credit because of Roy Williams and his background." Williams heard the charges that he felt guilty about beating Kansas after leaving there, so the Tar Heels did not come out with the killer instinct. "Biggest bunch of B.S. I've ever heard," he said.

Williams did allow that, for some reason he still can't explain, the Tar Heels ignored his weeklong instructions not to split a double-team by the Kansas guards or dribble more than once in the post because the Jayhawks were too quick and would take the ball away. "There were seven timeouts in the first half, and we went over all that each time," Williams said. "They looked at me like I was speaking a foreign language, and all of those we told them not to do, we did, and they resulted in turnovers."

Though the eventual 84–66 loss tore up Williams and his players, after they had gone back to Chapel Hill, he decided to attend the championship game and cheer for his old Jayhawks against Memphis. Two of his former players were on the Kansas staff, and many more of his KU alums were there with mixed emotions over the weekend. Now with Carolina gone, they could all root with a clear conscience.

Ryan Robertson, who played for Williams in 1996–99, stopped and hugged Williams as he walked to his seat in the Carolina section and Robertson handed him a Jayhawks sticker. Thinking nothing about it, other than that if his team couldn't win the national championship he wanted Kansas to do it, Williams slapped it on his chest.

When the CBS cameras caught him wearing it during the game, all hell broke loose from San Antonio to Chapel Hill and with Tar Heel alumni and fans in between. Williams was even asked about it during a national television interview at halftime and he said that with the season over for everyone else his heart was with the Jayhawks. "I have 19 former players at the game," Williams said. "I'm supposed to look down there and see Jacque Vaughn cheering for Kansas and I'm not supposed to cheer for them? I'm about people, not buildings…I was doing what I was taught to do by Coach Smith, supporting my former players."

73 A Season of Mourning

"That's what it's all about right there! That's on the floor, that's on your shirt, that's in your heart! That's why we're all here!"

The late Stuart Scott, UNC Class of 1987 and the beloved ESPN broadcaster, now begins every UNC home basketball game with those words on a video clip from when Scott hosted "Late Night with Roy" before he was stricken with cancer. Scott died Sunday morning, January 4, 2015, after a long battle with an undetermined type of cancer. Scott loved his life and job, his two daughters, and his alma mater, and he helped fill the Dean Dome for "Late Night with Roy" each time he hosted it between 2004 and 2009.

Scott, unfortunately, was one of three deaths that rocked the UNC community during the 2014–15 season. Roy Williams' longtime best friend and next-door neighbor, Ted Seagroves, succumbed to pancreatic cancer after a two-year battle in December.

Seagroves, 68, had known Williams since Roy was an assistant coach in the 1970s and '80s and was a member of Williams' famous golf posse. Seagroves, who owned a successful insurance agency in Chapel Hill, was so close to the coach that he often accompanied him on recruiting trips around the country to scout high school players. Williams spoke at Seagroves' service, which was basically 500 of his family, friends, and acquaintances gathering at the Chapel Hill Country Club, all toasting "Captain Teddy" with his favorite brew, Miller Lite.

Perhaps most tragically, Alina Kupchak, the 15-year-old daughter of former UNC All-American and current Los Angeles Lakers general manager Mitch Kupchak, died as a result of a rare form of cancer the morning after Scott passed away. Alina was a ranked junior tennis player in California, exemplary student, and the light of her father and mother's life. Many members of the Carolina basketball family traveled to Los Angeles for Alina's memorial service.

Then, of course, Dean Smith died on Saturday night, February 7, touching off two weeks of mourning and celebration over UNC's Hall of Fame coach, who had suffered from dementia for several years. Following the private service at Smith's Baptist church in Chapel Hill, the university staged a "Celebration of Life" for Smith on Sunday, February 22, which was attended by 7,500 people, including almost every player, coach, and manager under Smith and thousands of his fans from around the state and country. Thousands more watched on television and via the Internet.

Guest speakers included Billy Cunningham, Smith's first All-American; walk-on Mickey Bell who become a prominent reserve as a junior and senior; All-American and 1998 Player of the Year Antawn Jamison; UNC fund-raiser, broadcaster, and center on Smith's last NCAA championship team, Eric Montross; All-American Phil Ford, who popularized Smith's Four Corners offense; and, of course, Roy Williams, who concluded his remarks

Microcosm of a Season

In the 2015 NCAA Tournament, Carolina got back to the Sweet 16 for the first time in three years, but the two victories over Harvard and Arkansas and the loss to Wisconsin exemplified the inconsistencies the Tar Heels had shown since November.

They blew double-digit leads in both halves to Ivy League champ Harvard and were lucky to win the game after falling behind in the closing minutes. Roy Williams' strategy was called into question after the 67–65 victory against the Crimson because he stayed with a chasing man-to-man defense that Harvard continually foiled by getting good shots and turning what should have been a blowout into a nail-biter. "I'm stubborn," Williams said after the game. "I don't believe very much in sitting back in a zone or a sagging man-to-man. I always want to force offense from our defense."

The up-and-down Arkansas game in the second round was more to Williams' liking, and Carolina shot better and committed fewer turnovers (16 to 21) than the Razorbacks. The Tar Heels got 38 points from guards Marcus Paige and freshman Justin Jackson and 13 rebounds from Brice Johnson in the 87–78 victory in Jacksonville, Florida, sending them on to the West Regional Semifinals in Los Angeles. They had not advanced to the Sweet 16 since 2012. While Carolina did improve the last month of the season, losing second-half leads cost them in several very important games and, ultimately, in the final game of the 26–12 campaign. A 10-point lead with less than four minutes to play at Duke evaporated into overtime, where the Blue Devils won 92–90. The Tar Heels squandered a seven-point, second-half lead in the rematch with Duke in Chapel Hill. Earlier in the season, they were leading at Louisville by 18 points with 18 minutes left before losing that game in overtime as well. And despite terrific wins over No. 14-ranked Louisville and No. 3 Virginia in the ACC Tournament, they could not hold a nine-point lead midway through the second half against Notre Dame and stretched their ACC championship drought to seven years (last winning the ACC Tournament in 2008).

Carolina played gallantly against Wisconsin at the packed Staples Center and led by seven points midway through the second half.

> J.P. Tokoto had a run-out that could have stretched the lead to nine, but there was contact under the basket, no foul was called, and the ball went out of bounds off Tokoto. The Badgers promptly scored nine straight points and took control of the game, winning 79–72. Williams praised his team's improvement and said he could not wait for practice to begin for the 2016 season, when the Tar Heels had their top 10 players returning (except for Tokoto who declared for the draft).
>
> Williams hoped another summer of his team working on shooting, ball handling, and building strength would eliminate the rash of scoring cold spells, unforced turnovers, and playing soft in the paint that killed Carolina's chance of turning a good season into a great season.

by asking everyone to point to the heavens, giving Smith one last assist for helping everyone during his 83 years on Earth.

The day before, Williams had opened the home game against Georgia Tech with a tribute to the Four Corners by sending his team into that formation on its first possession. All-American Marcus Paige was in the middle dribbling the ball while wing players Justin Jackson and J.P. Tokoto stood in the back corners and post men Brice Johnson and Kennedy Meeks camped in the front corners. The tribute did not last very long before Johnson broke for the basket, and Paige hit him with perfect backdoor pass for a layup. The Smith Center crowd appreciated the testimonial moment and gave the Tar Heels a rousing ovation, as Williams sat down on the bench, dropped his head into his hands, and wept briefly for his old coach, considered the greatest innovator in the history of basketball.

74 Smith's Last Recruiting Class

Dean Smith's last recruiting year did not take him all over the country. With the return of four starters from the 1997 Final Four squad, there wasn't exactly a talent void in Chapel Hill. The biggest fish to jump in the boat—both literally and figuratively—was Greensboro (North Carolina) Dudley High's Brendan Haywood. The 7'0", 265-pound giant filled a pressing Tar Heel need at center. It was also an important commitment for another reason, as Smith continued his tradition of convincing the top in-state talent to wear Carolina blue.

The buzz on Haywood began in his junior year, when he led his team to the state 4-A championship with the finals being played in the Smith Center. Future teammate Vince Carter was on hand that afternoon and seemed to enjoy what he saw of the big center. Based on Haywood's performance in that tournament and the raw power he showed while competing with the AAU Carolina Warriors, he quickly was anointed one of the top 25 players in the country. While the status is an honor, it also meant that the 17-year-old would receive nightly calls from almost every school in the country.

Haywood's final choice came down to the Tar Heels and Tigers of Clemson, and the *Greensboro News & Record* received a flood of phone calls on the day he announced his decision. Everyone, it seemed, wanted to know where the local hero—who impressed everyone with his work ethic—would be attending school. "After school, when other people were hanging around and chilling, I was lifting weights and running sprints," Haywood said. "The coaching staff told me that if I come to Chapel Hill in shape, I have a great opportunity for playing time."

That opportunity was created by the departure of senior Serge Zwikker. With the only other experienced center on the roster being senior transfer Makhtar Ndiaye, Carolina expected to see Haywood on the court for plenty of minutes as a freshman.

Smith's next freshman signee was 6'9" Brian Bersticker. The Kempsville (North Carolina) High School star, who averaged 13 points, nine rebounds, and nearly six blocks a game during his senior campaign, wanted to benefit while under the tutelage of Smith and Bill Guthridge. "To be honest with you, Brian would run through a wall or die for Carolina," said his high school coach, Vernon King.

It's a reality that almost never happened. Carolina and Kentucky were Bersticker's final two schools, and despite a good experience on an unofficial visit to Chapel Hill during the summer of his junior year, there seemed to be a chance he would choose dark blue over light blue. His coach knew better. "I remember the day I knew when he was going to Carolina," King said. "He had just gone to Kentucky for his visit and he liked it. But then I think when he got home and got away from the rah-rah stuff, he started leaning to Carolina. Then one day when the team was lifting weights, he caught my eye and smiled and pointed to some UNC shorts he had on under his workout clothes. He still didn't announce it for a while, but I knew he was going to Carolina."

Orlando Melendez, a tremendous leaper who possessed a jumping ability that witnesses said eclipsed Vince Carter's, the 6'8" athlete was the last Tar Heel to sign on the dotted line without Smith having to leave the state. Born in Puerto Rico, he came to McDowell County High School in Marion, as an exchange student. He played only one year of basketball but made enough of an impression that he was named second team All-State.

It wasn't just his jumping ability, however, that endeared him to Carolina coaches. Melendez averaged 20 points a game and shot 60 percent from the field for a team that finished 24–5. Melendez said he learned that Smith "cared about his players and always looks for everything good for them and worries about them all the time." Because of his late arrival to the recruiting scene, Melendez's choice had to be put off until the last possible minute.

Fellow signee Max Owens got the decision out of the way early. Owens, a 6'5" shooting guard, was the first player to announce that he would attend Carolina, a rarity in today's hyperactive recruiting world. It caught almost everyone by surprise, and some analysts didn't even list Carolina as a school he was considering. Even if it was unexpected, Owens' decision was a boon for the Tar Heels. Not only did they steal away a player that Kentucky was almost sure they had locked up, but they also landed a guard with a feathery shooting touch and outstanding feel for the court.

Unlike most high school players, Owens did not experience culture shock when he arrived in the high-profile Carolina basketball world. After growing up in Macon, Georgia, he spent his last two seasons playing for Mount Zion Christian Academy in Durham, better known as the home of high-school-to-NBA phenom Tracy McGrady. The attention lavished on McGrady hurt Owens' stock somewhat, as his ranking slid slightly in the latter half of the season. "That had nothing to do with Max as a player," Mount Zion coach Joel Hopkins said. "If you've got a kid going to the NBA, obviously he's going to get more attention than anyone else on the team."

Carolina's four signees all played their high school basketball within a four-hour radius of Chapel Hill. When it came time to make their college decision, however, they were bound together by something more than just their location.

Little did they know that playing for Smith was not in the cards when the iconic coach retired in October just before practice for the 1997–98 season began. All four recruits played their entire careers at UNC—three seasons for Bill Guthridge and one for Matt Doherty.

75 Deanovations

Carolina introduced so many innovations to the college game during the Dean Smith years that they came to be known as "Deanovations." For example, Smith was the first to regularly take timeouts to stop the clock after a made basket in a close game, giving his team a chance to set up its defense. Teams still do that today, even though the college rule has changed to stop the clock after made baskets in the last minute until the other team takes the ball out.

That was another rule change brought on by Smith's creativity, the most famous being how the Four Corners eventually led to the shot clock in college basketball. But on the rare occasions Smith's team was behind in the final minutes, precious seconds could run off the clock while the other team was taking its time picking up the ball, stepping out of bounds, looking for someone to pass to, and finally throw it in bounds. All the while with the clock running.

So, it was not unusual to see all five Carolina players give the timeout signal after a made basket late in the game and then sprint to the bench to get the defense Smith was setting up. It got so commonplace among the knowledgeable Tar Heel fans that they, too, would raise their arms and signal for a timeout as the ball went in.

At about the same time, Smith instituted the huddle after his team was going to the free throw line. He never wanted to waste his precious timeouts, so he depended on his point guard to get the team together and call out the next defense. If the Tar Heel shooter missed the free throw, the team usually sprinted back and picked up their opponents in a man-to-man defense. But if he made the free throw, the point guard might have called for a full-court press, a run-and-jump trap, or a scramble where they were always double-teaming the ball trying to force a turnover. Like most of Deanovations, many college teams now huddle at their foul line before one of their players shoots free throws to set up the next defensive contingency plan.

Thanking the Passer

One of the most common gestures on the basketball court—from the high school level to the NBA—is when a player who makes a basket points to the teammate who threw him the pass. That started when Dean Smith wanted to show the world that an assist was as important as a basket because you couldn't have one without the other. And he was miffed that in the early years of the ACC, assists weren't even kept as an official statistic.

Under Smith, the Tar Heels were a selfless team where no one player deserved or received more credit than another. Of course, when superstars like Phil Ford and Michael Jordan began playing for Smith, he tried to utilize their skills to maximize the team's chances of winning. But even then it was within a team concept. Have you heard the old joke about the only person to ever hold Jordan under 20 points? Dean Smith (which wasn't true because Jordan averaged exactly 20 points a game during his sophomore season).

Pointing to the passer became such a part of Carolina basketball that it was not uncommon to see fans standing and pointing to the player who made an assist on the last basket. The UNC bench would stand together and all point to the passer as well.

So, now when you see it happening in a high school game, or Blake Griffin pointing to Chris Paul after slamming the ball home, you will know it all started with Carolina basketball.

76 Rick Fox

Rick Fox, a handsome Bahamian youngster, had taken up basketball late and defied all odds by playing only two years at an Indiana high school and then earning a scholarship to UNC.

When he arrived in the United States from Nassau, almost the only thing he knew about American college basketball was what he had seen on a large screen TV in the lobby of a resort hotel. He and some teenage friends had crossed the bridge to Paradise Island on the night of March 29, 1982. Bouncing from one hotel to the next, Fox stopped to watch the basketball game that was showing on the big tube. He saw No. 52 (James Worthy) in the white North Carolina uniform make a breakaway dunk against Georgetown in the dark uniforms. He watched No. 23 in white (Michael Jordan) sink a jumper from the left side of the basket with only seconds remaining. Fox was mesmerized by the victory celebration.

A few months later, the 13-year-old Fox played his first refereed game when an Indiana church ministry arrived in Nassau to conduct some basketball clinics. He got hooked on the sport and convinced his parents to let him attend the church's camp that summer back in Indiana. After returning home, Fox then begged his parents to let him transfer schools and play high school ball in America. In the summer of 1985 after his parents had conceded and Fox had played his sophomore season at Warsaw (Indiana) High School, his coaches took him to the Five-Star prep camp in Pittsburgh. Dean Smith sat down on a folding chair at courtside, ready to scout high school phenoms J.R. Reid and Lloyd Daniels, the two most heralded prep players in the camp's All-Star Game. About five minutes into the game, Smith began squinting at the typewritten lineup sheet. He had forgotten his reading glasses and had to ask the high school coach sitting next to him the name of the kid out there hounding Daniels into turnovers. "That's our player, Rick Fox, from Warsaw," said Pete Smith, one of Fox's coaches.

Less than a year earlier, Fox had humored Smith and Warsaw head coach Al Rhodes by stating his goal to play for North Carolina. They wanted Fox to walk away before rolling their eyes at each other. Now the head coach from North Carolina was asking them about the naïve youngster who had made them laugh. And sure enough, impressed by Fox's hustle and savvy for the game, Smith began recruiting him. By the end of Fox's junior year, Indiana, Purdue, and Georgia Tech were among the schools offering Fox a scholarship. Rhodes had worked overtime with Fox but remained flabbergasted by the youngster's improvement and natural gifts for the game. "He had the tremendous ability to learn in two or three weeks what might have taken other players several months," Rhodes said. "Across the U.S. and the world, there are lots of potential concert pianists who have never played the piano. Rick Fox was a basketball player who just had to start playing basketball."

Fox started his first game as a freshman at Carolina and went on to help the Tar Heels win two ACC championships and reach the 1991 Final Four. He went on to play for the Boston Celtics and Los Angeles Lakers and married former Miss America Vanessa Williams, with whom he had a daughter. Fox also became a movie and television actor, most notably starring in the HBO hit series *Oz*.

77 Football Stars— Julius Peppers and Ron Curry

When the 1999–2000 UNC season opened, the Tar Heels had a pretty solid starting lineup: senior Ed Cota, junior Brendan Haywood, sophomores Jason Capel and Kris Lang, and freshman hot shot recruit Joseph Forte. But with the graduation of All-ACC forward Ademola Okulaja, they were seriously lacking in depth, especially up front where 6'10" junior Brian Bersticker was the only reserve with any experience.

During preseason practice and throughout the first month of the schedule, the players kept telling head coach Bill Guthridge about Julius Peppers, the All-American defensive end on the Carolina football team who was also a star hoopster in high school in Bailey, North Carolina, and who held his own any time he showed up at the Smith Center for a pick-up game. Peppers was a 6'7", 270-pound beast of a man, no matter which sports he played.

Finally, to at least give his starters some competition in practice, Guthridge relented and invited Peppers to come out for the team. Peppers so impressed Guthridge that he played in UNC's last 31 games, providing key minutes and averaging 4.5 points and 3.5 rebounds with 19 steals and 17 blocked shots. As the up-and-down season wore on, Peppers got more minutes and helped the Tar Heels turn it around and eventually reach the Final Four in Indianapolis.

Guthridge retired that season, Matt Doherty became the new coach, and both Peppers and football quarterback Ronald Curry stayed with the hoops team. Peppers came off the bench, and Curry started at point guard after five games as the Tar Heels won 18 straight, upset Duke in Durham, and ascended to No. 1

A football star at North Carolina, Julius Peppers, who would become an eight-time Pro Bowler in the NFL, also was a valuable contributor to the UNC basketball team.

in the polls. In 25 games Peppers averaged seven points and four rebounds and shot 64 percent from the floor, improving from 57 percent during his first season on the college hardwood.

Curry, one of the greatest two-sport stars in Virginia high school history, returned to basketball after missing the entire 2000 season recovering from a football injury. He was a settling influence on the team, trying to be a facilitator rather than a scorer, and averaged 5.5 points and 4.3 assists in 28 games. Curry shot 35 percent from three-point range and added 34 steals.

Carolina skidded at the end of the season, splitting its last 10 games, dropping to No. 6 in the polls, and going out in the second round of the NCAA Tournament to unranked Penn State. With Curry facing his senior year in football and Peppers having redshirted as a freshmen, both were hoping to have a great 2001 season under new coach John Bunting and then to go high in the NFL draft. Thus both informed Doherty they would not play basketball in the season that ended up with the infamous 8–20 record.

On the gridiron Peppers and Curry led the Tar Heels to an 8–5 record in 2001, including a 41–9 upset of 1999 national champion Florida State and a win over Auburn in the Peach Bowl. Peppers was a first-round pick of the Carolina Panthers, for whom he began his All-Pro career that continued on to Chicago and Green Bay. Curry was picked in the seventh round by the Oakland Raiders, who used him as a wide receiver and kick returner for most of his seven seasons with the team.

78 Smith Center Seating

When the Smith Center was being conceived in the early 1980s, among Dean Smith's biggest concerns was that the fans would be as close to the court as they were in Carmichael Auditorium. He knew UNC needed a bigger arena, so more alumni and fans could see the Tar Heels play in person, but Smith worried about his team losing its home-court advantage. So he dispatched assistant coach Roy Williams with a tape measure to determine the distance between the closest seat and the sideline at Carmichael. And Smith told the architects to make sure that distance was upheld in the new building.

Carmichael was unique. It was not only small, fluctuating between 8,500 and 10,000 seats when taking out chair backs and replacing them with aluminum bleachers to squeeze in another thousand or so fans into "Blue Heaven," but that intimacy also made everyone from the first row to the last feel like a part of the game. The entire student seating was in the bleachers behind both benches. Because Carmichael was a three-sided building attached to Woollen Gym, the noise created by the fans sitting on the three sides would reverberate off the brick wall behind the students and make the place intolerably loud for visiting teams.

Smith believed that if the fans were as close to the court in the new, bigger building, they would make the same kind of noise. They did at times, but much of that noise rose like hot air toward the giant Teflon dome and could actually make the Smith Center seem quiet. One glaring difference between Carmichael and the Dean Dome was the location of student seating. It seemed like an afterthought when the Rams Club began raising the $32 million needed for the new basketball palace. So they sold seat licenses to people who could afford to purchase the best seats, and those seats were quickly scoffed up by wealthy alumni and donors.

But where to put the students, who could make more noise than anyone?

Over the years the students have sat in various locations, and the Carolina Athletic Association (CAA) has fought with the athletic department for better student seating. Some student sections were in the lower arena behind the baskets, but most of them were in the upper level where the student cheers went up in the air. It is 20/20 hindsight, but the Smith Center should have been built using the model of Cameron Indoor Stadium, which opened in 1940 and has not truly been replicated by any other school. At Duke the students surround the court on bleachers, and the reserved, theater-style seats are above the brass railings. Fans sitting in the reserve seats see the students going bonkers beneath them, and it helps them get excited, too, giving Duke one of the loudest home-court advantages in college basketball.

UNC could have done that, and Smith, who was helping to raise money for the new arena, could have easily convinced older donors and fans that truly the best seats in basketball are slightly elevated off the floor 12 rows up. Beneath those 12 rows could have been student seats ringing the court and giving the Tar Heels a much louder home court than they have had for most of the Dean Dome's 30 years in existence.

The student risers behind the home basket were implemented during Matt Doherty's three years as head coach from 2000–2003. About 200 students get to stand for the entire game on four rows of aluminum risers. A large section of the student seating is behind them in the comfy chairs. So that side of the building, cheering the Tar Heels on defense in the first half and offense in the second half, can get very loud. The rest of the student seating is still scattered throughout the arena, and that seems to change every year after the CAA meets with the athletic department. For some games the full student allotment of tickets of about 7,000 is not picked up, and many of those seats go unsold and remain empty for non-conference opponents and some of the ACC games, as well.

In 1992 Florida State guard Sam Cassell tagged the UNC fans as "kind of a cheese and wine crowd," and the stigma has held up. For many games the crowd does not give the Tar Heels much of a home-court advantage, and Coach Williams says so. But Duke, for example, always wonders what the "wine and cheese" talk is all about because the Blue Devils never see that crowd. When they come to Chapel Hill, every seat is occupied well before tip-off, and the building is 21,750 voices loud. During the 2005 Senior Day at the Dean Dome, Carolina scored the last 11 points of the Duke-Carolina contest. After Marvin Williams won the game with an offensive rebound and old-fashioned three-point play, Roy Williams called it the loudest crowd he had ever heard.

79 Coach K's Five-Step Program

The private funeral service for Dean Smith was held on Thursday, February 12, at the Binkley Baptist Church in Chapel Hill. A private email invitation was sent to family members, former lettermen, and close friends of Smith. About 350 of those emails went out, and the church sat about 400 people. Many uninvited guests—people who claimed to be Smith's friends and wanted to be there—were expected. The church was full, and speakers were Smith's son, Scott; his daughter, Kristen; longtime friend, Howard Lee; retired Reverend Robert Seymour; and current UNC coach Roy Williams.

Dean and Roy vs. Duke and K

The only coach Dean Smith had a career losing record against was Duke's Vic Bubas, who defeated Smith in their first seven match-ups from 1962–1964 before losing six of his last eight meetings with Smith, including the ACC championship games of 1967 and 1969. Bubas retired from coaching after the 1969 season.

Smith's 36-year career mark against Duke was 59–35, including winning 16 of 17 between 1972 and 1977 and eight of his last nine games against Mike Krzyzewski-coached Duke teams before he retired in 1997. Smith was 26–14 all time versus Coach K, though the Duke record books say 14–24 because Krzyzewski did not coach the two games against UNC in 1995, when he left the team in early January with a bad back.

Following the 2015 season, Roy Williams has a UNC record of 10–15 against Coach K's teams (while also going 1–3 against Duke when he was at Kansas, including 1–2 in NCAA Tournament meetings). A number of those 15 Carolina-Duke games went down to the last shot with the Blue Devils winning all but one of them. (UNC's 2005 dramatic comeback occurred in Chapel Hill.) But the NCAA Tournament comparisons between Krzyzewski and Williams are pretty even.

In the 12 seasons Williams has been at Carolina, he has taken three teams to the Final Four and won two national championships. Krzyzewski has had three Final Four teams and also won the NCAA title twice. And while Coach K has the most career wins in the NCAA Tournament with 88, Williams tied Smith for the second-most in 2015 with 65. And one of Williams' most sterling accomplishments is his ongoing 25-year NCAA Tournament record of winning at least one game. Coach K hasn't been as consistent in the Big Dance despite his five national championships. His teams were one-and-done five times (1984 vs. Washington, 1996 vs. Eastern Michigan, 2007 vs. VCU, 2012 vs. Lehigh, and 2014 vs. Mercer). Since 2001, Williams' record in the NCAA Tournament is 42–14; Krzyzewski's record is 38–12.

Among the invited guests was Duke coach Mike Krzyzewski, who wore a Carolina blue tie that his wife purchased for him the day before the service. Krzyzewski coached against Smith for 17 seasons in what was considered the most intense period of the Carolina-Duke rivalry. During those 17 years—from Krzyzewski's first season at Duke in 1981 through Smith's retirement in 1997—the teams combined to win four NCAA championships (two each), visit 13 Final Fours (Duke seven, UNC six), and win eight ACC championships (UNC five, Duke three). Smith retired with 879 career victories, the most among major college coaches at that time. Krzyzewski later surpassed both Smith and Bob Knight for the most career coaching victories.

Krzyzewski went through what might be termed as "Five Steps" in his relationship with Smith. As an unknown former head coach at Army and an unpopular choice to take over the storied Duke program, Krzyzewski had great **admiration** for Smith when he arrived in Durham and used the Carolina program as a measuring stick for where he wanted to take the Blue Devils. In Coach K's first three seasons, UNC won two ACC Tournaments, went to two Finals Fours, and won the 1982 National Championship. Duke meanwhile, had two seasons in which the Blue Devils lost 17 games and finished next-to-last in the ACC.

That admiration turned to **frustration** when Krzyzewski lost eight out of his first nine games against Smith, including two narrow losses (one in double overtime) in 1984. Duke earned what many consider to be a turning point victory in the rivalry with a 77–75 win in the semifinals of the 1984 ACC Tournament, beating the top-ranked Tar Heels who had Michael Jordan, Sam Perkins, Brad Daugherty, and Kenny Smith in their starting lineup.

The next step became competitive when Duke defeated UNC in Chapel Hill in 1985 for the first time in 19 years, and the Blue Devils and Tar Heels split their next 20 games during the most contentious period of the rivalry when the word **hate** was thrown around on both sides. The dislike for each other continued through Smith's retirement in 1997, when the Tar Heels defeated Duke in eight of the last nine meetings. Krzyzewski referred to Smith with great **respect**, reverence, and regret that he would no longer be competing with his old rival. That respect grew during Smith's retirement years when Krzyzewski insisted that he and Smith became great friends. They spoke on the phone occasionally, and Smith called Krzyzewski for a reference at the Duke Medical Center when Smith was planning to have knee replacement surgery.

During Smith's illness that was diagnosed by his family as progressive cognitive impairment, Krzyzewski often referred to the great **love** he felt for Smith after having built the Duke program into the same college basketball giant the Tar Heels were and resumed being so after Roy Williams returned to UNC as head coach in 2003. Krzyzewski was among the most quoted people after Smith died on Saturday, February 7, 2015, at 83 years old. He called Smith one of the great innovators in the history of the game and acknowledged he had used the UNC program as a blueprint in building the Blue Devils into a national power. "I loved competing against him," Coach K said. "I love Dean."

80 Tar Heel Testimonials

"I absolutely believe what I learned at Carolina is transferable to the business world," said Bill Harrison, class of 1964 and former CEO of JP Morgan/Chase. "When I became CEO, we did a lot of leadership training. In that training I talked a good deal about the values of the Carolina program and what I learned and how I apply it to business. The discipline, values, teamwork, and a lot of the organization can easily be applied to the business world from the culture that Coach Smith created and is still in practice at Carolina today."

"I like to believe I am an example of what the UNC system is all about," said John Skipper, UNC graduate and president of ESPN, "taking small-town kids and giving them worldly exposure so that they can contribute in their communities and wherever opportunities lead them."

"The Carolina fraternity exists," said Kenny Smith, UNC point guard and class of 1987. "I see it throughout my 30 years in basketball. I have guys who come up to me and played against us and never played for Carolina and ask, 'What's it like to be part of Carolina?' Because it is something special."

"Those are the best memories I have," said Danny Green of the 2014 NBA champion San Antonio Spurs. "The teams I've played with and the teammates I've played alongside, I can call those guys family and brothers. This is a second home to me."

"Carolina gets in your blood," said Vince Carter, an eight-time NBA All-Star. "You see all the former guys coming back and you want to be part of that. It just seems like something you're supposed to do as a Carolina guy, and no matter how long you stay in school, you always look forward to coming back. In the NBA Carolina guys look after each other. We're part of each others' lives."

"I didn't know it at the time, but when I chose to attend Carolina as a high school kid, it was the best decision I've ever made in my life," said Dick Grubar, class of 1969. "I loved playing basketball, yes. But it has opened doors for me every day of my life—from the day I graduated until today—that I never could have imagined would be opened."

"Playing basketball for Carolina is like playing baseball for the Yankees or playing in the NBA for the Celtics or the Lakers," said Mitch Kupchak, 1976 ACC Player of the Year and general manager of the Los Angeles Lakers. "It's right there with those programs in terms of their importance and the way that they sustain greatness over a long period of time."

"Every time I come in the Smith Center, I sneak a look up there every couple of minutes," said Antawn Jamison, 1998 ACC and national Player of the Year whose jersey hangs in the rafters of the Smith Center. "I just have to make sure it's still up there, that the big No. 33 is still hanging. When I see it up there, it takes me back to coming into Carolina with a bald head and a little mustache. Even at that time, you knew you were going to treasure those memories forever. When I was walking off the court the night of the alumni game in 2010, I grabbed my son and took a second to point out that jersey with 'JAMISON'. There are no words to describe what that felt like. I felt like I was showing him the past and the future all at the same time."

"What's unique is the unity and bond established in the short time you are at the university," Michael Jordan said. "It's a family atmosphere. You find yourself taking care of family members. It's something we cherish. No matter what happens to us or wherever we go, you will always cherish those relationships from the University of North Carolina."

81 The Voice of the Tar Heels

Woody Durham, the North Carolina native and 1963 UNC graduate, became known as the "Voice of the Tar Heels" when he did the play-by-play on Tar Heel football and basketball games from the fall of 1971 through the 2011 basketball season. Durham became the umbilical cord between the players and coaches and Carolina fans across the state in the days when far fewer games were televised.

When more games did get on TV, the alumni and fans who had to still hear Woody's magnetic voice would turn down the sound on television and watch while listening to Woody's broadcasts on the radio. That became less prevalent later in Durham's career when telecasts were transmitted by satellites that caused delays so Woody's words preceded what was being shown to happen on the field and court.

Like Kentucky's Cawood Ledford, Kansas' Max Falkenstien, and dozens of other "voices" of various big-time college athletic programs, Durham became a legendary fixture and one of the most recognizable figures in the state. Off the air, he represented UNC athletics at myriad alumni and donor functions from serving as emcee and guest speaker at dinners and banquets to accompanying alumni groups on trips around the globe with his wife Jean. Durham was behind the microphone for 13 Final Fours as well as four national championships (1982, 1993, 2005, and 2009). He also called 23 bowl games. Durham was inducted into the North Carolina Sports Hall of Fame in 2005 and was named North Carolina Sportscaster of the Year 12 times most recently in 2006.

Audiotapes and CDs of Woody's most famous calls have been produced. There was none more famous than when Walter Davis

Woody Durham, who announced UNC basketball games from 1971 to 2011, interviews Dean Smith.

capped a furious Carolina comeback against Duke in 1974 by hitting a 30-foot bank shot that tied the game. "UN-BE-LEEEEV-ABLE!!!" Durham bellowed into the microphone as UNC's Carmichael Auditorium erupted.

After Durham's retirement he was awarded the Priceless Gem, one of the highest athletic honors at the university. He was also inducted into the Stanly County Hall of Fame where his hometown of Albemarle is located. (Interestingly, longtime radio voice of archrival Duke, Bob Harris, is also from Albemarle, and they went to high school together.) On December 3, 2012, Durham received the first ever Lombardi Excellence in College Broadcasting Award.

241

In 2015 it was announced that he would receive the Curt Gowdy Media Award by the Naismith Basketball Hall of Fame.

Durham also generously gave his time to many charities, most notably the Carolina Kids Klassic that he created and hosted with the university's head football and basketball coaches for more than 30 years. That event raised hundreds of thousands of dollars for the UNC Children's Hospital and related entities that are part of the UNC healthcare system.

Broadcasting became a family affair for the Durhams. Jean was always present at UNC home games and most road contests, wearing an ever-present earpiece so she could hear Woody's calls. Their oldest son, Wes, got the bug from an early age and served as play-by-play man for Radford College, Marshall, Vanderbilt, Georgia Tech, and currently the NFL Atlanta Falcons. Wes Durham left Georgia Tech to remain with the Falcons and do TV for FOX Sports and occasionally a national radio broadcast of big college games.

Woody's younger son, Taylor, also got into the radio business first as an affiliate manager for ISP Sports, which later became part of IMG College, and eventually began calling the games for Elon University. In a big golfing family, Taylor has the distinction of being the best golfer.

Woody Durham has remained very close to the UNC athletic department and all of its coaches and administrators as he continued to emcee events such as the Fast Break for Cancer breakfast originated by Roy Williams in 2003 and special occasions like after the passing of his close friend and frequent golf partner, coach Dean Smith.

Although Durham is the "voice" most associated with Carolina sports, there were broadcasters before him and obviously since. Durham, then 29, left his job as sports director of WFMY in Greensboro to succeed Bill Currie, the sometimes controversial and always entertaining "Mouth of the South." Currie took a job at KDKA radio in Pittsburgh. He was succeeded during the 1971 basketball season by Charlotte broadcaster Bob Lamey. Then UNC athletic director Homer Rice hired Durham for the job in the spring of 1971.

In the maiden days of college radio before Currie, Bill Jackson and Wally Ausley called the Carolina and N.C. State games. Ausley eventually moved to N.C. State permanently. Over the years Durham worked with many color analysts on the UNC broadcasts, including Bob Quincy, Jim Heavner, Henry Hinton, Freddie Kiger, and Mick Mixon—currently play-by-play man for the NFL's Carolina Panthers—and former Tar Heel hoops star Eric Montross.

When Durham retired, studio host and UNC graduate Jones Angell beat out a number of outside candidates with more play-by-play experience. The hard working and talented Angell was barely 32, but he had become a favorite among UNC coaches and athletes. And the Carolina Way was always to promote from within when a capable candidate sought the job.

82 The 2005 Duke-Carolina Game

Perhaps the single most important game of the Roy Williams era at Carolina was the March 6, 2005, comeback win against Duke. The 75–73 victory was not only Williams' first over the Blue Devils as UNC's head coach, it also reversed a disturbing trend in the rivalry and gave the Tar Heels favorable seeding for the NCAA Tournament.

When Williams returned to Chapel Hill as head coach in 2003, Carolina had lost 12 of its last 14 games to Duke during one of the Blue Devils' most dominating runs in their basketball history. Duke had won the 2001 national championship and was in an amazing 10-year stretch during which it won the ACC regular season and/or ACC Tournament championships. It was another pendulum swing in the rivalry, which saw similar stretches of dominance by Tar Heel teams under Dean Smith. And when Williams lost his first three games to Duke, Carolina had gone 2–15 against the Blue Devils, even though Williams' first three defeats were by a total of eight points. It would not be an understatement to say that Duke was in Carolina's head—from the players and coaches to the respective fan bases.

So how was it looking with three minutes left in the March 6, 2005, game? *Not good.*

Duke had broken open a close game behind All-ACC stars J.J. Redick and Shelden Williams and had built a 73–64 lead with three minutes left after a three-ball by reserve Lee Melchionni. And much of the Tar Heels' offensive fire power was missing as they played their fourth straight game without the ill Rashad McCants. At the next timeout, Williams yelled at his players to "get your heads up" and promised that "if you do exactly what we say and give me a total commitment on every possession—not to do well but to do the best—we're going to win this game." Williams admitted later that it might have been a desperate coach trying anything in that situation, "But I really believed it."

Jawad Williams' tip-in of a Sean May miss, a turnover by Duke's Daniel Ewing, Marvin Williams' two free throws, a missed one-and-one by Duke's Demarcus Nelson, and an old-fashioned three-point play by May had cut the deficit to 73–71 with 1:44 remaining. The Smith Center was going crazy. After both teams missed shots, Ewing turned it over again, and Raymond Felton came up with the ball and called timeout.

Felton drove left and went up to shoot, drawing a foul. He made the first but missed the second, and somehow the ball wound up with Marvin Williams on the right block. He went up strong and banked it in to give Carolina a 74–73 lead and virtually no one heard the whistle for an and one. Marvin made the free throw, and after Redick and Ewing missed on the other end, Carolina fans flooded both the court and Franklin Street to celebrate the most improbable victory.

The win not only swung the rivalry back toward UNC, which won six of the next eight games against Duke, including four straight in Cameron Indoor Stadium. But more importantly, it gave the 2005 Tar Heels the No. 1 seed in the NCAA East Regional, where they defeated Villanova and Wisconsin, while Duke went to the South and lost to Michigan State. So without a miracle 11–0 run in the regular-season finale, the immediate future might have been very different for both teams.

83 The Beginning

The story of the North Carolina basketball program begins on December 21, 1891. It was on that day that James Naismith introduced a new game to his physical education class at the YMCA International Training School (now Springfield College) in Springfield, Massachusetts. Naismith had been assigned the task of developing a new indoor game in order to keep the class busy during the winter months. Up until then, nothing had captured the students' interest, and the 30-year old Naismith was becoming increasingly frustrated.

Naismith wrote down the games' rules. He then turned the handwritten rules over to the departmental secretary and had her type them up. Typed and ready to go, Naismith excitedly headed to the gym and thumb tacked the rules to the gymnasium bulletin board. As is the case with most classes, Naismith's physical education class had a leader, and the teacher knew that if the class leader liked the new game, the rest of the class would fall in line. Naismith wrote in his journal, "Frank Mahan, a football tackle from Charlottesville (sic), North Carolina, was the ringleader of the group. He saw me standing with a ball in my hand. He looked up at the basket on one end of the gallery, and then his eyes turned to me. 'Huh! Another new game,' Mahan muttered."

But despite that comment, Mahan, was so sure that the game would be a success that he took the rules from the gymnasium bulletin board for a souvenir. Several days later, Mahan returned the would-be-collector's item to its rightful owner, saying, "I took these as a souvenir. I think you should have them." Naismith considered the typewritten sheets to be among his most prized possessions.

Following the Christmas break, Mahan returned to Naismith's office to again talk about the new game. Over the Christmas holidays, many of the students had returned home and started playing the game in their hometown YMCAs. However, the game had yet to be named, and Mahan wanted to know what his teacher was going to call it. Naismith hadn't given the matter much thought, so Mahan offered, "How about Naismith ball?" The humble teacher laughed and said, "That name would kill any game." Mahan then suggested, "Why not call it Basket Ball?" Naismith responded, "We have a basket and a ball, and it seems to me that would be a good name for it." Naismith would later write, "It was in this way that basketball was named."

From there, basketball became somewhat of a fad and experienced tremendous growth. Due to its invention at the YMCA Training School in Springfield, the game spread rapidly through the YMCAs around the world. Dr. Naismith's nine original players did their part in basketball's growth as one player took it to India, another to China, and another to Japan. Interestingly enough, Mahan, the leader of the original nine and the man who named the game of basketball, ended up not in some far corner of the world but in Charlotte, North Carolina. After graduating from the YMCA Training School, Mahan became the director of the Charlotte YMCA and directed the YMCA in Charlotte from 1893–1899. During his six years in Charlotte, he taught the game to many children and adults in the Queen City. The children that Mahan taught and influenced would include Marvin Ritch, Junius Smith, Will Tillett, Roy McKnight, and Cy Long. These five men would be instrumental in starting the Carolina basketball program in 1910.

A year after UNC opened Bynum Gym, the game began to take off locally as Trinity (which would become Duke University in 1923), Wake Forest, and Guilford each started varsity basketball teams in 1906. Elon began playing the sport in 1907, and Davidson followed suit in 1909. N.C. State (known as the North Carolina College of Agriculture and Mechanic Arts during the early part of the 20th century) started its program in 1911, the same year as Carolina. The first game between two area schools was played on March 2, 1906, in Durham when Wake Forest defeated Trinity 24–10.

By 1910 nearly every college in the state was fielding a varsity basketball team. Only Carolina and N.C. State had yet to play a varsity basketball game. On December 3, 1910, *The Daily Tar Heel* voiced the feelings of the UNC student body when it wrote, "Basket ball is a rattling good game; if it weren't, 99 per cent of the colleges in the country wouldn't be playing it. Why, even the calico colleges have taken it up in a modified chocolate fudge form. Surely we doughty Tar Heels are not going to permit the ladies to outdo us in the athletic line; it would be a disgrace; we must have basketball." Ritch, a Charlotte sophomore, would lead the way in making the dream of basketball become a reality at UNC.

With Ritch leading the way, the group approached UNC athletic director Dr. Robert Lawson with the idea of starting a varsity basketball team. Roy McKnight related to Ken Rappoport in the 1976 book *Tar Heel* that, "The boys from Charlotte just got together one day and started it. We set up poles in front of Bynum Gymnasium and mounted the backboards and baskets on the poles because Dr. Lawson didn't want his pretty [gym] floor messed up. After playing outside for several days, we went to university president Francis Venable about the situation, and he told Dr. Lawson to let us use the gym."

Dr. Lawson gave the go-ahead to Ritch to start playing varsity basketball at UNC. Lawson then approached Carolina track coach Nat Cartmell about coaching the team, and Cartmell agreed. December 1910 and January 1911 saw Coach Cartmell, Ritch, and the newly formed basketball team preparing for the season. *The Tar Heel* reported on December 12, 1910, that, "Basketball work has started off in nice style; the apparatus has been placed in the gymnasium, and there has been night practice this week. Things are getting in good shape and there will be strenuous work after the holidays." On January 14, 1911, *The Tar Heel* announced that the team would play an 11-game schedule and that its first game would be on January 27, 1911, against Virginia Christian College.

84 Hansbrough and the Memory Makers

Over and above a sensational season and almost every accolade imaginable, Tyler Hansbrough's performance against Louisville in the 2008 NCAA Tournament ushered him across a rarified threshold of Tar Heel history. Hansbrough's 28 points and daggers down the stretch in Carolina's 83–73 win joined some of the greatest game-changing performances in the annals of Tar Heel hoops. These are cherished moments to never be forgotten, when one player was mighty enough to carry an entire team over the finish line in a championship-caliber game.

In 1967 All-American, ACC Player of the Year, and all-around campus hero Larry Miller made 13-of-14 shots in the ACC Tournament final, lifting the Tar Heels over Duke and giving Dean Smith his first postseason title of any kind. Miller played with a column written by the late Smith Barrier of the *Greensboro Daily News*, predicting Carolina couldn't beat Duke for a third time that season, folded up in his sneaker. After the game he proudly showed it to sportswriters who jammed around his wire locker in the bowels of the old Greensboro Coliseum.

A warrior like Hansbrough, Miller played all out every minute and lived to grab the big rebound or make the last driving basket of the game. Midway through the second half, when Duke had erased Carolina's lead and Smith tried to settle the team as he drove by the bench, the lefty with the floppy hair shouted, "Don't worry, coach, we got it!" Indeed he did, and Carolina basketball was reborn with the first of three consecutive ACC titles and Final Four berths under Smith. That game will always reside close to the hearts of Tar Heels who have reached their 50th birthday.

Two years later, after Miller was gone on to the old ABA, Charlie Scott etched the next magical moment in Carolina lore. In the ACC championship, the Tar Heels trailed Duke by nine points at halftime and had lost senior point guard Dick Grubar to a knee injury that ended his college career. Still down by double digits midway through the second half, Scott began calling for the ball and telling his teammates to clear out. Twenty-eight points (40 for the game) later, Carolina had won going away and advanced to a third consecutive Final Four.

Larry Miller cuts down the nets after scoring 32 points on 13-of-14 shooting to lift the Tar Heels past Duke and give Dean Smith his first ACC Tournament title.

In 1971, after they had lost a heartbreaker to South Carolina in the ACC Tournament final, the Tar Heels needed someone to carry them through the still-prestigious NIT after All-ACC forward Dennis Wuycik tore up his knee against UMass and Julius Erving in the opener at Madison Square Garden. That's when junior Bill Chamberlain thrilled his New York hometown fans with an MVP performance, averaging 22 points for the tournament and ringing up 34 points and 10 rebounds against Georgia Tech for the NIT title.

One regular season game that belongs in this category came in 1978, when Phil Ford gave the virtuoso performance of his college career in his last home game against Duke. Ford, himself recovering from a wrist injury, pushed the rest of his banged-up team past the Blue Devils as Carolina clinched first place in the ACC. Anyone who watched Ford spin, bob, drive, and shoot his way to 34 points that day will never forget it.

In 1981 Carolina had lost to Virginia and Ralph Sampson twice during the season before their bitter rivalry resumed at the Final Four in Philadelphia. Who can forget Al Wood exploding in the semifinals for the 39 points that propelled the Tar Heels into the championship game against Indiana? Thousands of fans flooded Franklin Street that afternoon and painted "39" on walls, windows, and sidewalks.

The next year James Worthy helped the Heels avenge the eventual loss to Indiana (and Smith win his first NCAA title) with the signature—and last—game of his college career, hitting 13-of-17 shots on the way to 28 points and Carolina's pulsating 63–62 win against Georgetown in New Orleans. Michael Jordan hit the shot that ignited his star, but every serious UNC fan knows that Worthy was the undisputed, indispensable leader of that team.

Smith's second national championship 11 years later could not have been won without sophomore guard Donald Williams, who began hitting three-pointers in the NCAA Tournament and did not stop until the Superdome nets were taken down. Williams hit three treys each against East Carolina, Rhode Island, Arkansas, and Cincinnati and then five each against Kansas and Michigan in the Final Four. Every Carolina fan will treasure forever the Donald's shining MVP moment.

Two other games belong in the same category, the 1998 ACC Championship against Duke in Greensboro, North Carolina, when Antawn Jamison shook off a sore groin to score 22 points and pull down 18 rebounds, and Sean May dropping 26 points and grabbing 24 rebounds on the Dukies in the 2005 regular season finale in the Smith Center. Both big victories wrapped up No. 1 seeds in the NCAA Tournament for the Tar Heels.

Hansbrough wrote his own chapter by strapping the Tar Heels to his back in the final, frenzied minutes of the 2008 East Regional against a fast-closing Louisville team. Hansbrough's slam-dunk follow and driving layup kept the Cardinals at bay, and his last two face-up jumpers sent them packing back to Kentucky and his own team onto San Antonio for the Final Four.

Fans watching in person or on TV drew collective breaths on his last two field goals as the shot clock wound down. Like he had done two weeks earlier in the same building with the winner over Virginia Tech, Tyler the Terrific simply squared his body to the basket, rose straight up, and calmly let fly with perfect form. Everything else he did before and after—that night and in his career—was something special. And those last acts of grace under fire put him in the most extraordinary class of Carolina basketball players.

85 To Build or Not to Build

One of the continuing debates over Carolina basketball is what to do with the Smith Center, which is more than 30 years old. Once a state-of-the-art arena that opened in 1986 (with a win over Duke, no less), the Dean Dome has become antiquated with narrow concourses and actually *too many seats*, so that the stadium doesn't reach capacity except for a few games each season.

The Smith Center court area has been renovated cosmetically over the years—changing out the padded light blue seats, upgrading the lighting and four video boards, and adding an LED ribbon around the fascia of the upper deck. The storage is inadequate because the ground floor goes only halfway around the building due to rock that wasn't blasted during construction. But the biggest drawback of the basketball arena for an elite program is that it is no longer an increasing revenue stream for the athletic department.

Alumni and donors who pledged money to build the Smith Center were given the deal of a lifetime—in fact, two lifetimes. The more money pledged, the more season tickets could be purchased in the best locations. Some wealthy alums pledged enough money to buy four, eight, or 12 season tickets. And their pledge was good for their lifetime *and* the lifetime of their oldest child. This sweetheart deal was offered because the Smith Center was the first on-campus arena financed privately, and UNC wanted to make sure the necessary $32 million was raised (in fact, more than $36 million was pledged).

But the two-lifetime seat licenses kept Carolina from being able to refinance the building every 10 years or so, and wealthy younger alumni, who were willing to give the university millions, refused to do so because there were no premium seats available. The right to buy them by the original donors seemed like it would last in perpetuity. So many potential donors instead bought tickets on the secondary market from season ticket holders who sold a portion of their seats to pay for having to buy them all each year.

Something needs to be done with the Smith Center—either extensive renovations that would cost hundreds of millions of dollars or tearing down the dome and building a new arena for close to $1 billion with fewer seats and more luxury suites that would attract corporate dollars. Ultimately, a decision has everything to do with the future of UNC athletics and the 28 sports Tar Heel teams now play.

If another Smith Center were built, the Tar Heels could continue to play in their current home until the new arena was finished. The original seat licenses would no longer be valid, and hundreds of thousands could be generated each year through private suites and increasing Rams Club dues to be eligible to purchase any tickets in the building. With less general seating, the supply and demand would change to UNC's advantage. Then there are the premium seats—lower level and on the first few rows of the balcony—that would require new seat licenses to purchase.

UNC would be able to tell the original season ticket holders what the right to keep their seats now cost, and it would be at least 10 times what they paid more than 30 years ago. The new seat licenses could be paid annually, creating a brand new revenue stream that could generate between $25 and $50 million each year and not only help pay for construction of the building but also increase the annual athletic budget that is now stagnant at about $80 million.

For example, if 10,000 premium seats (not counting faculty and student seating) were subject to a private seat license each year and the average seat license, depending on location of the seats, was $5,000, that could generate a maximum of $50 million *each year* of new revenue. That money could help pay for the long-term construction and also bump the athletic budget over $100 million a year. Rumored locations for a new Smith Center are in the Bowles lot adjacent to the current building, on the proposed North Campus, or on the site of Granville Towers in downtown Chapel Hill.

Every alternative is being considered with various estimates commissioned for renovation and new construction. But the big problem is perception. With the NCAA yet to rule on athletic and academic scandal by the end of the 2015 school year, the UNC administration would get massive pushback from certain corners of the university to commit to raising and spending $1 billion on the construction of a new basketball arena.

86 Steve Bucknall

The toughest kid to ever play at Carolina? Most fans would say Tyler Hansbrough, but some veteran observers might say it was Steve Bucknall, the London native from a Massachusetts prep school whom Bill Guthridge discovered at an All-Star tournament in Dayton, Ohio, while he was scouting another recruit. It took Guthridge only two minutes to decide he wanted the 6'6", 220-pound senior from Governor Dummer Academy to wear Carolina blue. During those two minutes, Bucknall muscled up for one rebound and fell on his head going for another. Bucknall had to leave the game, but Guthridge had seen enough. "He had caught my eye in warm-ups," Guthridge recalled. "When Steve got in the game, he played very hard from the start. I liked the way he went after that rebound, even though he got knocked in the head."

Bucknall grew up in south London playing soccer. He only fooled around with basketball until one of his chums beat him in a game of horse. That challenged Bucknall, who was better than his friend in soccer and was determined to be better in everything. Five years and dozens of recruiting letters later, Bucknall was considered one of England's best basketball players.

And he did it by honing his game at a small prep school in the United States, where he hadn't been long enough to be classified as a five-star recruit. After Bucknall was voted MVP at the Five-Star camp in Pittsburgh the summer before his senior year at Dummer, Big East schools joined the smaller programs that had been watching him. But Bucknall also knew about UNC, which had played two exhibition games in London in 1979, and the 13-year-old Bucknall had listened to those games on the radio. Carolina was the first American college program he had heard of, and then in Bucknall's first year in the United States, the Tar Heels won the 1982 national championship. After Dean Smith watched Bucknall play and agreed with Guthridge, he signed the player whose American family had moved to London when he was a toddler.

Bucknall got into 24 games as a freshman and by his junior year he was an integral part of Carolina's nationally ranked program. He played on UNC teams that won back-to-back ACC regular season titles, including the 1987 Heels that went 14–0 in conference play. He was joined by J.R. Reid as the two enforcers on a team that had as much toughness as talent.

As a senior Bucknall helped Carolina break a six-year drought and win the 1989 ACC Championship against Duke in a physical game at the old Omni in Atlanta. Bucknall had the key three-point play late in the 77–74 victory by muscling into the lane, faking Duke's Phil Henderson off his feet, and drawing the foul while making the bank shot. Bucknall wasn't an NBA talent but returned home to play professionally in England and later coach semipro teams in Europe. Throughout his coaching career, Bucknall preached the same kind of hard-nosed basketball that he played when he first caught Bill Guthridge's eye many years before.

87 Madden Takes the Gamble

Kevin Madden was at the crossroads of his college basketball career and he chose what might have been the more difficult path. When Madden did not meet UNC's standards for progress toward graduation after his freshman year, coach Dean Smith gave him a choice. He could sit out the 1986–87 season to work on his academics or he could transfer to another school.

It might have been the easy way out to go play and study elsewhere, but Madden had made a commitment to his terminally ill mother, Helen, after his freshman year at Robert E. Lee High School in Staunton, Virginia, where as a four-year starter he helped Lee win 52 straight games. She wanted him to go to UNC, play basketball, and earn a degree.

Madden chose to remain in Chapel Hill and be redshirted, taking a substantial gamble with his basketball future. Had Madden transferred to a less-strenuous academic environment, he would have had to sit out a year under NCAA rules. And he would have had three seasons of eligibility left and resumed play in 1987–88. Had he not gotten his academic house in order, Madden would still have had to transfer, and it might have cost him two seasons of eligibility. "He could have left, but he is staying here," Smith said at the time. "He knew it was going to be a tough year in school, and I think he was relieved when I told him he couldn't play."

Madden was expected to contend for the starting small forward position after showing flashes of brilliance as a freshman. He appeared in all 34 of Carolina's games in his first year, averaging almost five points and shooting nearly 60 percent from the floor. His best game was against Rutgers early in the season when he had

18 points and six rebounds and later against Virginia when he had 10 points filling in for the injured Steve Hale.

In between, Madden had his moments, making the decision to sit out his true sophomore season a difficult one for him and his coaches. They considered Madden to have as much physical talent as anyone on the team, but they believed his work habits could improve on and off the court. "He is so gifted that in high school he was automatically better than anyone he played against," said Roy Williams, then an assistant on Smith's staff. "But in college he played against people who are just as athletic and he had to learn to work harder on his game."

So Smith was faced with a decision that might have been the best in the long run for Madden but not necessarily the best for his team. It turned out the best for both, as Madden boosted his GPA to where it needed to be, and the 1987 Tar Heels went undefeated in the ACC (14–0) for the second time in four years.

Madden returned as a redshirt sophomore in 1987–88 and went on to finish with a career scoring average of just under 10 points and scored 14.6 a game in 1989, when he helped Carolina win its first ACC championship in seven years and was named second-team All-ACC. He never shot below 57 percent in his four years in college.

Undersized at 6'4", Madden never made the NBA but played more than 10 years professionally in Europe. He remained part of the Carolina basketball family long after his decision to stick it out at UNC. "He could have gone somewhere else and averaged a lot more points," said Edwin Caldwell, a Raleigh supporter who mentored Madden, Kenny Smith, and Charlie Scott when they were in Chapel Hill. "But he chose to stick it out with this program."

88 The Heroes of 2009 Return

The chartered jet carrying the 2009 national champions broke through the clouds on its approach to Raleigh-Durham Airport and entered a wide expanse of Carolina blue sky. The team, coaches, support staff, and university administrators aboard were finally home after six days of sun, cold, and snow in Detroit and the NCAA Final Four.

Their approach was smooth—not aborted twice, which had happened 52 years before when North Carolina's first national championship team returned from Kansas City on an Eastern Airlines propjet. That plane almost did not land because an estimated 5,000 fans had broken through whatever security they had in those days and swarmed near the runway.

This time the North Carolina Tar Heels were greeted by the high-tech stuff of the 21st Century. Cameras replaced people for the moment. The ABC Chopper 11 hovered in the airspace above the terminal, waiting for the team and travel party to board three buses for the 30-minute trip back to Chapel Hill. The TV helicopter would trace every mile of the ride down Interstate 40 and their victory lap snaking through the UNC campus.

By then the lower-level Dean Smith Center had filled with about 12,000 people of all ages, thanks to the afternoon schedule and public school vacation that allowed excited Tar Heel fans from seven months to 70 years old a chance to welcome their latest hoop heroes. Inside the light blue arena, four large video screens were showing the live coverage of the buses accompanied by their police escorts fore and aft as they traveled the last mile up Manning Drive.

Tyler Hansbrough celebrates winning the 2009 National Championship, Roy Williams' second title at UNC.

The biggest roar came when the three tiny white rectangles on the screen turned down Skipper Bowles Drive and parked behind the huge octagon in which their celebrated passengers had won 14 games on the way to first place in the ACC and another No. 1 seed in the NCAA Tournament. In the arena, the four fascia scoreboards had been lit up with: UNC 89, Michigan State 72. Adjacent electronic signs read: 2009 NATIONAL CHAMPIONS.

Finally, the buses emptied out, heightening the anticipation inside, as video cameras now scanned the crowd. They panned up to the five national championship banners hanging from the rafters and then focused on the empty space next to 2005, which would be filled in a few months.

The crowd cheered impatiently.

How long would it take the team to walk the few hundred feet through the tunnel and climb up on the stage where 24 chairs had been arranged in a perfect oval?

At the other end of the court, a media platform had already filled with a phalanx of cameras ready to record the moment. On the wooden playing floor in between, covered by a blue tarp, students clustered toward the stage while behind them children cavorted with their parents and cheerleaders-to-be cartwheeled the time away in the open areas.

The portion of the UNC pep band that had not made the bus trip to Detroit set up in a corner of Section 105, ready to sub for the regulars still on the road *from* the Final Four. They blurted out the Tar Heels' fight song and "Rah, Rah, Carolina." People waiting at three open concession stands in the concourse scurried back inside when they heard Woody Durham, voice of the Tar Heels, bellow: "Isn't this great?"

Durham said he told the players on the plane ride that they had had a pretty good party the night before on the court at Ford Field and afterward in the hotel, but it was nothing compared to what was going on at home. Then he walked off the stage. Durham returned a few minutes later with a small table he set down right in front. "We have something to bring out and we need a place to put it," he said. At long last he introduced the traveling party, one by one. The Tar Heels, all looking weary, wore coats and ties. It wasn't the blue blazers and gray slacks of the McGuire era, but they looked classy by modern standards.

Some of them carried camcorders pointed at the crowd. Bobby Frasor cradled the game ball from the national championship game. Danny Green cracked everybody up when he said, "But did you see *how* we won it?" and then got provoked into his jersey-pulling

ART CHANSKY

"Jump Around" dance. Girls in the front row held up "Marry Me" signs as the last player called, Tyler Hansbrough, walked out to the biggest roar of all.

Finally, Roy Williams arrived holding the national championship trophy draped by one of the nets that had been stripped about 14 hours earlier. He put it down on the table. "It doesn't get any better than this," UNC's favorite son said to cheers, "winning a national championship for *our* alma mater. These guys took me for one fantastic ride."

Williams looked up at the video boards as Carolina's own version of "One Shining Moment" played. It showed Tar Heel highlights only, which Williams watched with misty eyes.

89 Freshmen Eligibility

In 1972 the NCAA voted to allow freshmen to participate in varsity sports. The vote was the last in a series of votes concerning freshman eligibility dating back to the 1920s.

From 1911–1919 every student was eligible to play varsity basketball. During those nine seasons, a total of 26 true freshmen played basketball for UNC. Out of that group, nine were starters, and four—Meb Long, Raby Tennent, Billy Carmichael, and Bailey Liipfert—went on to be four-year starters, a rare feat in the history of Carolina basketball.

With interest in the sport growing by 1919, schools saw the need to offer both freshman and varsity basketball teams. During the 1919–20 school year, Carolina fielded its first freshman basketball team led by Durham's Cartwright Carmichael (Billy's brother), Charlotte's Monk McDonald, and Wilmington's Howard "Fats"

Hanby. Interestingly, playing freshman basketball did not mean one less year of varsity eligibility. Cart Carmichael and Monk McDonald both played four years for the UNC varsity—in 1921, 1922, 1923, and 1924—and were also four-year starters.

The rule to reduce the number of years of varsity eligibility from four to three would not take place until 1922–23. The rule change would have an adverse effect on future Carolina superstar Jack Cobb, a freshman in the fall of 1922. Cobb played on the freshman team in 1923 and on the varsity in 1924, 1925, and 1926. Had Cobb been eligible in 1927, it is likely that the Tar Heels would have won a fourth straight Southern Conference championship and competed for national honors.

The most interesting case involving eligibility, however, was that of Bill Dodderer, who entered school in the fall of 1920 and played for Billy Carmichael on the 1921 freshman team. He sat out of school in 1922 and 1923 but returned in 1924. He played on the varsity in 1924, 1925, and 1926. He then sat out of school in 1927 and returned in 1928. Since he began school in 1920, which was before the eligibility rule went into effect, Dodderer was grandfathered in on the old rule and was eligible to play a fourth varsity season in 1928. The old man was the heart and soul of the '28 White Phantoms, playing the best ball of his career before being sidelined by an ankle injury prior to the Southern Conference tournament.

Freshman eligibility returned during World War II due to the loss of so many college men to military service. On December 12, 1942, the Southern Conference voted to allow freshmen to once again play varsity athletics. Fritz Nagy and Edgar Lougee were the first true freshmen to play varsity basketball for Carolina since Robert Griffith and Sanford Brown in 1919. Nagy, who had been an All-State performer at Akron (Ohio) South High School in 1942, was the first true freshman to lead the Tar Heels in scoring since Long in 1913. For six seasons from 1943–1948, Carolina fans watched true freshmen such as Nagy, Soc Creticos, John Dillon, and Nemo Nearman start for the varsity and help the team win games and championships.

Freshmen were again ruled ineligible prior to the 1949 season, and the change couldn't have come at a worse time for Carolina head coach Tom Scott. After losing eight lettermen from the 1948 team, Scott could have used some freshmen help, particularly from an outstanding prospect from Potsdam, Pennsylvania, named Dick Harter. The 6'1" Harter led the 1949 Carolina freshman team in scoring before transferring to Penn where he would graduate in 1953. He would go on to have a successful coaching career at both the college and professional levels and is remembered for being the first coach of the NBA's Charlotte Hornets.

In the spring of 1951, the Southern Conference once again voted to allow true freshmen to play varsity sports due to the Korean War. Paul Likins, the tallest player for Carolina up to that time at 6'9", and Al "Fuzzy" Lifson both started as true freshmen for the 1952 Heels. Lifson became the third true freshman, along with Long and Nagy, to lead the team in scoring. In 1953, with the rule still in effect, no less than six true freshmen—Jerry Vayda, Hal Bowden, Gene Glancy, Gerry McCabe, Jack Powell, and Tony Radovich—played on Frank McGuire's first UNC team. The 1953 season would end with an 86–54 loss to N.C. State in the Southern Conference tournament with Vayda, Radovich, and Glancy each playing in that game. These three were the last freshmen to play in a UNC varsity basketball game until 1972.

Following the 1953 season, Carolina left the Southern Conference to join the newly formed Atlantic Coast Conference. Though the Southern would continue to allow freshmen to play varsity sports, the ACC would not. This policy continued until January 8, 1972, when the NCAA voted to once again allow freshmen to play varsity basketball and football. The ACC adopted the new rule at its annual spring meeting in May and on November 25,

1972, against Biscayne in Carmichael Auditorium, Mitch Kupchak and Bill Chambers were the first UNC freshmen to play varsity basketball since 1953. In 1975 Phil Ford became the first Carolina freshman to start since Jerry Vayda in 1953. In 2000 Joseph Forte was the first Carolina freshman to lead the team in scoring since Lifson in 1952.

"We're No. 4!"

The signs in Chapel Hill read, "Remember '57 in '67!" When the Tar Heels advanced to the Final Four in Louisville, it was 10 long years since they had been there to complete the legendary undefeated season of 1957.

"McGuire's Miracle" had so fixated the state that Smith had an awful time digging his way out of Frank McGuire's shadow. After taking his own team to the last weekend of the season for the first time, Smith was compared to his colorful predecessor. Fortunately, UNC fans were just happy to be back in the Final Four, and they weren't devastated when their team played poorly and lost the national semifinal game to Dayton. "Coach Smith zoned early against Dayton because he was worried about how to stop their athletes," recalled assistant coach Larry Brown. "We got the lead and then went back to man-to-man. After they beat us, Coach said, 'Larry, we might have been better off if we had stayed in the zone, but I'm not a zone coach.'"

Larry Miller, for one, doesn't think it would have made any difference. He was the Tar Heel trying to stop Dayton All-American Donnie May, who scored 34 points. "It was my fault because I was guarding him," Miller said. "I ran into him years later and I told him, 'You just beat the crap out of us.' He was hitting 25-footers and he was 6'7"!"

In the third-place game against Houston the following night, Smith let his seniors play longer than normal as a reward for sticking it out after the younger stars moved into the lineup. Another lopsided loss ensued, but another Carolina party broke out after the game. "After we lost the game, our fans took over Louisville, yelling 'We're Number 4,'" Brown remembered. "I knew then that things had changed. There was so much appreciation for what had been done. Something special happened there."

Smith brought the 1967 team, plus the '68 and '69 Final Four members, back to Chapel Hill in 1997 for a grand reunion. Miller was there, heavier at 50 years old, with graying hair and thick glasses. Lewis made a rare appearance in Chapel Hill and joined his former teammates at midcourt of the Smith Center.

91 Multimedia Mess

Prior to 1992 each of UNC's athletic media properties had been contracted out separately, essentially leaving Carolina with several different media partners that paid the school a rights fee. Each of those properties, such as the Tar Heel Sports Radio Network and the football and basketball coaches' radio and TV shows, had advertising inventory that was now owned by the rights holder to sell and, theoretically, make more than the rights fees they paid and their operational costs so they could turn a profit.

As for basketball this method played nicely into Dean Smith's philosophy—like in *The Godfather*—because he could "throw a carrot" to a number of people who had been loyal to him and his program over the years. For example, Woody Durham had been UNC's play-by-play announcer—the Voice of the Tar Heels— since 1971. They were social friends and golf buddies who often took trips together after the season. Smith had also developed a fierce loyalty to John Kilgo. A UNC graduate like Durham, Kilgo had covered the Tar Heels for years as a radio and TV commentator and columnist in Charlotte. When Jefferson-Pilot Communications bought the rights to produce the coaches' weekly television shows in 1983, Smith allowed J-P employee Kilgo to replace Durham as host of his weekly TV show.

Though Smith did not mind having "two sons" and ostensibly treated them equally, the arrangement created growing controversy and fractious feelings within the Carolina camp. Durham and Kilgo were professional rivals who each wanted the other's job. Plus, having to bid out the rights to the radio and TV properties separately and accepting smaller rights fees from several other companies for the gameday programs and magazines covering the Tar Heels, UNC had little leverage or synergy with any of its rights vendors.

Meanwhile, athletic director John Swofford had learned about the concept of "one-stop shopping" developed by Jim Host and his company who owned *all* the media rights at the University of Kentucky. Host had paid Kentucky a large rights fee for the exclusive multimedia rights at Kentucky and later other Southeastern Conference schools. With only one media rights holder, UNC could build a true partnership and be more involved with specific advertisers to help drive the sponsorship dollars higher than they had ever been. That meant a bigger rights fee in years to come. In 1992 Swofford received approval from UNC to bundle all of the schools' athletic media rights into one package and put it out to bid.

When he heard about it, Smith objected. He knew that it meant that either Durham or Kilgo could be out of a job if

Durham's employer, the Tar Heel Sports Radio Network, or Kilgo's J-P Communications won the multimedia rights. Smith had liked the routine he had developed with both men and was a creature of habit. As his basketball program grew into a nationally known juggernaut, Smith's workload increased, and he abhorred any change that would require more of his time. He did virtually no preparation for his weekly TV and radio shows, walked in, taped the interviews or took the calls, and walked out. And he preferred it that way.

As unquestionably the most powerful man at the university, Smith could kill the multimedia concept before it ever got off the ground. And he threatened to do it.

Still unclear why this system had to change, he reluctantly allowed Swofford to proceed with bidding out the exclusive, packaged rights—with one very specific stipulation: nothing would change for Smith unless he agreed to it. That meant, no matter which company won the rights, Kilgo would be retained as host of his weekly radio and TV shows, and the new owner of the Tar Heel Sports Network would keep Durham as the play-by-play voice of the basketball program (as well as football). Kilgo would continue to produce the shows in exactly the same manner, would have the same budget as always, and still be able to travel with the basketball team to any away games he deemed important.

The bid was won by the local Village Companies, which had owned the radio play-by-play rights since 1975. And Smith often reminded employees and producers that everything would remain the same as it applied to basketball. Even though Durham was on the payroll of the company, Kilgo had to be paid extra to keep hosting and producing Smith's weekly shows. Meanwhile, football coach Mack Brown immediately dumped Kilgo as host of his shows and, with Durham now hosting, agreed to a more contemporary format that went beyond the host and coach sitting side by side and going over the highlights of the previous game.

Eventually, Kilgo lost the TV show to Durham and eventually the radio show, too, after Smith retired in 1997 and the entire multimedia rights contract was sold to Learfield Communications of Jefferson City, Missouri. That company had a policy of having one announcer at each of its schools and paid that announcer by the game or the show he was broadcasting. So Kilgo, though he would later receive a reported $850,000 to write Smith's autobiography, lost the income he had generated directly from Smith's support.

Learfield remains UNC's multimedia rights holder and partner and, as of 2014, was paying the athletic department a guaranteed annual $7.5 million rights fee. Durham also retired after the 2011 basketball season and was succeeded by the former host of the game broadcasts, Jones Angell, who calls the games and hosts the weekly football and basketball shows.

92 Dean's Kansas Roots

Dean Smith's roots ran deep in Kansas, even with the 50-plus years he spent in North Carolina. There remained something very Sunflower State-like in the man. After all, he brought Kansan Bill Guthridge to work for him at UNC and sent Larry Brown and Roy Williams out west to coach at the University of Kansas, his alma mater.

Smith's parents moved from Emporia to Topeka in 1947, Dean's sophomore year in high school. His father, once a high school basketball coach, had taken a job as recreation director for the Veterans Administration Hospital near Topeka. He missed coaching and he missed his players. Alfred Smith was a champion, too. His lone state title had been won on the same cavernous

Topeka High School court, where his son would play varsity basketball.

On a visit there on a cold and windy day, he talked about that championship game. One player was missing from the 1934 Kansas State High School tournament that year. Paul Terry was African American, and his coach could not take him to Topeka, or his entire team would be disqualified. Dean Smith, who would become a champion of civil rights, recalled, "I remember so well the experiences Dad would have with former players. Almost as soon as one would come home from the war, *boom*, he'd be over at the house."

Smith and his sister, Joan, were simply never given a chance to doubt themselves growing up. The pretty white house built in 1951 remained full of testaments to the children and grandchildren long after they had all grown up. Dean's mom, Vesta Smith, who taught at Emporia State Teachers College in the early years, confided, "If either one of them turned a somersault, we were there to see it." His parents kept their son's room ready for Dean's visits, most of them short. There was a Carolina blue dresser and a simple, wooden bed. There were two framed resolutions from the Kansas House of Representatives praising their son, this child of a teacher and a coach.

The Smiths had been in the Superdome when the most emotional game in UNC history had been played and somehow won by their son's Tar Heels. The 64-team NCAA Tournament pairings sheet from 1982 was also framed and on the wall, but Dean's accomplishment at the Olympics was even more memorable for them. The elder Smith recalled, "Seeing Dean win the gold medal in Montreal was probably the biggest thrill his mother and I have had in his career. I remember telling him I was the proudest father alive that night. There were some tears, I'll tell you."

Alfred Smith, silent for a bit, looked out the window into the grey February dusk. He said, "You know, Dean's forgotten more about basketball than I ever knew. But we gave him the atmosphere to love coaching. And…Dean's always had a knack for putting things in the places they belonged."

93 Where's Wayne?

One of the most invisible characters in the UNC athletic and academic scandal that raged on between 2010 and 2015 was Wayne Walden, the longtime academic advisor to head basketball coach Roy Williams at Kansas and North Carolina. Walden joined the Carolina academic advisory staff in the summer of 2003 after spending 16 years in the student support services office at the University of Kansas.

At both schools he worked with multiple sports but was most tied to men's basketball under Williams. At Carolina Walden's title was associate director of the academic support program for student-athletes (ASPSA). He coordinated and oversaw scheduling, registration, structured study halls, tutorial services, and progress toward degrees for the student-athletes in several programs but primarily men's basketball.

A native of Topeka, Kansas, who received bachelor's and master's degrees from Kansas, Walden was director of degree and career counseling at KU and worked with the baseball, tennis, and volleyball programs, as well as men's basketball. He was also an instructor in the School of Education, where he taught a course designed to help seniors make the transition to post-college experiences.

There was never a hint of impropriety in Williams' program at KU, but both the head coach and Walden were eventually swept up in the academic scandal at UNC that began with football but later implicated the men's and women's basketball teams. When

Williams returned to Chapel Hill as head coach in April of 2003, he soon hired Walden to handle many of the same duties he had at Kansas.

It was a strange juxtaposition of jobs for Williams, who as an unknown UNC assistant was named head coach at Kansas in 1988 after the Jayhawks had won the national championship under Larry Brown (another former Tar Heel player and assistant coach under Dean Smith) who also left the program under NCAA investigation that later turned into a one-year probation and ban from postseason play in 1989, Williams' first season at KU. So the scrutiny of the Kansas program had already been finished when Williams arrived there.

At Carolina, Williams inherited a roster of talented players who had been recruited, signed, and coached by his predecessor Matt Doherty. When Walden began reviewing the academic standing of the 2003–2004 Tar Heels, he found that at least half of the players were majoring in Afro and African American (AFAM) studies and that many of the classes those players were taking were independent studies that required little class attendance and the writing of a term paper to determine final grades.

Walden said he informed Williams that a certain amount of "clustering" was going on amongst his new players and that Williams discouraged that because he wanted all students to pick their own majors and favored more lecture-style classes than independent studies. So Walden began weaning players out of the AFAM major, and by the time the Tar Heels won their second NCAA championship under Williams in 2009, no men's basketball players were AFAM majors. After that season Walden got married, left UNC, and moved to Dallas. That timing was never questioned until the academic scandal broke at UNC in 2010 and the infamous Wainstein Report tracked Walden down for one of the 126 interviews conducted by Kenneth Wainstein and his staff of lawyers.

Before that interview, no reporters (or anyone, for that matter) could find Walden, though he was living in Dallas all that time. Walden had worked with longtime basketball tutor Burgess McSwain. When Walden found out about the so-called paper classes, he thought they had been approved by the university (which they were) because they were open to all students (which they were). He said Williams was more concerned with developing a culture in the basketball program that depended too much on these classes. According to the Wainstein Report, "Walden did not know [AFAM department chairman Julius] Nyang'oro but he would work with [Nyang'oro assistant Deborah] Crowder to enroll his students in the AFAM...classes. He knew that students enrolled in paper classes had no contact with faculty and he said that he thought Crowder was probably doing some of the grading, though he never knew for sure. Walden did not feel that there was anything wrong with these courses, however, because they were open to and taken by regular students in addition to student-athletes."

Easy classes were not unique to UNC, and neither was limited faculty involvement in certain classes that were taught, administered, and graded by teaching assistants or graduate students. Walden remained one of the many people who could have had more knowledge of academic irregularities in the basketball program and athletic department but was never proven to be complicit in any way beyond his statements in the Wainstein Report.

When UNC received its Notice of Allegations from the NCAA in May of 2015, Roy Williams and men's basketball did not receive charges, which left fans hopeful that it would not result in serious sanctions.

94 The German Influence

Starting with Randy Wiel from the island Curacao in the 1970s, Dean Smith made it a habit of bringing international players into his program. Timo Makkonen from Finland, Steve Bucknall from England, Rick Fox from the Bahamas, and Serge Zwikker from the Netherlands followed, but perhaps the "truest" foreigner was Ademola Okulaja, who never played at a prep school in the United States and arrived in Chapel Hill from a club team career in Berlin, Germany.

Overshadowed by the more highly recruited classmates Vince Carter and Antawn Jamison, Okulaja had a solid career that culminated with his making the All-ACC team as a senior in 1999 after Carter and Jamison had turned pro the year before. Born in Nigeria to a German mother and Nigerian father, Okulaja moved to West Berlin when he was three. It was there that Okulaja began developing skills that would earn him spots on prestigious German club teams and eventually a scholarship to UNC.

He was not a serious basketball player until the fourth grade, concentrating more on swimming, handball, and rugby. Then Okulaja kept growing toward his 6'7" frame until he spent most of his time on the basketball court. At 14 he made the best youth club team in Germany and eventually the Alba Berlin team took a chance on Okulaja and signed him as its only amateur player.

An 18-year-old starting on a team with all other veteran professional players, Okulaja helped Alba win the Kovac Cup as the best club team in Europe. One of the players on that team was yet another former Tar Heel foreigner, Chapel Hill High School graduate Henrik Rodl, who returned to his native Germany after playing for North Carolina's 1993 NCAA Championship team.

The friends on Alba Berlin spent time talking about American college basketball, and Rodl sent his scouting report on his teammates back to Smith and Bill Guthridge. The UNC coaches traveled to Germany to watch Okulaja play and meet his family. They schooled the family on the success of former Carolina players on and off the court. Smith was already a recognized figure around the globe, having taken his teams to play in Spain, England, Japan—and eventually—Germany. Several fans in Berlin recognized him and asked for his autograph.

Carter, Jamison, and Okulaja bonded as friends and teammates as freshmen, even though they all played basically the same interchangeable positions. The Americans ingrained their traditions into the German, whose experience playing with pros overseas made him tougher than most publicized and coddled high school stars brought to colleges in this country.

Okulaja also experienced some things few youngsters see, such as the fall of the Berlin Wall and the symbolic end of the Cold War, one of the most important events of the 20th century. He shared with teammates how the reunification of Germany opened markets and created new opportunities with companies such as Mercedes-Benz and Sony taking advantage of the new business climate.

Like Wiel, who came to Carolina as an accomplished guitar player and singer who often serenaded male and female students at Granville Towers, Okulaja arrived in Chapel Hill as a polished cello and clarinet player. By the time he finished at UNC, Okulaja also mastered the saxophone—and college basketball, averaging 14 points and 8.4 rebounds as a senior while leading the Tar Heels in three-point shooting for Bill Guthridge's 24–10 team.

Following graduation in 1999, Okulaja tried to make several NBA rosters but eventually played for seven professional teams in Germany, Spain, and Italy, winning the Most Spectacular Player award in the 2002 Spanish All-Star Game. He also played for the

German national team and competed in the 2006 FIFA World Cup in Japan on the same team as NBA All-Star Dirk Nowitzki.

95 Buddy Baldwin

Roy Williams was the first in his family to attend college. He did his schoolwork and used sports as his lifeblood. He played little league and pony league baseball and discovered basketball and ping pong (interestingly, Dean Smith's childhood game, too) at the local YMCA, where he spent his Saturdays. Basketball was his favorite because, even alone, he could still work up a sweat on the court by running incessantly, shooting, and fetching the ball. He got so competent with the round ball that he finally found his first mentor and the man who changed his life in Buddy Baldwin, the coach at T. C. Roberson High School, which had opened after the merger of Valley Springs and Biltmore in 1962.

Baldwin met Williams as a freshman and loved his work ethic, his sincerity, and the manners his mother, Mimmie, taught him. "I liked Roy's attitude, his competitiveness, the way he always said 'Yessir!' and 'Nosir!' and how he played both ends of the floor and tried to do everything you told him," said Baldwin, who became a best friend for life.

In turn, Williams says Baldwin was the "first person to give me confidence, to believe in me." Williams grew into a solid, though small basketball player at 5'9" and 135 pounds, who hustled and squeezed every ounce out of his ability to earn a starting position as a sophomore at Roberson, where he went on to average 16 points a game and be named team captain as a senior. "He was pretty hard-headed even back then," Baldwin said. "He knew what to do on the court, what was needed, and I didn't need to call a timeout to tell him."

An avid golfer, Baldwin introduced Williams to the game that turned into a second love. Baldwin's regular foursome often drove out to Sapphire Valley, a new course that required carts to stay on path, so they brought Roy and a buddy along to carry their bags. Years later, when it dawned on Williams that the group could have easily hired caddies at the course, he realized "Coach just wanted to put a few dollars in our pockets more than anything. But I was intrigued with the game."

Idolizing Baldwin, who had graduated from UNC and briefly played freshman basketball, Williams decided he, too, wanted to coach. He first discussed it with Baldwin during his sophomore year in high school. "He started talking to me about college, something as fundamental as that," Williams said. "It became the first thing I thought about in the morning and the last thing I thought about at night...the most important thing in the world to me."

Baldwin, of course, displayed North Carolina bias because he had grown up a basketball fan and enrolled at UNC a year after Frank McGuire's 1957 team finished undefeated and won the national championship. "The reason I went to Chapel Hill was to watch great basketball," said Baldwin, who had played on Spring Valley's 1-A state champs his senior year.

When Williams eventually joined the UNC staff as a part-time assistant in 1978, he talked incessantly about "my high school coach, Buddy Baldwin." After Baldwin visited Chapel Hill, Smith then realized it was the same Buddy Baldwin who had to drop off the freshman team so he could stay in school, graduate, and someday become a mentor to other young coaches and give someone like Roy Williams the chance of a lifetime.

96 Tricky Ricky Webb

Ricky Webb, who was a reserve in the late 1960s, tried to take advantage of coach Dean Smith's system of allowing players to take themselves out of the game if they were tired by raising a closed fist toward the bench. Smith always wanted his players going 100 percent, and, if they were getting tired, they could take themselves out of the game and put themselves back in when they told Smith on the bench, "I'm ready."

Webb didn't play much and he decided that when he did get in the game, he was going to try to accumulate as many minutes as possible by taking himself out and putting himself back in as many times as he could. He would be getting more minutes than usual and still be playing by Smith's rules. Webb got his chance in the very next game, but he made the mistake of telling a couple of teammates what he was planning.

After Smith subbed him in, Webb ran up and down the court as fast as he could a couple of times and then flashed the first toward the bench. After coming out, sitting for a few minutes, and putting himself back in, Webb gave the tired signal again. Smith took him out, but by this time he was on to Webb, probably with the help of some guys on the bench who were watching and laughing so hard. When Webb tried to put himself back in, Smith said, "Sit there!"

The next day Webb spent the entire practice running up and down the stairs at the old Carmichael Auditorium with weights strapped around his ankles and wearing a weighted vest. Every other player had finished practice and gone in to shower while Webb was still running the stairs.

Finally, Smith came out of the locker room and approached the exhausted and sweat-soaked Webb, who thought for sure he was getting thrown off the team. So he took another chance and gave Smith the tired signal. Smith broke into laughter and told Webb to hit the showers. "Whenever I saw a player giving the tired signal," Webb said years later, "I always wonder if the guy was really tired or trying to control his playing time. I always thought the idea would work. My technique was just bad!"

97 Dean's Impact on George Karl

George Karl, a point guard for Carolina from 1970–73, played professionally for the San Antonio Spurs before going on to coach six teams in the NBA. "I've never been in the company of another basketball coach like Dean Smith," said Karl, reflecting on his former mentor's philosophy of the game of basketball and of life itself. "I've never known anyone who believed more in his team and his coaching staff to the final minute."

Recently hired as Sacramento Kings head coach, Karl, whose successful but turbulent career includes being fired five times, said he learned from Smith throughout his career. Karl coached five NBA teams for 25 seasons and had a career record of 1,131–756 for a .599 winning percentage. "Coach was always around much more when you were down and losing," Karl recalled, "calling, watching your games, helping you at times. It's amazing what he knew. I think the more failure and problems you had, the more he was around. I now believe that to coach, you must be highly motivated by losing."

Before he became a longtime NBA head coach, George Karl played point guard at North Carolina under Dean Smith. (Getty Images)

Karl explained one of the many elemental bits of wisdom he acquired from Smith over the years: "Not to yell and scream and condemn but to coach. I realized that the one time in coaching when your team will probably listen to you more often, and with more intensity, is in losing. Coach Smith could be critical, but never, ever did he reach negative. It was always positive. I did that as a coach but not every day. I couldn't even come close to it every day."

The comments indicate a sense of reverence from the man who changed considerably since he first visited Chapel Hill as a cocky teenager from Pennsylvania in 1969. "The player today has an individuality that has been developed by the game," Karl said. "You've got to react to it and learn to relate in the system, which I think Coach Smith proved. That might have been his greatest accomplishment: to change, to constantly change."

Smith helped Karl, who returned to coaching following bouts with prostate, neck, and throat cancer, to grow not only as a coach, but as a person. "He believed life is spiritual, and life is important, and there's a bond in the soul," Karl said. "There was one phrase he said to me more than anything else in my life: 'Isn't that we, George?' I'll say, 'I did this.' 'Don't you mean *we* did this?'"

Even though Smith retired in 1997 and passed away in 2015, Karl said "you still can't mention Carolina basketball without mentioning Dean Smith."

98 Kirkpatrick and Gammons

Two of the best sportswriters of all time, Curry Kirkpatrick and Peter Gammons, cut their teeth covering Carolina basketball in the 1960s. Kirkpatrick was from St. Louis, Gammons was from

Boston, but both found their way to Chapel Hill for college and began writing for *The Daily Tar Heel*. They went on to distinguished careers in journalism, including writing best-selling sports books.

Kirkpatrick was the more flamboyant one with an entertaining style that eventually made him the lead college basketball writer for *Sports Illustrated* in the 1970s, when he showed up to cover games wearing the flashiest clothes of that decade. Known for his clever leads and anecdotes, Kirkpatrick's college basketball stories in *SI* were must-reads for more than a decade. He won numerous national sports writing awards and earned special recognition in the Basketball Hall of Fame. He briefly came out of retirement to cover The 2014 French Open for ESPN.com.

Gammons was more conservative, professionally and personally, and became known as a great baseball reporter who was a special category inductee into the Baseball Hall of Fame. Gammons started his career at *The Boston Globe* and later worked for *Sports Illustrated*, ESPN, and MLB Network. He is a longtime Boston Red Sox season-ticket holder and played guitar in a rock-and-roll band with several members of the team, including former general manager Theo Epstein.

Kirkpatrick's freshman year at UNC was Dean Smith's first season as head basketball coach, having succeeded the legendary Frank McGuire. He covered Smith's early travails, including the 8–9 record his inaugural season and the criticism that engulfed Smith as he tried to rebuild the Tar Heel program after the 1961 NCAA probation that chased McGuire away. Although he also covered pro basketball, tennis, and golf for *Sports Illustrated* and later worked for CBS, ESPN, *ESPN The Magazine*, and ESPN.com, Kirkpatrick's first love remained college hoops, and his favorite team was the Tar Heels. Now 72, he still travels to many Carolina games in Chapel Hill and on the road from his home on Hilton Head Island, South Carolina.

Gammons, now 70, was Kirkpatrick's protégé at *The Daily Tar Heel* and decided he wanted to make sportswriting his profession with the encouragement of Smith. Gammons, in fact, was on the team bus in 1965, when it returned from a loss at Wake Forest and students had hung an effigy of the embattled Smith from a tree across the street from Woollen Gym. But as a senior in 1967, Gammons also witnessed and covered Smith's first ACC championship and Final Four appearance. Smith once invited him to sit in on an interview being conducted by Frank Deford of *Sports Illustrated* and later told Gammons he was good enough to write sports for a living. Gammons was covering baseball for ESPN in 2006 when he was stricken with a brain aneurysm. He survived and returned to the broadcast booth the following season.

99 Oldest Living Tar Heel

At 94 years young and still going strong, Bob Gersten remains the oldest living Tar Heel basketball player. He and his wife, Libby, who met while at UNC in the early 1940s, have moved from New York back to Chapel Hill and now live in a retirement community.

Gersten was an unsung star for the Tar Heels of coach Bill Lange, as he played tenacious defense while getting the ball to All-American George Glamack. But Gersten was good enough and popular enough to win the Patterson Medal, awarded to the best all-around UNC athlete each year, in 1942.

When he returned for the program's 100th birthday celebration in 2010, the then 89-year-old Gersten joined Sherman "Nemo" Nearman and other Tar Heel seniors in a true old-timers half-court game in the packed Smith Center. Gersten's picture was in every newspaper the next morning, and he was mobbed on Franklin Street as he walked to breakfast.

As a high school coach on Long Island for almost 40 years, Gersten was not shy about steering players to his alma mater. He coached Larry Brown at Long Beach High School, and there was never a doubt where Brown was going to college—to Carolina and play for Frank McGuire. Gersten had several chances to become a college coach, but he turned them all down to continue running his family's Brant Lake Camp for boys each summer in the Adirondacks.

100 Tallest Tar Heel

Seven-foot-five Neil Fingleton was not only the tallest basketball player ever at UNC, he also is in the *Guinness World Records* as the tallest British-born man in history. Since he stopped growing, Fingleton's height has been listed as seven feet, 7.56 inches, and he is also among the tallest 25 men in the history of the world. He reached the seven-foot mark when he was 13 and made the British tabloids that tracked his height through high school.

At 16 Fingleton came to America from Durham, England, to Worcester, Massachusetts, and attended Holy Name Central Catholic High School, graduating in 2000. Fingleton helped the Holy Name basketball team to the Central Massachusetts Division I title and a berth in the Massachusetts final game in 1999 and a 22–4 record in 2000.

After signing with UNC, Fingleton appeared in only one game for the Tar Heels, redshirted as a freshman and, after back surgery that summer, played four minutes against Davidson on November

20, 2001, in the Smith Center. He attempted two shots and missed them both, had one defensive rebound, and committed one turnover.

He never played another minute for Carolina and after the fall semester transferred to Holy Cross, where he played in the 2003 NCAA Tournament for the Patriot League champion Crusaders. He graduated in 2004 with a degree in history and kicked around semipro basketball and the NBA Developmental League and for several European pro teams before retiring in 2007 and returning to his hometown of Durham to pursue a career in show business.

He is now the tallest actor in England. Fingleton has appeared in popular shows playing suitable characters like the Giant Blunderbore in *Jack and the Beanstalk* and has been in several movies, plus the HBO series *Game of Thrones*. He remains a very tall footnote in the history of Carolina basketball.

Sources

A Century of Excellence, 2010 (UNC Press)

March to the Top, 1982 (Four Corners Press)

Return to the Top, 1993 (Four Corners Press)

GoHeels.com (UNC website)

Blue Blood, 2005 (St. Martin's Press)

Chapelboro.com (WCHL website)

Ron Smith, from his forthcoming book on the history of Carolina basketball

Carolina Court magazines, 1986–2000 (Four Corners Press)

Dean's Domain, 1999 (Longstreet Press)

Light Blue Reign, 2009 (St, Martin's Press)

Greensboro News Record (News-Record.com), February 16, 2015

UNC media guides and basketball brochures, 1968–2015

UNC website

What It Means to Be a Tar Heel, 2010 (Triumph Books)